The Ultimate Interactive Revision Book

Advanced Higher

CHEMISTRY

Written by:

Peter & Lesley Johnson

Published by

Kitchen Chemistry

23 Edderston Road

Peebles

ISBN 978-0-9934494-3-7

© Peter & Lesley Johnson, 2021

Images Credits:

The majority of images are taken from Wikimedia Commons. Every effort has been made to contact the copyright holder for images, if you identify your work and it has not been credited please contact Peter & Lesley Johnson (kitchenchemistry@tiscali.co.uk)

Acknowledgement:

The authors would like to thank Charlie Kerr & Liz Thompson of Stewart's Melville College for their support in developing the activities in this book and for their helpful feedback. Also Fiona Neave of The Mary Erskine School for proof reading and feedback.

Note that answers to all the games, activities and practice questions can be found at the following website:

www.ultimate-revision-books.co.uk

Contents Page

How to make the most of this book

Lets face it……. revision can be boring!!!

Reading your notes or a textbook, copying facts and information out, then turning these into shorter notes may help you remember information but it can be slow, tedious and boring! More importantly it's not the most effective way of learning as you don't have to think much. Thinking is key to remembering information, the more you have to think about something the more you are going to remember it. **Active learning** is about getting you to look at and think about the information in lots of different ways; and then using that information in a variety of activities that are much more interesting than sitting looking at pages & pages of writing.

This book is split up into short topics, with summary pages of the key ideas at the start. You should look through this information and make sure you understand what it's about. If you don't understand it look back at your own notes or textbook; even better speak to your teacher and ask them to explain it to you. Once you understand the material it's time to learn it. To help you there are pages with different activities all linked to those key ideas. Keep flicking back to the summary pages to check you are getting it right, as none of the activities are there to test you, they are all about getting you to use the correct information in lots of different ways.

Once you have completed all the activities on a particular topic there are some practice questions to try. Again don't be afraid to check your answers as you go by either looking back at some of the activities or even your own notes or textbook. It is far better to put the right answer down having looked at your notes than it is for you to guess incorrectly. The correct answers are all available on our website (**www.ultimate-revision-books.co.uk**).

Once you have done all this try making your own games and activities as this is an even better way of getting you to remember the information. You can convert the summary pages into mind maps or spider diagrams. You can also make flash cards with the question on one side and the correct answer on the other.

So to recap.
- **Read and make sure you understand the key ideas at the start of each topic.**
- **Work through the different activities, checking the summary pages as you go.**
- **Try the practice questions using your own notes or summary pages to help.**
- **Create your own mind maps, flash cards, games and activities.**

It is recommended that you use a pencil rather than a pen to complete the activities so you can easily correct any mistakes you make.

4

Unit 1 Electromagnetic Spectrum

Visible light is part of the electromagnetic spectrum. The electromagnetic spectrum consists of photons or packets of energy travelling with a particular wavelength, frequency and energy. **The photons can act as both waves and particles and this is known as wave-particle duality.**

Visible light has a wavelength between approximately 400-700nm.

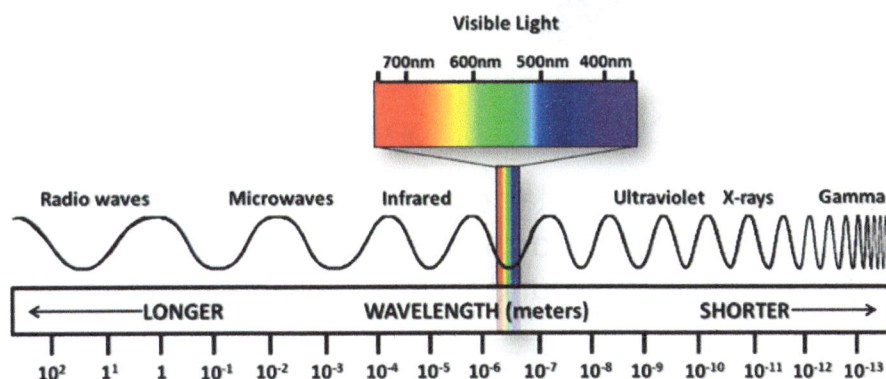

Frequency is measured in Hz and energy measured in joules, both increase as the wavelength gets shorter.

$$f = \frac{c}{\lambda}$$

where:
f = frequency(Hz),
c = speed of light (3×10^8 ms^{-1}),
λ = wavelength(m) **note 1nm = 1×10^{-9}m**

The energy of a mole of photons with a particular wavelength can be calculated in kJmol^{-1} using either:

$$E = \frac{Lhf}{1000} \quad \text{or} \quad E = \frac{Lhc}{\lambda 1000}$$

Where:
L = Avogadro's number (6.02×10^{23} mol^{-1}),
h = Planck's constant (6.63×10^{-34} Js^{-1}),
f = frequency (Hz)
c = speed of light (3×10^8 ms^{-1}),
λ = wavelength(m) **note 1nm = 1×10^{-9}m**

Example
Potassium salts impart a lilac colour to a Bunsen flame. The lilac light has a wavelength of 405nm. Calculate the energy associated with one mole of photons of lilac light.

$$E = \frac{6.02 \times 10^{23} \times 6.63 \times 10^{-34} \times 3 \times 10^8}{405 \times 10^{-9} \times 1000}$$

$$E = \underline{295.65 \text{ kJmol}^{-1}}$$

Emission spectroscopy

Heat or electrical energy is used to excite electrons in an atom to a higher energy level (excited state). Here they are unstable and fall back down to the original energy level (ground state) releasing a photon of light of a particular wavelength corresponding to the energy gap it fell.

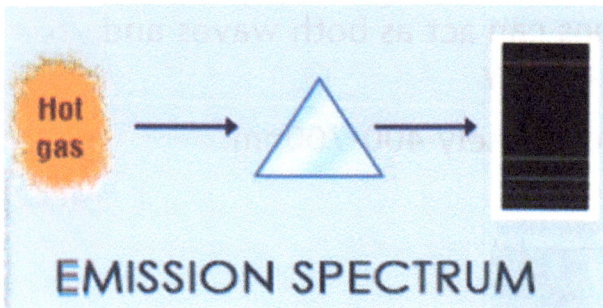

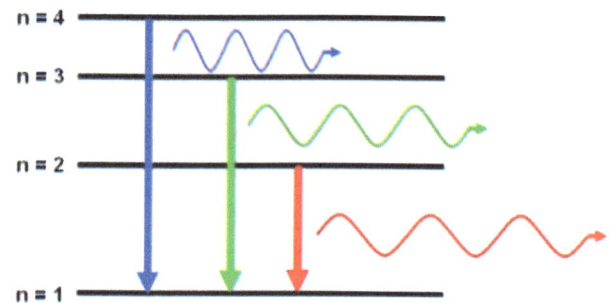

EMISSION SPECTRUM

The spectra produced for a particular element is a complex series of coloured lines due to the many electrons and the number of possible ways the excited electrons can fall back to their ground state.

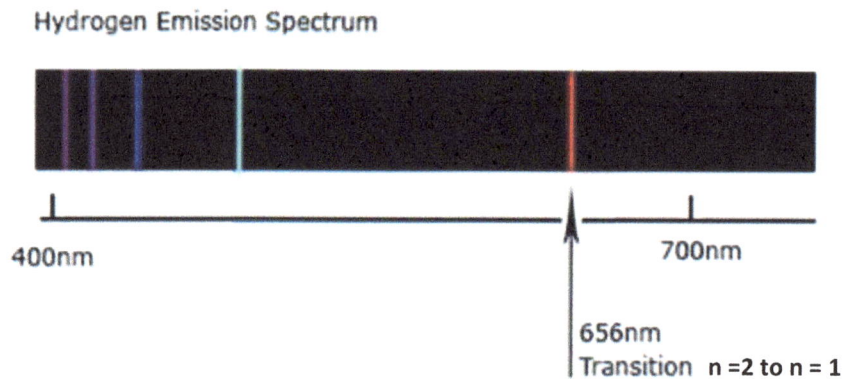

Hydrogen Emission Spectrum

400nm   700nm

656nm
Transition n = 2 to n = 1

Absorption spectroscopy

Light is shone at a sample and the resulting spectra analysed which shows dark bands corresponding to the wavelengths of light absorbed by the electrons to move to an excited state. (These bands are exactly the same wavelength as the coloured lines produced in the emission spectroscopy for the same element.)

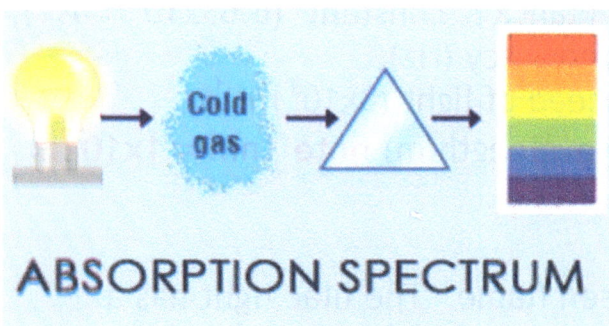

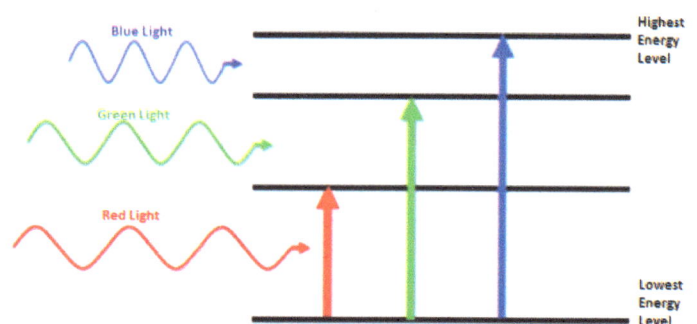

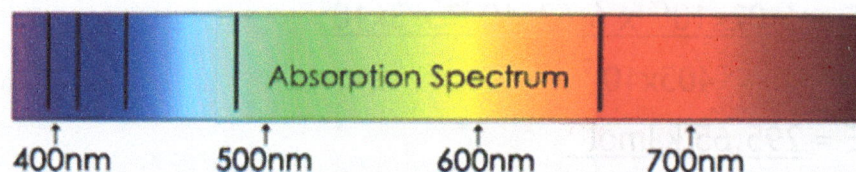

ABSORPTION SPECTRUM

Absorption Spectrum

400nm   500nm   600nm   700nm

Electromagnetic Radiation

Connect the different types of radiation to their appropriate wavelength, frequency and relative energy. The first one has been done for you:

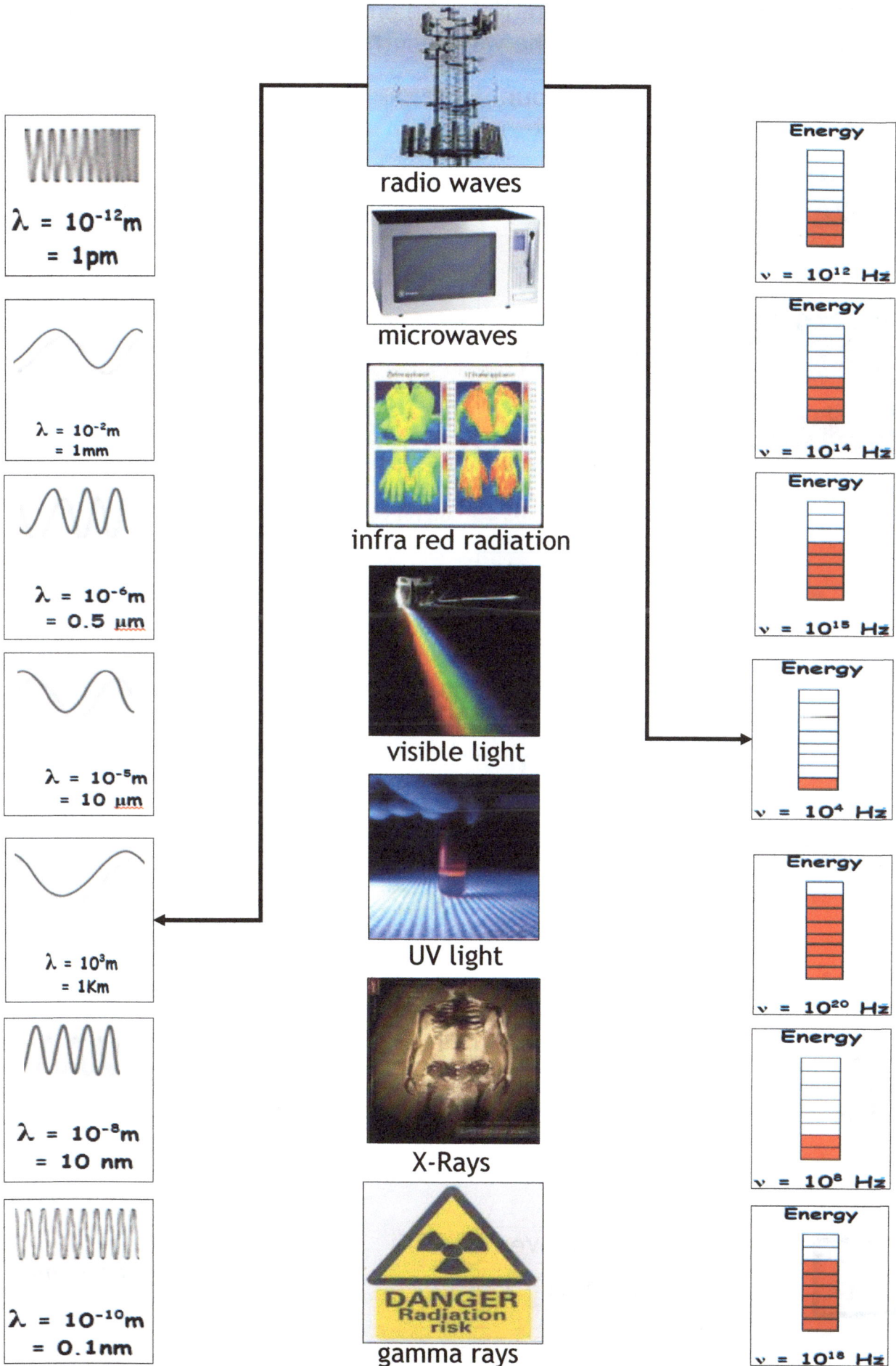

radio waves

microwaves

infra red radiation

visible light

UV light

X-Rays

gamma rays

$\lambda = 10^{-12}$m
= 1pm

$\lambda = 10^{-2}$m
= 1mm

$\lambda = 10^{-6}$m
= 0.5 μm

$\lambda = 10^{-5}$m
= 10 μm

$\lambda = 10^{3}$m
= 1Km

$\lambda = 10^{-8}$m
= 10 nm

$\lambda = 10^{-10}$m
= 0.1nm

Energy
$\nu = 10^{12}$ Hz

Energy
$\nu = 10^{14}$ Hz

Energy
$\nu = 10^{15}$ Hz

Energy
$\nu = 10^{4}$ Hz

Energy
$\nu = 10^{20}$ Hz

Energy
$\nu = 10^{8}$ Hz

Energy
$\nu = 10^{18}$ Hz

Energy, Wavelength and Frequency

Connect the correct energy value for either the frequency or wavelength of electromagnetic radiation given. Use p22 of your data booklet to help work out the values for the frequencies given. Note the energy values for the frequencies are in Jmol^{-1} and the energies for the wavelengths are in kJmol^{-1}.

Sodium vapour streetlight 589nm		**126 kJmol^{-1}**
Strontium red distress flare 650nm		**0.96 Jmol^{-1}**
Submarine sonar 30Hz		**203 kJmol^{-1}**
TV infra red remote 950nm		**0.36 Jmol^{-1}**
WIFI Signal 2.4GHz		**1.2 x10^{-8} Jmol^{-1}**
Microwave oven 900MHz		**184 kJmol^{-1}**

Quiz Word

Answer the following questions to complete the quiz word and then try to work out what the key phrase in the **bold** boxes should be.

1. Constant that relates to the energy of a photon of light. (7)
2. Produced when an element is heated in a Bunsen flame. (8,8)
3. A measure of the number of waves passing a fixed point per second. (9)
4. Constant that relates to the number of moles of photons. (9)
5. This is the state that the electron rises to when heated. (7)
6. This is the state that the electron falls back to releasing a photon of light. (6)

Quiz Word Clue: Has a value of 3 x10⁻⁸ ms⁻¹

Chemical Misconceptions

A student wrote the following into their notebook as a set of definitions for **emission spectroscopy:**

- Wave / particle duality -   This is the idea that photons act as waves of energy but not as particles.

- Emission spectroscopy -   Electrons in atoms are heated by electricity and they move to the ground state emitting photons of light.

- Photon   -   A packet of light found in energy.

- Energy   -   As the wavelength of electromagnetic radiation increases the energy also increases, but the frequency decreases.

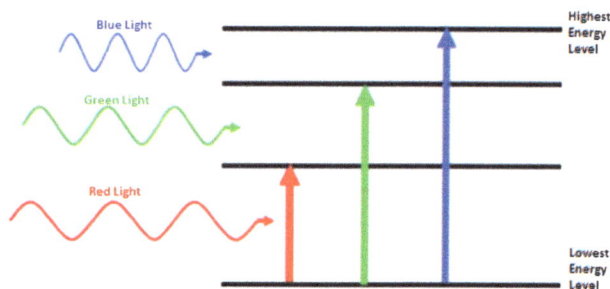

Identify their mistakes and write the correct definitions in the space below:

- Wave / particle duality -

- Emission spectroscopy -

- Photon   -

- Energy   -

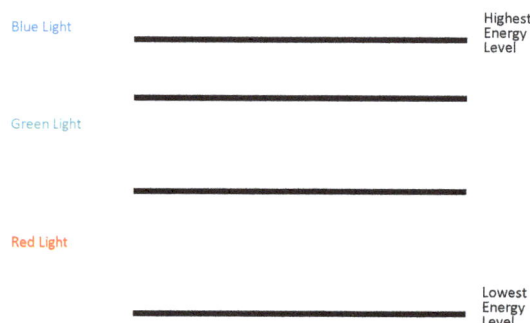

Practice Questions

1. Light from a sodium street lamp is found to have a frequency of 5.09×10^{14} Hz. Calculate the wavelength of this light in nanometres.

2. Data booklet information records that the flame colour of potassium is lilac and has a wavelength of 405 nm. Calculate the frequency of this radiation.

3. Use the data booklet to find the wavelength of light emitted by a sample of copper in a flame and thus calculate the energy of this light in $kJmol^{-1}$.

4. Explain how the red flame colour of strontium salts occurs.

5. The red line in the hydrogen spectrum has a wavelength of 656.3 nm. Calculate the energy value in $kJmol^{-1}$ for one mole of photons at this wavelength.

6. Which of the following lists electromagnetic radiation bands in order of increasing wavelength?

A   X-ray, infrared, ultraviolet, radio

B   Infrared, ultraviolet, X-ray, gamma

C   Ultraviolet, visible, infrared, radio

D   Radio, infrared, visible, gamma

7. Many old paints contained lead compounds. These can be analysed by emission spectroscopy.

a. Explain how a line in emission spectroscopy is produced.

b. Explain why there is a series of lines at discrete wavelengths in the emission spectrum of lead.

c. The lead emission spectrum has a line at 644 nm.

Calculate the energy, in kJ mol^{-1}, associated with this wavelength.

Unit 1 Atomic Orbitals

The lines observed in atomic emission spectra of elements can be explained if electrons display the properties of both waves and particles. Electrons are quantised, meaning they possess fixed amounts of energy. According to Heisenberg's Uncertainty Principle the exact position of an electron cannot be known but its believed they have >90% probability of being found in spaces called atomic orbitals and these spaces can have a variety of shapes from simple spheres to quite complex multilobed shapes. However no matter what the size or shape; an atomic orbital can only hold a maximum of 2 electrons.

Atomic Orbital Shapes:

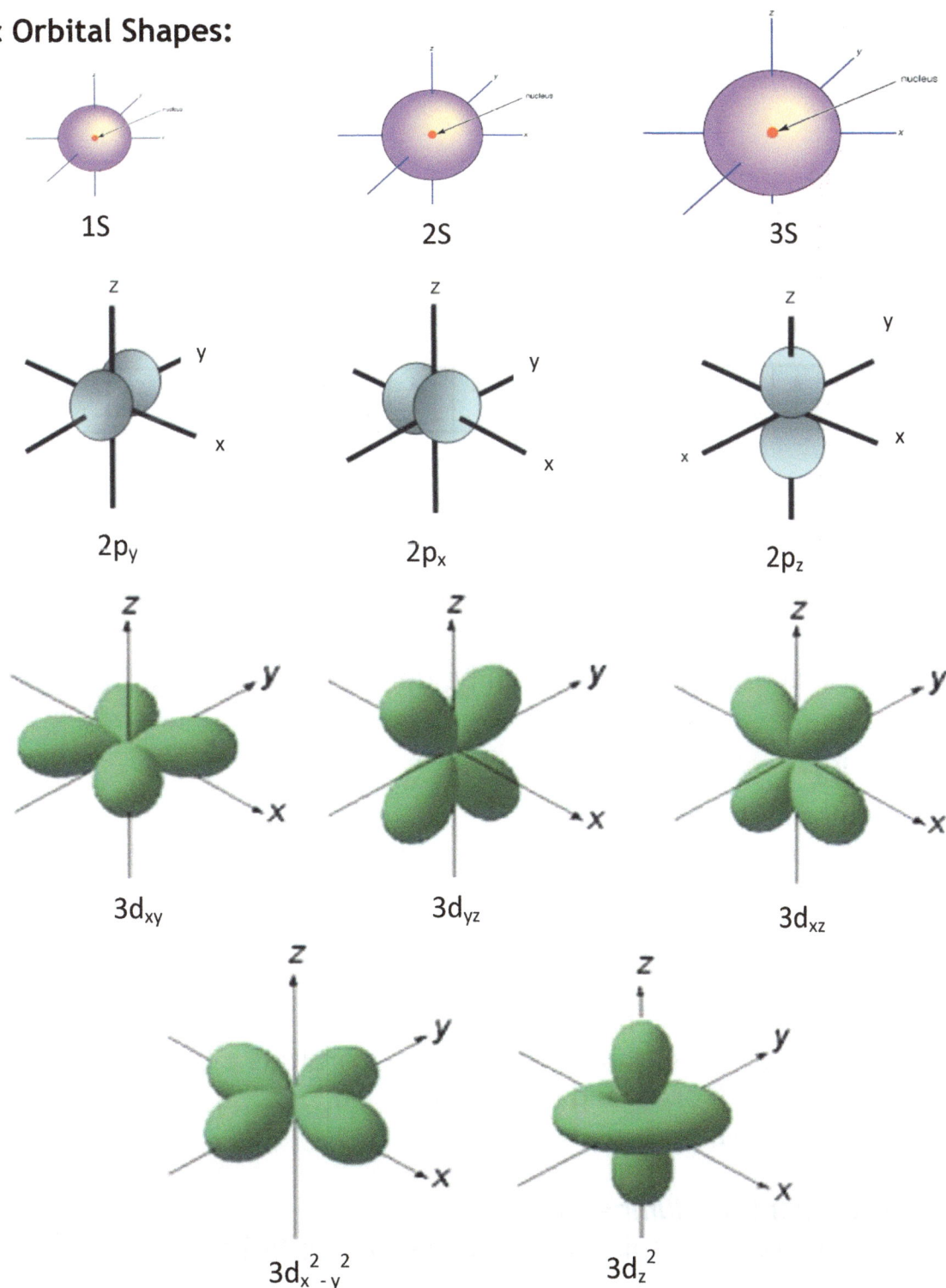

1S

2S

3S

$2p_y$

$2p_x$

$2p_z$

$3d_{xy}$

$3d_{yz}$

$3d_{xz}$

$3d_{x^2-y^2}$

$3d_{z^2}$

Previously electrons were described as being in energy levels, but its now been shown that these energy levels have sublevels e.g. s, p, d, f & g; the further from the nucleus the more sublevels an energy level has.

Electrons fill the atomic orbitals according to the Aufbau Principle where electrons fill sub-levels in order of increasing energy starting with sub-levels of lowest energy first, i.e 1s before 2s, before 2p, etc. Note that the 4s orbitals are filled before the 3d, except in the case of chromium and copper.

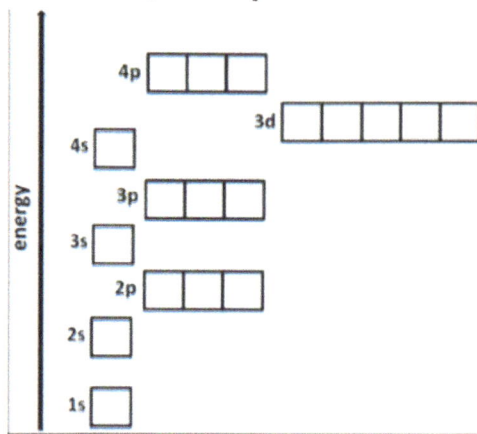

Hund's Rule of Maximum Multiplicity means that electrons fill all the orbitals in a particular sub-level singularly, spinning in the same direction before pairing up. It also states that ½ filled or completely filled sub-levels are more stable than partially filled sub-levels, e.g. chromium with atomic number 24.

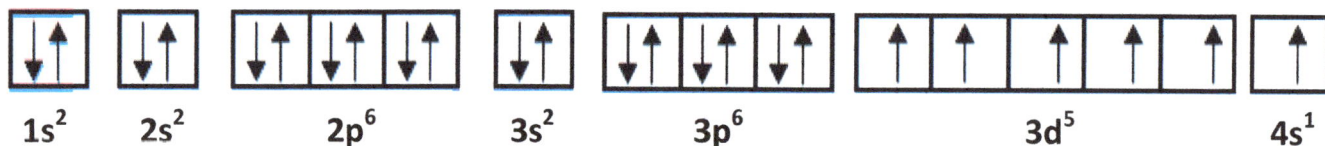

$1s^2$ $2s^2$ $2p^6$ $3s^2$ $3p^6$ $3d^5$ $4s^1$

Pauli's Exclusion Principle states that no two electrons can have exactly the same 4 quantum numbers which essentially means that the two electrons in a particular orbital must spin in opposite directions, see diagram above.

The position of electrons in an atom can be defined by a series of quantum numbers.

Quantum Numbers Definitions:

Principle Quantum Number, n
The energy level or period on the Periodic table either 1, 2, 3,4, 5, 6 or 7

Angular Momentum Quantum Number, l
The sub-level s, p or d; where s = 0, p = 1 and d = 2

Magnetic Quantum Number, m_l
The particular orbital within a sub-level; where s orbitals = 0, p orbitals (p_x, p_y or p_z) can be either -1, 0 or +1 and d orbitals (d_{xy}, d_{yz}, d_{xz}, d_{x2-y2} or d_{z2}) can be either -2, -1, 0, +1 or +2.

Spin Magnetic Quantum Number, m_s
The direction the electrons spins in the orbital can be either +½ or -½

Iron has an atomic number of 26, so therefore 26 electrons:

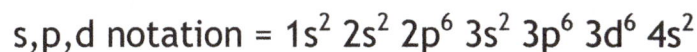

s,p,d notation = $1s^2\ 2s^2\ 2p^6\ 3s^2\ 3p^6\ 3d^6\ 4s^2$

Box notation = ↓↑ ↓↑ ↓↑ ↓↑ ↓↑ ↓↑ ↓↑ ↓↑ ↓↑ ↓↑ ↑ ↑ ↑ ↑ ↓↑

The table below gives the position of each electron and its four quantum numbers:

Electron	Orbital Position	Principle Quantum Number n	Angular momentum Quantum Number l	Magnetic Quantum Number m_l	Spin magnetic Quantum Number m_s
1	$1s^1$	1	0	0	+½
2	$1s^2$	1	0	0	-½
3	$2s^1$	2	0	0	+½
4	$2s^2$	2	0	0	-½
5	$2p^1$	2	1	-1	+½
6	$2p^2$	2	1	0	+½
7	$2p^3$	2	1	+1	+½
8	$2p^4$	2	1	-1	-½
9	$2p^5$	2	1	0	-½
10	$2p^6$	2	1	+1	-½
11	$3s^1$	3	0	0	+½
12	$3s^2$	3	0	0	-½
13	$3p^1$	3	1	-1	+½
14	$3p^2$	3	1	0	+½
15	$3p^3$	3	1	+1	+½
16	$3p^4$	3	1	-1	-½
17	$3p^5$	3	1	0	-½
18	$3p^6$	3	1	+1	-½
19	$4s^1$	4	0	0	+½
20	$4s^2$	4	0	0	-½
21	$3d^1$	3	2	-2	+½
22	$3d^2$	3	2	-1	+½
23	$3d^3$	3	2	0	+½
24	$3d^4$	3	2	+1	+½
25	$3d^5$	3	2	+2	+½
26	$3d^6$	3	2	-1	-½

For example the 26th electron found in a 3d orbital could have its position described by the following quantum numbers:

3, 2, -1, -½

Orbital Shapes

Connect the orbital box with the potential shape of the orbital. The first one has been done for you:

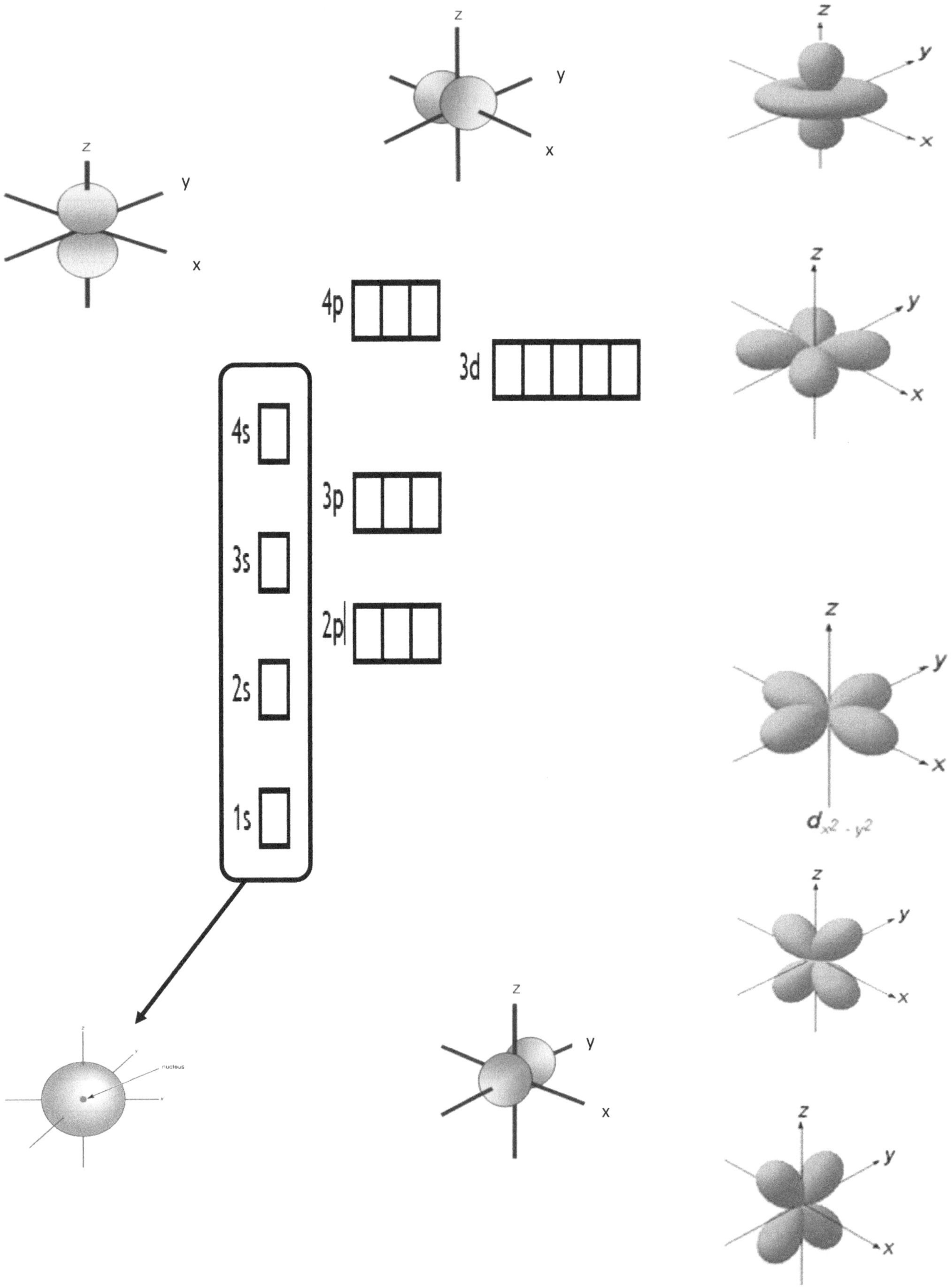

4p ▢▢▢

3d ▢▢▢▢▢

4s ▢

3p ▢▢▢

3s ▢

2p ▢▢▢

2s ▢

1s ▢

$d_{x^2 - y^2}$

Chemical Misconceptions

A student wrote the following into their notebook as a set of definitions for the quantum numbers:

- Principal, m_s -   This is the number that defines what sublevel the electron is in.

- Angular Momentum, n -   This is the number that tells you what direction the electron is spinning.

- Spin, m_l -   This is the number that tells you what specific orbital the electron is in.

- Magnetic, l -   This is the number that tells you what energy level the electron is in.

- Example Scandium has 21 electrons, its last electron has the following quantum numbers: 4, 0, -3, -½

Identify their mistakes and write the correct definitions in the space below:

- Principal,   -

- Angular Momentum,   -

- Spin,   -

- Magnetic,   -

- Example Scandium has 21 electrons, its last electron has the following quantum numbers :

Electronic Configuration

Match the element to its correct electronic configuration.

Li	
Ar	
S	
P	
Cu	
Na	
C	
Mn	
O	
Ca	

$1s^2 2s^2 2p^6 3s^2 3p^6 3d^{10} 4s^1$

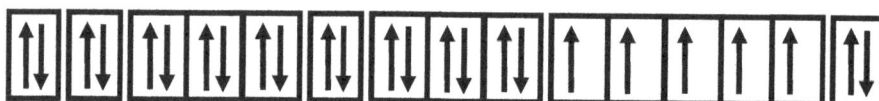

$1s^2 2s^2 2p^6 3s^1$

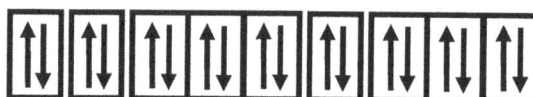

$1s^2 2s^2 2p^6 3s^2 3p^4$

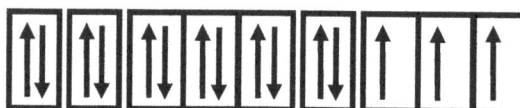

$1s^2 2s^2 2p^4$

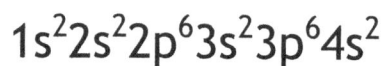

$1s^2 2s^2 2p^6 3s^2 3p^6 4s^2$

Hund's Rule of Maximum Multiplicity

Hund's rule plays an important role in explaining patterns in the Periodic Table and the electron arrangement of certain atoms and ions.

Match the correct explanation to the corresponding diagram.

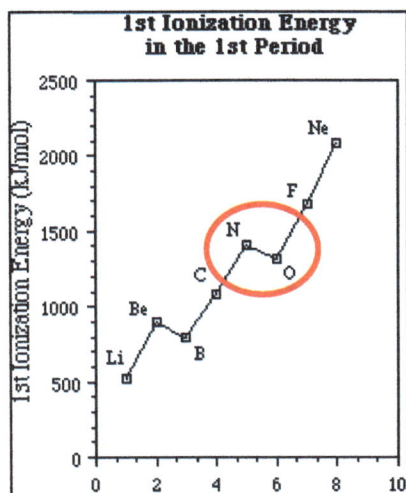

One of the 4s electrons is promoted to the 3d sublevel which is more stable than the expected partially filled 3d and the completely filled 4s.

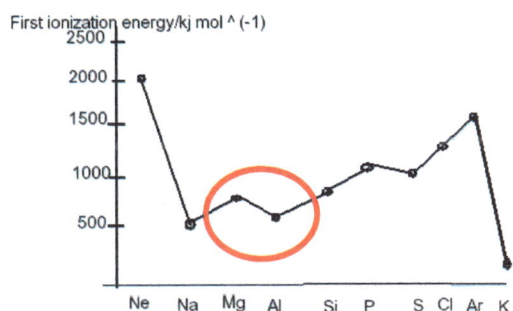

Removing an electron from a partially filled sublevel takes less energy than taking it from a half filled sublevel.

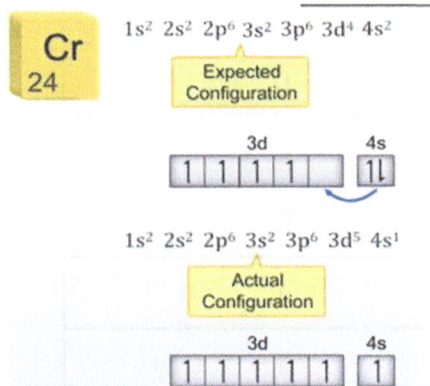

Cr
24

$1s^2\ 2s^2\ 2p^6\ 3s^2\ 3p^6\ 3d^4\ 4s^2$

Expected Configuration

3d   4s

$1s^2\ 2s^2\ 2p^6\ 3s^2\ 3p^6\ 3d^5\ 4s^1$

Actual Configuration

3d   4s

Due to the promotion of a 4s electron to completely fill the d sublevel, the atom is able to form a 1+ ion.

Cu₂O

Removing an electron from a completely filled sublevel takes more energy that taking it from a partially filled sublevel.

Practice Questions

1. Transition metals, such as vanadium and copper, can have variable oxidation states and a wide range of uses.

(a) Write the electronic configuration of copper atoms in terms of s, p, and d notation.

(b) Complete the table giving the 4 quantum numbers for the 23rd electron in a vanadium atom.

Principle Q N^0 n	Angular Momentum Q N^0 l	Magnetic Q N^0 m_l	Spin Q N^0 m_s

(c) Vanadium dioxide, VO_2, can be used to coat glass. Using orbital box notation, write the electronic configuration for the **vanadium ion** in VO_2.

2. In the periodic table, period 2 is comprised of the elements lithium to neon.

The following table shows two of the quantum numbers for all 7 electrons in a nitrogen atom.

Electron	Principle Q N^0 n	Angular Momentum Q N^0 l
1	1	0
2	1	0
3	2	0
4	2	0
5	2	1
6	2	1
7	2	1

(a) The angular momentum quantum number, l, is related to the shape of an orbital. Draw the shape of an orbital when l has a value of 1.

(b) The magnetic quantum number, l_m, is related to the orientation of an orbital in space.

State the values of l_m for the orbital which contains the seventh electron.

(c) The trend in 1st ionisation energy is that it increases as you go across the Periodic Table. Explain why the 1st ionisation energy of nitrogen is higher than that of oxygen even though oxygen is positioned further to the right.

3. A representation of a d-orbital is shown:

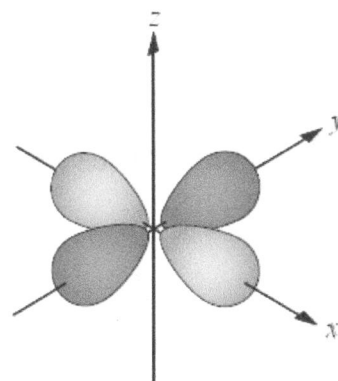

(a) What is the maximum number of electrons this orbital can hold?

(b) Suggest the angular momentum and magnetic quantum numbers for an electron in this particular orbital.

4. Aluminium has the following electronic configuration.

$$1s^2\ 2s^2\ 2p^6\ 3s^2\ 3p^1$$

(a) This electronic configuration is consistent with the Aufbau principle.

State the Aufbau principle.

(b) For the 3p electron in aluminium, complete the table to show one possible set of values for the four quantum numbers.

Quantum Number	n	l	m_l	m_s
Value				

Unit 1   Shapes of Molecules

The shapes of molecules and polyatomic ions are determined by the repulsion of electron pairs. Lewis electron dot diagrams can be used to show the valence electrons.

$$H:\ddot{\underset{..}{Cl}}: \qquad \text{or} \qquad H-\ddot{\underset{..}{Cl}}:$$

Valence Shell Electron Pair Repulsion theory, VSEPR, is used to work out the number of electron pairs and hence the shape.

1. Count number of electrons in outer shell of central atom.

2. Add 1 for every negative charge and minus 1 for every positive charge.

3. Count number of atoms bonded to central atom and add to total.

4. Divide total by 2 to get number of electron pairs.

The following table gives the names and shapes corresponding to the number of electron pairs:

Example: NH_4^+

1. N = 5 outer electrons

2. +1 = -1

3. 4 x H = 4

4. 8 $\div$ 2 = 4

Shape = tetrahedral

Example: PCl_5

1. P = 5 outer electrons

2. no charge = 0

3. 5   x Cl = 5

4. 10 $\div$ 2 = 5

Shape = trigonal bipyramidal

Lone pairs of electrons can cause the bond angles to be smaller than expected.

NOTE: Read questions carefully, sometimes they ask for the shape of the **electron pairs**; other times they ask for the shape of the **molecule.** This is especially the case where there are 4 electron pairs but one or two are a lone pair.

Electron groups	Bonding electron groups	Lone pairs	Electron group geometry	Molecular geometry
2	2	0	Linear	Linear 180°
3	3	0	Trigonal planar	Trigonal planar 120°
4	4	0	Tetrahedral	Tetrahedral 109.5°
4	3	1	Tetrahedral	Trigonal pyramidal 107°
4	2	2	Tetrahedral	Angular 104.5°
5	5	0	Trigonal bipyramidal	Trigonal bipyramidal 120° 90°
6	6	0	Octahedral	Octahedral 90° 90°

Shape of Molecules

Match the shape of the molecule to the name of that shape:

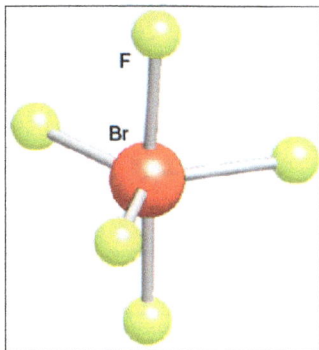

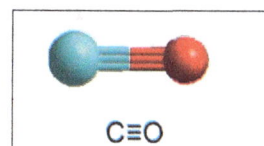

linear

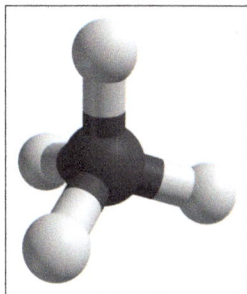

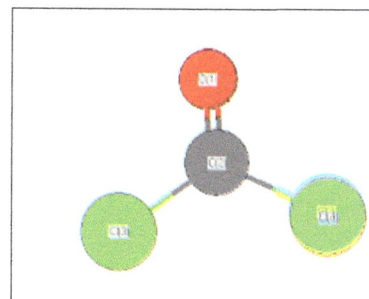

trigonal planar

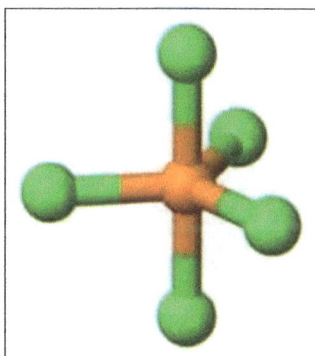

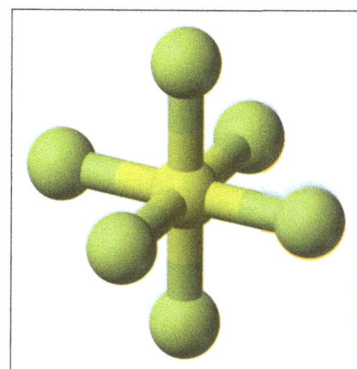

tetrahedral

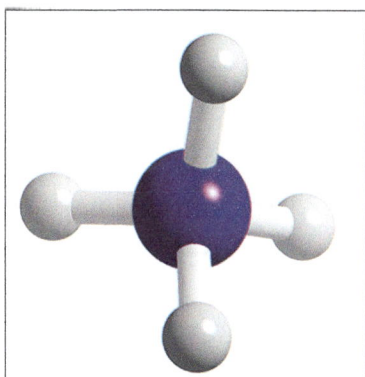

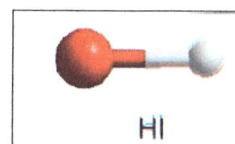

trigonal bipyramidal

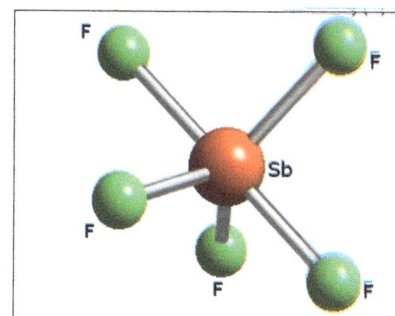

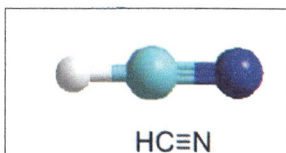

octahedral

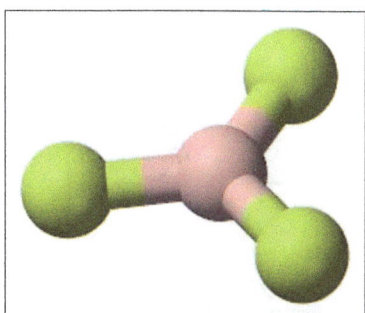

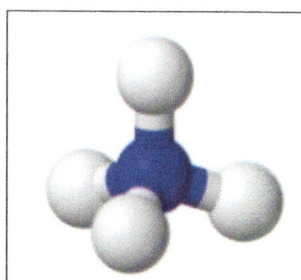

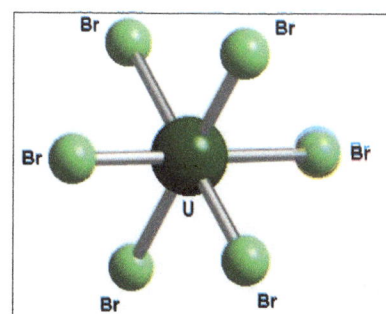

VSEPR

Use VSEPR to identify the number of electron pairs and then match the shape of the molecule to the structure shown:

NH_4^+

$BeCl_2$

SF_6

$SiCl_4$

PH_3

$AsBr_5$

BF_4^-

H_3O^+

BI_3

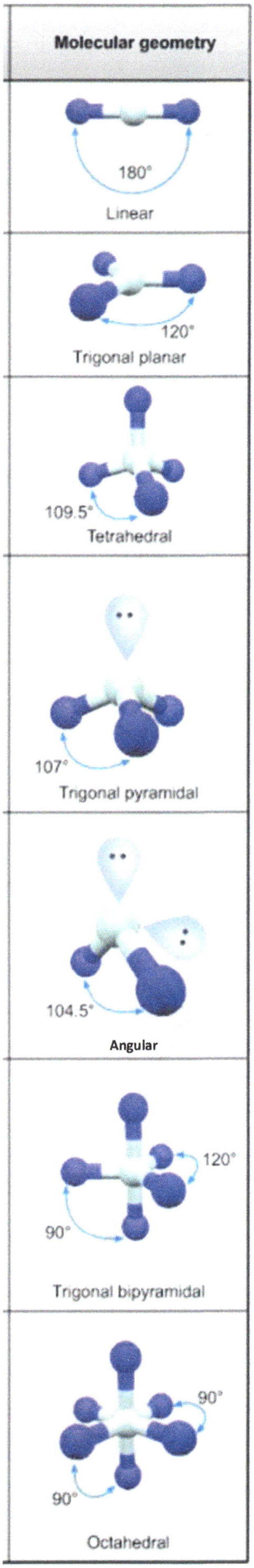

Molecular geometry
180° Linear
120° Trigonal planar
109.5° Tetrahedral
107° Trigonal pyramidal
104.5° Angular
120° 90° Trigonal bipyramidal
90° 90° Octahedral

Quiz Word

Answer the following questions to complete the quiz word and then try to work out what the key phrase in the **bold** boxes should be.

1. Flat shape with three bonds. (8, 6)
2. Number of electron pairs with a linear shape. (3)
3. Common shape adopted by electron pairs in silicon compounds. (11)
4. These electrons cause the bond angle for tetrahedral shapes to be smaller than expected. (4, 5)
5. Acronym given to the theory explaining molecular shapes. (5)

Quiz Word Clue: Shape formed by 6 electron pairs.

Chemical Misconceptions

A student wrote the following into their notebook as a set of notes on the shapes of molecules and polyatomic ions, however they got some of their shapes and examples wrong. Replace the shapes with the correct ones and the examples given with new ones not given on the page:

- Linear shapes - When there are two or three atoms with one or two electron pairs.

  Example BF_3

- Trigonal planar shape - When there are four atoms with three electron pairs.

  Example BCl_3

- Tetrahedral shapes - When there are three to five atoms with four electron pairs. Lone pairs of electrons can make the bond angle smaller than expected.

  Example $BeCl_2$, PH_3, NH_3^+ or CH_4

- Trigonal bipyramidal shapes - When there are six atoms with five electron pairs.
  Example PCl_5

- Octahedral shape - When there are seven atoms with six electron pairs.

  Example ICl_5

Practice Questions

1. For the reaction shown below:

    BF_3 + F^- → BF_4^-

    Complete the following table:

Molecule or polyatomic ion	BF_3	BF_4^-
Name of shape	Trigonal planar	
Shape		

2. Two phosphorus chloride compounds exist. They are phosphorus trichloride and phosphorus pentachloride.

    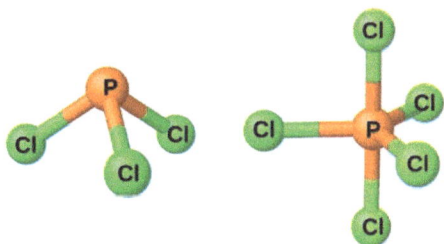

a. Name the shape adopted by both the phosphorus trichloride and phosphorus pentachloride molecules.

    phosphorus trichloride

    phosphorus pentachloride

b. Using VSEPR theory explain why phosphorous trichloride is not trigonal planar even though there are only three atoms bonded to the central phosphorous atom.

3. Phosgene is the chemical in Mustard Gas that killed and injured thousands in World War I.

Phosgene has the chemical formula $COCl_2$. VSEPR theory breaks down when trying to work out the number of electron pairs, but it has a similar shape to BCl_3.

a. Draw a structural formula for phosgene and work out the name of the shape the molecule takes.

b. Suggest a reason why the bond angle between the two chlorines in phosgene is smaller than the bond angles between the chlorines in BCl_3.

Unit 1   Transition Metals

Transition metals are defined as having a partially filled d sublevel as either atoms or ions. Technically zinc shouldn't be classed as a transition metal as it has a complete d sublevel as both an atom and ion.

Element	Atomic No	Electron Arrangement					
		'other' electrons	3d electrons				
Sc	21	(20) [Ar] $4s^2$	↑				
Ti	22	(20) [Ar] $4s^2$	↑	↑			
V	23	(20) [Ar] $4s^2$	↑	↑	↑		
Cr	24	(19) [Ar] $4s^1$	↑	↑	↑	↑	↑
Mn	25	(20) [Ar] $4s^2$	↑	↑	↑	↑	↑
Fe	26	(20) [Ar] $4s^2$	↑↓	↑	↑	↑	↑
Co	27	(20) [Ar] $4s^2$	↑↓	↑↓	↑	↑	↑
Ni	28	(20) [Ar] $4s^2$	↑↓	↑↓	↑↓	↑	↑
Cu	29	(19) [Ar] $4s^1$	↑↓	↑↓	↑↓	↑↓	↑↓
Zn	30	(20) [Ar] $4s^2$	↑↓	↑↓	↑↓	↑↓	↑↓

Transition metals exhibit variable oxidation states because they not only lose their $4s$ electrons but some or all of their $3d$ electrons as well.

The table below shows some of the more common oxidation states of the transition metals.

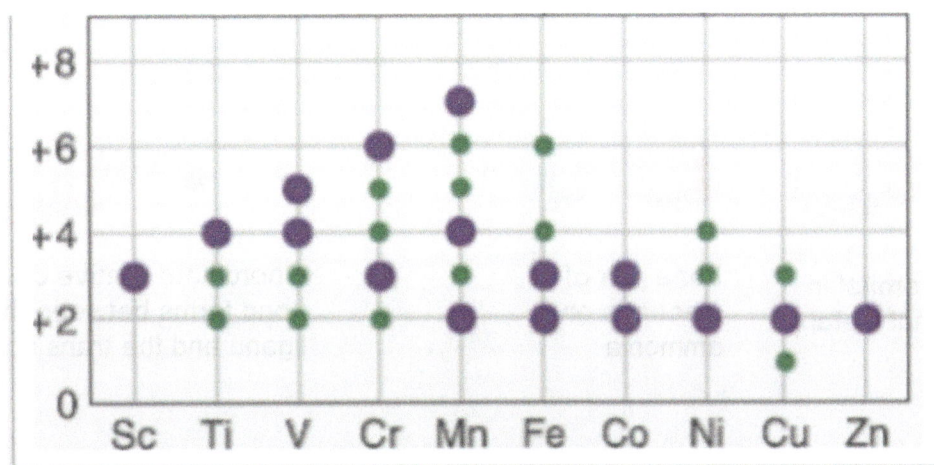

Manganese has the most oxidation states:

Oxidation Number	Transition metal Ion	Colour
+7	MnO_4^-	Purple
+6	MnO_4^{2-}	Green
+5	MnO_4^{3-}	Blue
+4	MnO_2	Brown
+3	Mn^{3+}	Violet
+2	Mn^{2+}	Pink

Working out oxidation numbers in ions with more than one element:
Non-metals always have their usual negative charge i.e. O^{2-}, Cl^- etc. Add up the total amount of negative charges. The oxidation number is the number of positive charges the metal needs to give the overall ion its correct overall charge.

E.g. MnO_4^{2-}
Total negative charge from O = -8, overall charge on ion = -2
So Mn must have a +6 oxidation number sometimes written as manganese(VI)

Transition Metal Complexes
Due to the vacant or partially vacant d-orbitals transition metal atoms and ions can form coordinate (dative covalent) bonds with ions and molecules that have a lone pair of electrons.

These molecules or ions are called **LIGANDS** and anything from 2 to 6 can bind to the central transition metal, forming what is known as a **COMPLEX**.

Often the resulting complex has an overall charge and is therefore called a **COMPLEX ION.**

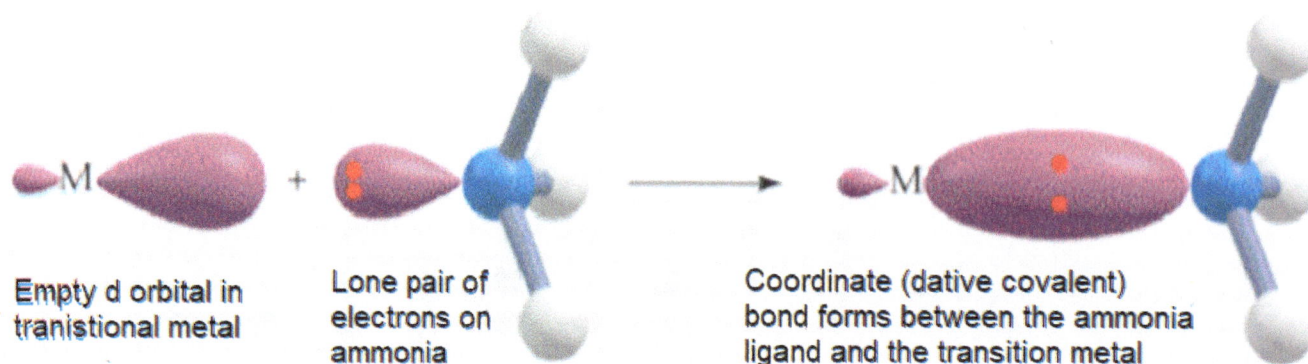

Empty d orbital in tranistional metal

Lone pair of electrons on ammonia

Coordinate (dative covalent) bond forms between the ammonia ligand and the transition metal

If the ligand has 1 lone pair it is called a monodentate ligand, 2 lone pairs are bidentate and 6 are called hexadentate ligands.

Ligand	Type	Prefix in name of complex
H_2O	Monodentate	aqua
NH_3	Monodentate	ammine
Cl^-	Monodentate	chlorido
CN^-	Monodentate	cyanido
$NH_2CH_2CH_2NH_2$	Bidentate	1,2-diaminoethane
EDTA	Hexadentate	EDTA

Naming Transition Metal Complexes:

Decide whether you are naming the whole complex or just the complex ion.
If it's the whole complex, remember the positive ion comes before the negative ion in the name, like sodium chloride Na^+Cl^-
The complex ion is always in a [ ] the other ion can be before it if its positive or after it if its negative.
The other ion will help you to work out the charge on the complex ion if it's not given.
e.g
$[Fe(NH_3)_2(OH_2)_4]Cl_3$ = diamminetetraaquairon(III) chloride

$[CuCl_4]^{2-}$ = tetrachloridocuprate(II)

Step 1 – The number and type of ligands are given first. If there is more than one type of ligand they go in alphabetical order e.g. diamminetetraaqua = 2x NH_3 and 4x H_2O in the first example. **In their formulae the ligand's binding atom is written first and the order is then based on this atom alphabetically, i.e. ammine comes before chloride in the name but Cl comes before NH_3 in the formula. Aqua is written (OH_2).**

Step 2 – Name the metal, if the complex ion is positive just use the normal name, if the complex ion is negative use the Latinised name and end in -ate e.g. cuprate in the second example as the complex ion is negatively charged.

Step 3 – Work out the oxidation number of the transition metal by looking at the overall charge on the ion and looking at whether the ligands are charged or neutral molecules. Iron(III) in the first example as NH_3 and H_2O molecules are neutral and yet you have 3 Cl^- ions joined to the complex ion.

Worked Example:
$K_3[Fe(CN)_6]$ = potassium hexacyanidoferrate(III)

$[Cr(Cl)_2(NH_3)_4]Cl$ = tetraamminedichloridochromium(III) chloride

$[Mn(CN)_2(OH_2)_4]Cl_2$ = tetraaquadicyanidomanganese(IV) chloride

Shapes of Complexes

The shape of the complex depends upon the number of coordinate bonds formed with the ligands. The bonding electron pairs will repel each other and take up a position so they are as far away from each other as possible.

The shapes are therefore similar to the molecules you saw in an earlier section.

The **number of coordinate bonds** is called the **coordination number**. Monodentate ligands can only form one coordinate bond, bidentate ligands can form 2 and hexadentate ligands can form 6.

Coordination Number	Shape	Example
2	linear	diammine silver(I)
4	square Planar	tetracyanidonickelate(II)
5	trigonal bipyramidal	pentacarbonyliron(II)
6	octahedral	hexacyanidoferrate(III)

Colour in Transition Metal Complexes

A white object will reflect all colours of the visible spectrum and therefore appear white.

A black object absorbs all colours of the visible spectrum and therefore appear black.

A coloured object absorbs some colours of the visible spectrum and therefore appears as the opposite colour on a colour wheel.

e.g. a blue object absorbs yellow light.

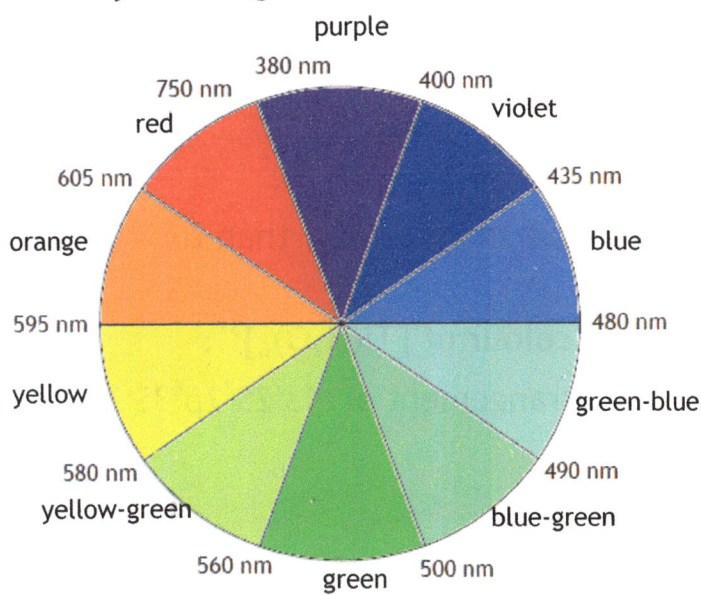

Transition metal complexes produce colour because of the interaction of ligands (L) with the d-orbitals (shown in blue).

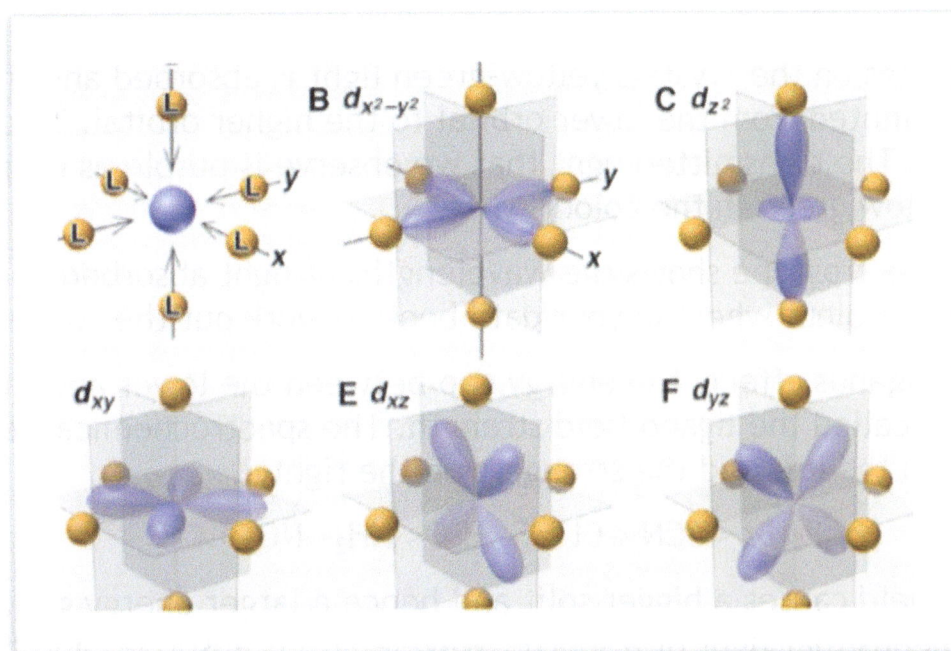

The ligands affect the $d_{x^2-y^2}$ and d_{z^2} orbitals making them less stable and therefore more energetic. This causes **d orbital splitting**.

Splitting of d-orbital energies by an octahedral field of ligands.

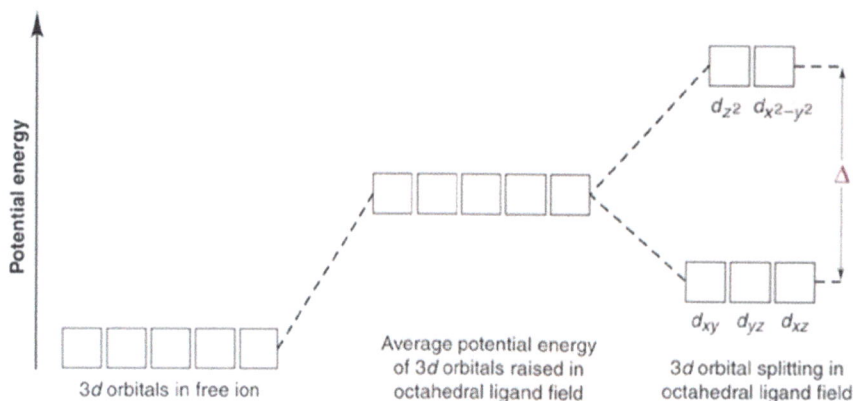

3d orbitals in free ion	Average potential energy of 3d orbitals raised in octahedral ligand field	3d orbital splitting in octahedral ligand field

The two higher d-orbitals have more energy than the three lower d-orbitals given by symbol Δ.

Explanation of the purple colour of $[Ti(H_2O)_6]^{3+}$:

Ti^{3+} ions have an electron arrangement of $1s^2 2s^2 2p^6 3s^2 3p^6 3d^1 4s^0$

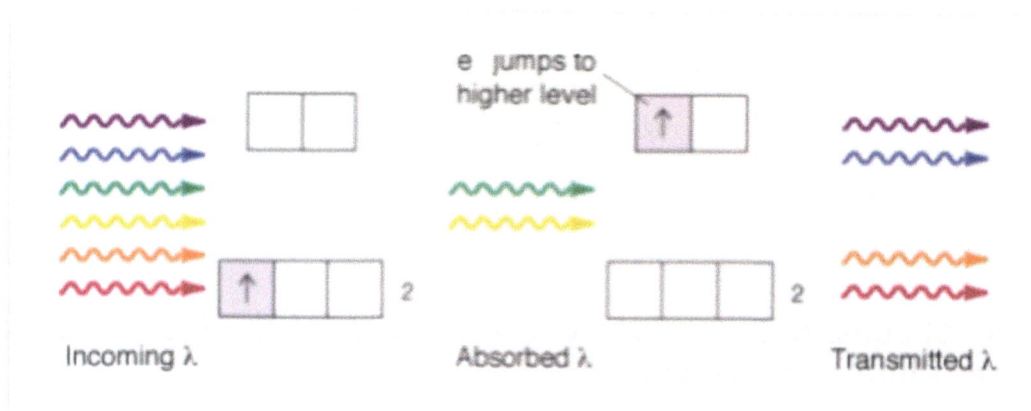

Incoming λ	Absorbed λ	Transmitted λ

When light shines on the crystals yellow-green light is absorbed and the 3d electron is promoted from the lower orbital to the higher orbital. This is called a **d-d transition**. The transmitted light that we observe is purple as purple (violet) is opposite yellow green in the colour wheel.

A UV-Visible spectroscope shows the wavelengths of light absorbed and from this you can use the colour wheel in your data book to work out the colour seen.

Changing the ligands affects the energy gap between the lower and the higher orbitals and is called the ligand field strength. The spectrochemical series shows the weakest on the left and the strongest on the right:

$$I^- < Br^- < SCN^- < Cl^- < F^- < H_2O < NH_3 < NO_2^- < CN^-$$

The stronger field causes a bigger split and hence a larger energy gap. A bigger energy gap means that light of a shorter wavelength is absorbed and the colours seen move closer to the red end of the visible spectrum.

Electron arrangement

Match the transition metal atoms or ions to the correct electron arrangement, using either spd or box notation.

manganese
$$1s^2\ 2s^2\ 2p^6\ 3s^2\ 3p^6\ 3d^2\ 4s^2$$

cobalt(II)
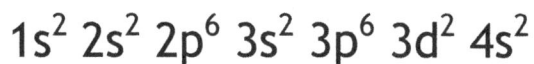

Cr^{3+}
$$1s^2\ 2s^2\ 2p^6\ 3s^2\ 3p^6\ 3d^3\ 4s^2$$

titanium

iron(III)
$$1s^2\ 2s^2\ 2p^6\ 3s^2\ 3p^6\ 3d^2$$

V
$$1s^2\ 2s^2\ 2p^6\ 3s^2\ 3p^6\ 3d^7$$

Sc

Ni^{2+}
$$1s^2\ 2s^2\ 2p^6\ 3s^2\ 3p^6\ 3d^3$$

manganese(III)

Ti^{2+}
$$1s^2\ 2s^2\ 2p^6\ 3s^2\ 3p^6\ 3d^{10}$$

copper
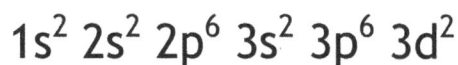

Fe^{2+}
$$1s^2\ 2s^2\ 2p^6\ 3s^2\ 3p^6\ 3d^8$$

zinc
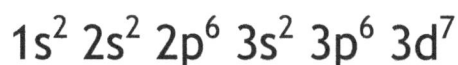

nickel
$$1s^2\ 2s^2\ 2p^6\ 3s^2\ 3p^6\ 3d^1\ 4s^2$$

Cu$^+$

Oxidation Numbers

Match the transition metal complex to the correct oxidation number of the metal.

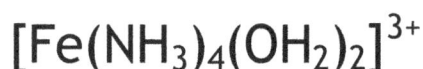

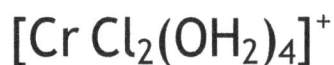

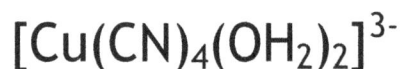

$[Ni(OH_2)_6]^{2+}$ +1

$[Co(CN)_6]^{4-}$

                                                           +2

$[Fe(NH_3)_4(OH_2)_2]^{3+}$

$[Co(OH_2)_6]^{3+}$ +3

VO_2

                                                           +4

$[Cr\,Cl_2(OH_2)_4]^+$

$[MnO_4]^-$ +5

$[Cr_2O_7]^{2-}$

                                                           +6

$[Cu(CN)_4(OH_2)_2]^{3-}$

$[Cr(Cl)_6]^{2-}$ +7

Quiz Word

Answer the following questions to complete the quiz word and then try to work out what the key phrase in the **bold** boxes should be.

1. All ligands contain these type of electrons. (4, 4)
2. Transition metals and ligands form these type of ions. (7)
3. Name given to the ammonia ligand. (6)
4. Useful hexadentate ligand used in complexometric titrations. (4)
5. The number used to help name the shape of a transition metal complex. (12)
6. Ligands interfering with the dz^2 and dx^2-y^2 orbitals causes this. (1-9)

Quiz Word Clue Shape formed with a coordination number of 6.

Colour

Match the colour of the transition metal complex ion to the correct light being absorbed by the complex ion and its energy, use p20 of your data booklet to help. The first one has been done for you.

Complex ion	Wavelength absorbed	Energy
$[Cu(OH_2)_6]^{2+}$ 450nm	390nm	247 kJmol^{-1}
$[Cr_2O_7]^{2-}$ 600nm	450nm	242 kJmol^{-1}
$[Ni(OH_2)_6]^{2+}$ 550nm	495nm	210 kJmol^{-1}
$[Fe(CN)_6]^{4-}$ 570nm	585nm	266 kJmol^{-1}
$[CrO_4]^{2-}$ 585nm	550nm	307 kJmol^{-1}
$[Cu_2(OH_2)]^{2+}$ 650nm	485nm	205 kJmol^{-1}
$[Cu(NH_3)_2(OH_2)_4]^{2+}$ 420nm	420nm	184 kJmol^{-1}
$[MnO_4]^{-}$ 390nm	650nm	218 kJmol^{-1}
$[Ni(NH_3)_2(OH_2)_4]^{2+}$ 495nm	570nm	285 kJmol^{-1}

The first worked example connects $[CrO_4]^{2-}$ (585nm) to the 585nm box and then to 205 kJmol^{-1}.

Transition Metal Complex Names

Match the correct name of the transition metal complex using both the positive ion and negative ion names given. The first one has been done for you.

$K_3[Cr(Cl)_6]$	tetraamine diaqua iron(II)	bromide
$Na_2[Cu(CN)_4]$	tetraamine dichlorido titanium(III)	chloride
$[Fe(NH_3)_4(OH_2)_2]Br_2$	potassium	hexachlorido chromate(IV)
$Mg_2[Ti(OH)_6]$	tetraamine diaqua iron(III)	chloride
$K_2[Cr(Cl)_6]$	tetraamine dichlorido titanium(IV)	bromide
$[Ti(Cl)_2(NH_3)_4]Cl$	magnesium	hexahydroxido titanate(II)
$[Fe(NH_3)_4(OH_2)_2]Br_3$	potassium	hexachlorido chromate(III)
$[Ti(Cl)_2(NH_3)_4]Cl_2$	sodium	tetracyanido cuprate(II)
$[Fe(NH_3)_2(OH_2)_4]Br_3$	diamine tetraaqua iron(III)	bromide

Ligand Type & Coordination Number

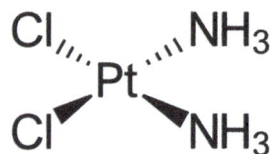

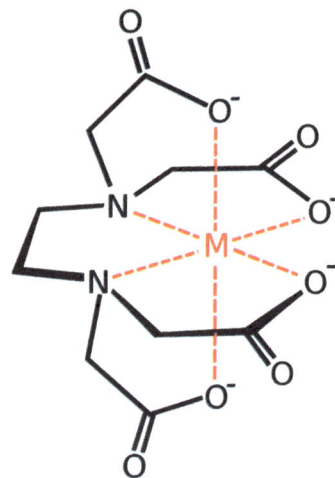

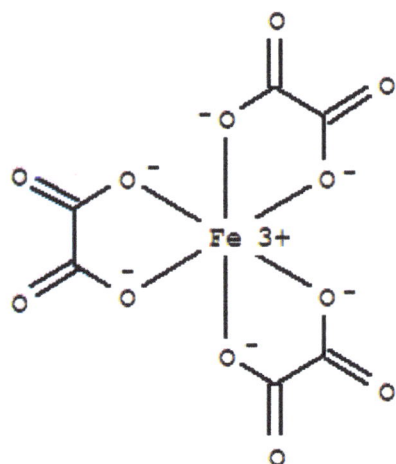

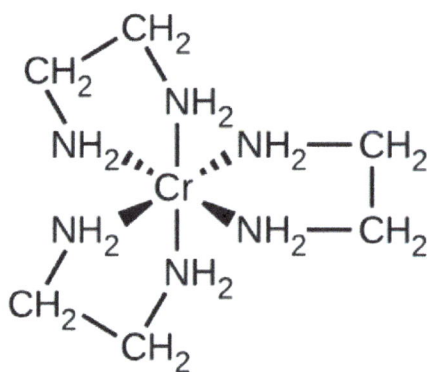

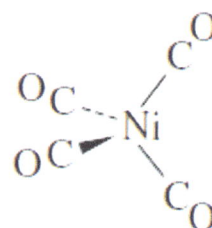

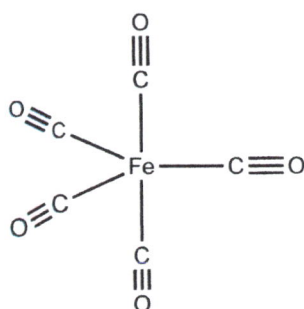

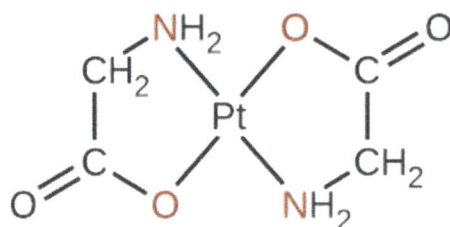

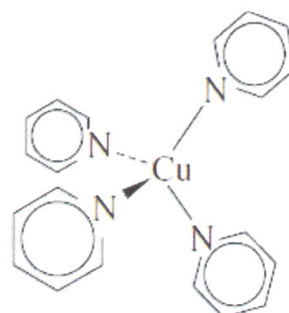

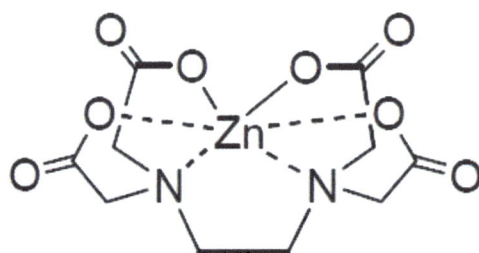

Identify the ligand type and coordination number for each of the complexes.

The first one has been done for you:

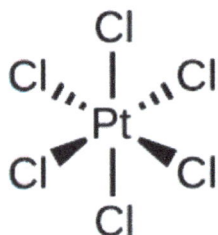

Monodentate ligand

Coordination N° = 6

Wordsearch

Complete the wordsearch below using the clues given to identify the correct words(s) that can be found in the wordsearch.

```
C F N H E X A D E N T A T E N
O F O B X H T A C L X C B O D
M D I E S U U U O A S D I P H
P K T G N Q A N A T W T K J F
L G I M A I E G F Y A N L S H
E B S F O P M J R N F X F P F
X B N R A N T M I R E B M U N
I K A I W E O D A Q U W D H K
O M R S Z U R D A K K I N F P
N N T Z V O L E E T G D A Q Y
H K D X O E P Q U N A A G T S
U G D C V J L W N Z T Z I N F
I V H V U U P P Q W X A L J P
P C T S Q X Y N K O O D T E T
W A I V Z V Y J Q H J S C E V
```

1. When electrons undergo this in metal complexes a wavelength of light is absorbed and the complementary colour is seen. (1-1,10)

2. Many ligands contain one of these types of electrons. (4,4)

3. Tells you how many coordinate bonds there are in the complex. (12,6)

4. $[Ni(OH_2)_6]^{2+}$ and $[Cu(CN)4]^{2-}$ are examples of this. (7,3)

5. The name of the water ligand. (4)

6. A ligand able to bind to a metal ion in 6 places. (11)

7. Name of the NH_3 ligand. (6)

8. H_2O, NH_3, Cl^-, CN^- and OH^- are examples of this. (11,6)

Practice Questions

1. Titanium (IV) chloride dissolves in concentrated hydrochloric acid to give the ion $[TiCl_6]^{2-}$.

a) What is the cordination number of the titanium ion ?

b) What is the oxidation number of the titanium ion ?

c) Suggest a name for the $[TiCl_6]^{2-}$ ion.

d) Draw the square planar structure for this ion.

2. Consider the following reactions.

$[Co(OH_2)_6]^{2+}$ $\xrightarrow{\quad NH_3 \quad}$ $[Co(NH_3)_4(OH_2)_2]^{2+}$

$\downarrow$ NaCN

$Na_4[Co(CN)_6]$ $\xrightarrow{\quad Cl_2 \quad}$ $Na_3[Co(CN)_6]$

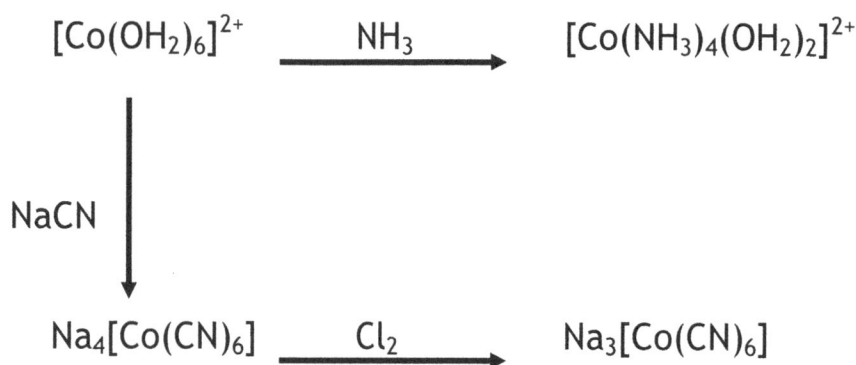

a) Write the electronic configuration of the cobalt (II) ion in terms of s, p and d orbitals.

b) Name the $[Co(NH_3)_4(OH_2)_2]^{2+}$ ion.

c) What is the function of the chlorine in the following reaction:

$Na_4[Co(CN)_6]$ $\xrightarrow{\quad Cl_2 \quad}$ $Na_3[Co(CN)_6]$

d) There is a colour change when NH_3 is added to the $[Co(OH_2)_6]^{2+}$. Why does this change in ligand result in a different wavelength of light being absorbed?

e) The complex ion $[Co(OH_2)_6]^{2+}$ absorbs at 560nm. Calculate the energy in $kJmol^{-1}$ corresponding to this absorption.

Unit 2   Equilibrium

An equilibrium occurs when you have a reversible reaction and the following.

rate of the forward reaction = rate of the reverse reaction

The concentration of reactants and products remains constant.

Equilibrium Law:

For a reaction

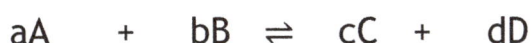

$$aA \quad + \quad bB \rightleftharpoons \quad cC \quad + \quad dD$$

$$K = \frac{[C]^c[D]^d}{[A]^a[B]^b} \qquad \text{where [ ] = concentration at equilibrium}$$

The value of K tells you whether the equilibrium lies towards the reactants or products side.

If K >1 equilibrium lies to the right and favours the products

If K <1 equilibrium lies to the left and favours the reactants

In the following reaction the concentrations of the substances were found to be $N_2 = 1.5$, $H_2 = 3.0$ and $NH_3 = 0.3$

e.g. for $N_2 + 3H_2 \rightleftharpoons 2NH_3$

$$K = \frac{[NH_3]^2}{[N_2][H_2]^3}$$

$$K = \frac{(0.3)^2}{(1.5)(3.0)^3}$$

$$K = 0.0022$$

The equilibrium therefore lies to the left and favours the reactant side

Calculating equilibrium concentrations:

When **2.00** moles of hydrogen gas and **1.00** mole of iodine gas are mixed together in a flask and left to reach equilibrium at 490°C.

It is found that at equilibrium, **1.86** moles of hydrogen iodide gas is present.

Calculate the equilibrium constant, K for the reaction at 490°C, using **RICE**.

	$H_2(g)$	+	$I_2(g) \rightleftharpoons$	$2HI(g)$
Ratio	1	:	1 :	2
Initial	2moles		1moles	0
Change	-0.93		-0.93	+1.86
Eqm	1.07moles		0.07moles	1.86moles

> If 1.86 moles of HI was made, then half that, 0.93 must have been used up of the H_2 and I_2 according to the balanced chemical equation.

$$K = \frac{[HI]^2}{[H_2][I_2]}$$

$$= \frac{(1.86)^2}{1.07 \times 0.07}$$

$$= \underline{46.2}$$

Equilibrium lies to the right and favours the product side.

Le Chatellier's Principle

When a system is at equilibrium making a change causes the equilibrium to shift to counteract that change.

Effects on equilibrium constant K.

Changing the concentration or pressure has no effect on K.
Changing the temperature changes the value of K.
If the temperature change favours the forward reaction the value of K goes up.
If the temperature change favours the reverse reaction the value of K goes down.

Influence	Equilibrium position	Rate at which equilibrium position is achieved	Equilibrium constant
change in concentration	changes	changes	no change
change in pressure	changes	changes	no change
change in temperature	changes	changes	changes
Use of a catalyst	no change	changes	no change

Acids and Bases

Bronsted-Lowry definition:

Acid = anything that can donate a proton (H^+)

Base = anything that can accept a proton (H^+)

General Equations:

Acids

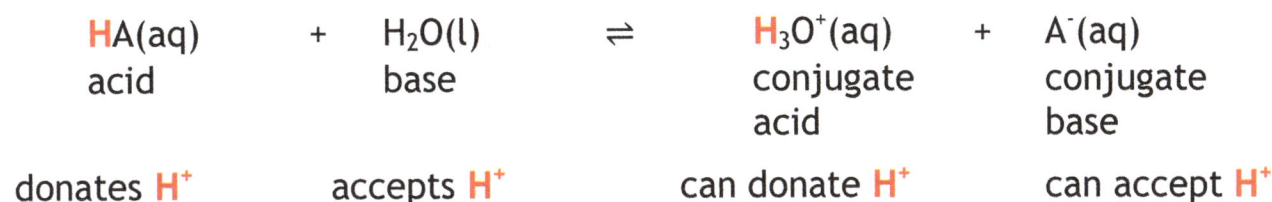

$HA(aq)$	+	$H_2O(l)$	$\rightleftharpoons$	$H_3O^+(aq)$	+	$A^-(aq)$
acid		base		conjugate acid		conjugate base
donates H^+		accepts H^+		can donate H^+		can accept H^+

Bases

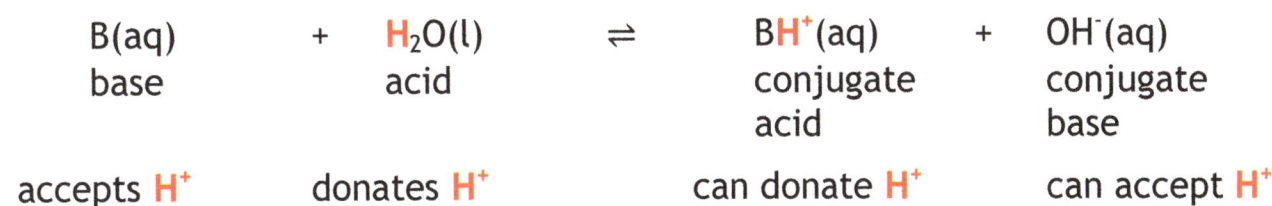

$B(aq)$	+	$H_2O(l)$	$\rightleftharpoons$	$BH^+(aq)$	+	$OH^-(aq)$
base		acid		conjugate acid		conjugate base
accepts H^+		donates H^+		can donate H^+		can accept H^+

The H_3O^+ ion is called the hydronium ion; it is often simplified to $H^+(aq)$ you must be able to recognise it and use it when appropriate. A proton in water will always form a dative covalent bond with the lone pair of electrons on the oxygen atom in a water molecule.

Examples:

Ethanoic acid

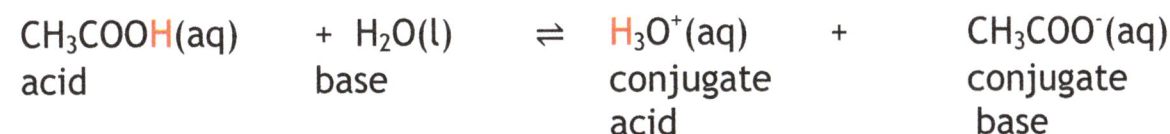

$CH_3COOH(aq)$	+ $H_2O(l)$	$\rightleftharpoons$ $H_3O^+(aq)$	+	$CH_3COO^-(aq)$
acid	base	conjugate acid		conjugate base

Ammonia

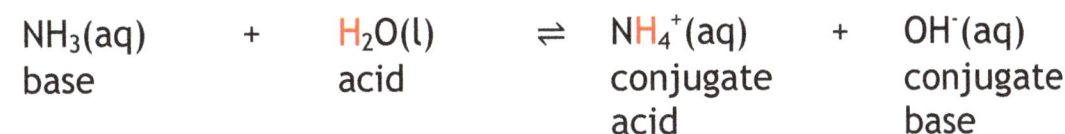

$NH_3(aq)$	+	$H_2O(l)$	$\rightleftharpoons$ $NH_4^+(aq)$	+	$OH^-(aq)$
base		acid	conjugate acid		conjugate base

Water equilibrium

You can see from these equations water can act as both a base and an acid, this is known as being amphoteric. In normal water two water molecules can combine.

$$H_2O \quad + \quad H_2O \quad \rightleftharpoons \quad H_3O^+ \quad + \quad OH^-$$

The equilibrium constant for this is called the water product K_w

where $K_w = [H_3O^+][OH^-] = 1 \times 10^{-14}$.

At room temperature water has a pH of 7 and $[H_3O^+]$ and $[OH^-]$ are 1×10^{-7} moll^{-1}.

Strong acids like HCl, H_2SO_4 and HNO_3 undergo complete dissociation.

Strong bases like NaOH, KOH and $Ca(OH)_2$ undergo complete dissociation.

pH of strong acid = -log[H_3O^+]

For a strong base [H_3O^+] = $\dfrac{1\times10^{-14}}{[OH^-]}$

Weak acids like CH_3COOH, H_2CO_3 and H_3PO_4 undergo partial dissociation and set up an equilibrium with an associated equilibrium constant called the dissociation constant K_a. **The smaller the value of Ka the weaker the acid.**

pK_a = -logK_a

pK_a is often used as it makes the very small numbers easier to understand. **The bigger the value of pK_a the weaker the acid.**

pH of a weak acid = ½ pK_a - ½ log C

where C = concentration of the weak acid

Weak bases like NH_3, CH_3NH_2 and $C_6H_5NH_2$ undergo partial dissociation and set up an equilibrium with an associated equilibrium constant called the dissociation constant K_b.

Indicators

Indicators are just weak acids that have a different colour for the acid molecule and the conjugate base:

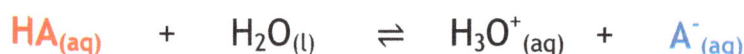

$HA_{(aq)}$ + $H_2O_{(l)}$ ⇌ $H_3O^+_{(aq)}$ + $A^-_{(aq)}$

acid molecule   **conjugate base**

In an acidic environment there will be an increase in the $H_3O^+_{(aq)}$ concentration and so the equilibrium will shift to the left and the red colour will be predominant.

In an alkali environment there will be an decrease in the $H_3O^+_{(aq)}$ concentration and so the equilibrium will shift to the right and the blue colour will be predominant.

The pH range that this change in colour occurs is dependent upon the equilibrium constant for the indicator called K_{In}. This can be converted to pK_{In} to make the numbers more manageable and we use the following expression to work out the pH range:

pH range = pK_{In} +/- 1   where pK_{In} = -log K_{In}

e.g methyl red has a pK_{In} of 5.1 and a pH range of 4.2 – 6.3

The end point of an acid / base titration should occur around the pK_{In} value for the particular indicator being used.

Titration Curves

If a titration is set up but a pH probe used to monitor the pH as the base is added and the results plotted on a graph, then a titration curve is produced. These are really useful for identifying the end point and the appropriate indicator to use. The titration curve shows a rapid change with an almost vertical line and half way up this is the end or equivalence point. The indicator pH range must lie within this rapid change to be useful.

Strong acid/strong base – neutral salt

Most indicators can be used as their pH range lies within the vertical section of the titration curve.

Their salts are always neutral, as the positive and negative ions of the salt have no effect on the water equilibrium.

Weak acid/strong base—basic salt

Only indicators with a higher pH range can be used as the vertical section begins above pH 6.

Their salts are basic due to the conjugate base of the weak acid joining up with H_3O^+ ions of the water equilibrium, causing there to be more OH^- ions compared to H_3O^+ ions.

e.g. $CH_3COO^-Na^+_{(aq)}$ $\rightarrow$ $CH_3COO^-_{(aq)}$ + $Na^+_{(aq)}$

$2H_2O_{(l)}$ $\rightleftharpoons$ $H_3O^+_{(aq)}$ + $OH^-_{(aq)}$

$\downarrow\uparrow$

$CH_3COOH_{(aq)}$

Strong acid/weak base—acidic salt

Only indicators with a lower pH range can be used as the vertical section ends above pH 8.

Their salts are acidic due to the conjugate acid of the weak base joining up with OH^- ions of the water equilibrium, causing there to be more H_3O^+ ions compared to OH^- ions.

e.g. $NH_4^+Cl^-_{(aq)}$ $\rightarrow$ $Cl^-_{aq)}$ + $NH_4^+_{(aq)}$

$2H_2O_{(l)}$ $\rightleftharpoons$ $H_3O^+_{(aq)}$ + $OH^-_{(aq)}$

$\downarrow\uparrow$

$NH_{3(aq)} + H_2O_{(l)}$

Buffer Solutions

A buffer solution is one in which the pH of the solution does not change even when small amounts of acids or alkalis are added.

A buffer solution is made by adding an appropriate salt to a weak acid or a weak base.

e.g. sodium ethanoate added to ethanoic acid or ammonium chloride added to ammonia solution.

A buffer solution has an excess (XS) of the acid or base molecules and the corresponding conjugate ion.

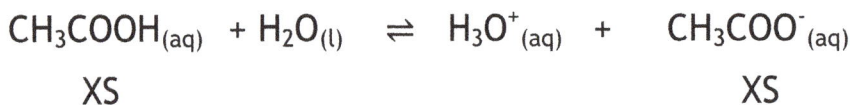

$$CH_3COOH_{(aq)} + H_2O_{(l)} \rightleftharpoons H_3O^+{}_{(aq)} + CH_3COO^-{}_{(aq)}$$

XS   XS

When more H_3O^+ ions are added the equilibrium shifts to the left and mops them up to produce more ethanoic acid molecules. The pH stays the same.

If OH^- ions are added these neutralise the H_3O^+ ions but the equilibrium shifts to the right producing more of them. The pH stays the same.

In a titration involving a weak acid and a strong base the area before the sharp rise is called the buffer zone because here you will have an excess (XS) of acid molecules and an excess of conjugate ions.

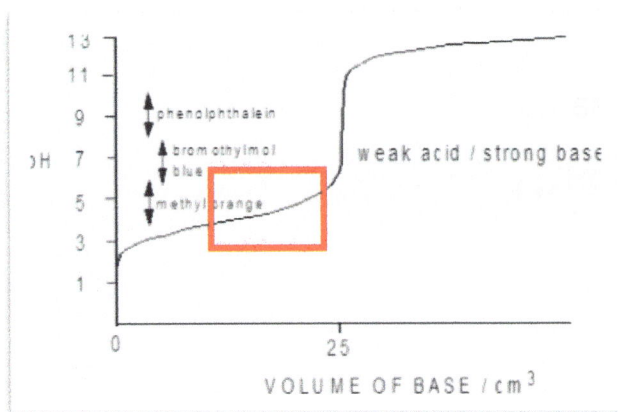

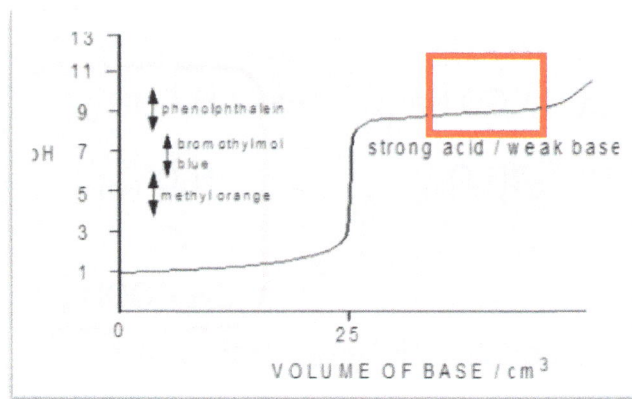

= buffer zone

The pH of a buffer solution can be calculated by using:

pH = pK$_a$ − log$_{10}$ [acid]
                          [salt]

where pK$_a$ = pK$_a$ of the weak acid
               [acid] = concentration of weak acid
               [salt] = concentration of the salt

The Equilibrium Constant

Use the balanced chemical equation and other information to write an expression for the equilibrium constant K and calculate its value.

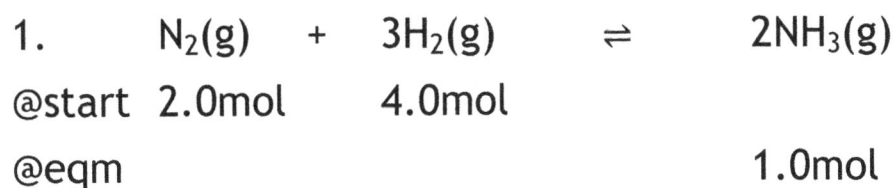

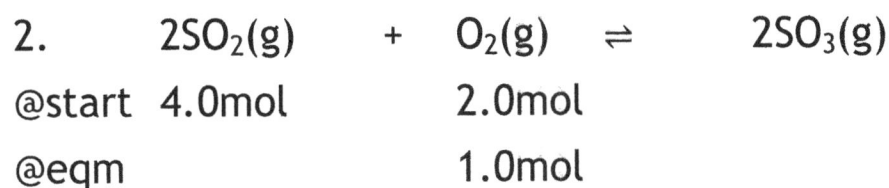

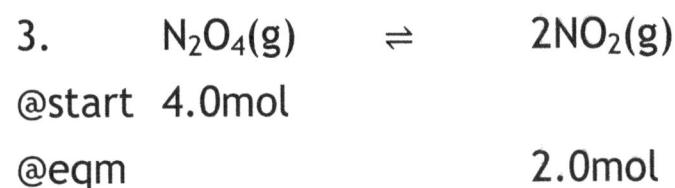

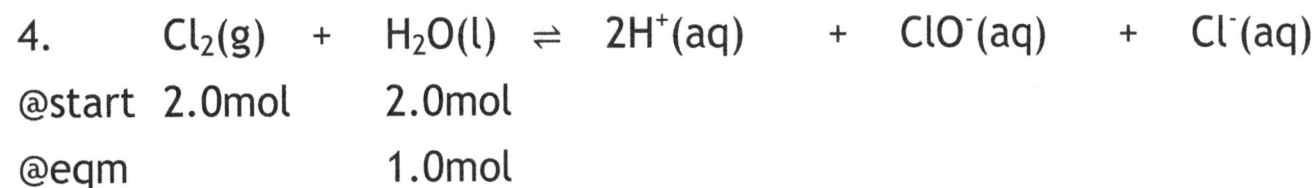

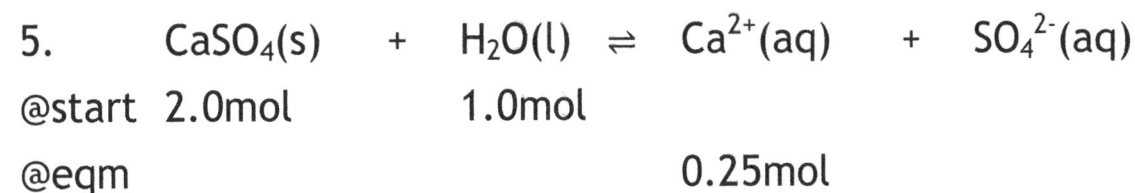

1. $N_2(g)$ + $3H_2(g)$ $\rightleftharpoons$ $2NH_3(g)$

@start 2.0mol   4.0mol

@eqm   1.0mol

2. $2SO_2(g)$ + $O_2(g)$ $\rightleftharpoons$ $2SO_3(g)$

@start 4.0mol   2.0mol

@eqm   1.0mol

3. $N_2O_4(g)$ $\rightleftharpoons$ $2NO_2(g)$

@start 4.0mol

@eqm   2.0mol

4. $Cl_2(g)$ + $H_2O(l)$ $\rightleftharpoons$ $2H^+(aq)$ + $ClO^-(aq)$ + $Cl^-(aq)$

@start 2.0mol   2.0mol

@eqm   1.0mol

5. $CaSO_4(s)$ + $H_2O(l)$ $\rightleftharpoons$ $Ca^{2+}(aq)$ + $SO_4^{2-}(aq)$

@start 2.0mol   1.0mol

@eqm   0.25mol

Chemical Misconceptions

A student created a summary table of factors affecting the position of equilibrium. Unfortunately they made a number of mistakes. Can you identify all of the mistakes in their table, circle them and complete the second table so that all the information is correct.

Variable	Change	Side of reaction favoured	Effect on the value of K
Concentration of reactants	Increase	Reactants	Decrease
Concentration of products	Decrease	Reactants	Decrease
Pressure	Decrease	Side with fewest gaseous molecules	Increase
Pressure	Increase	Side with most gaseous molecules	No effect
Temperature Forward reaction is exothermic	Increase	Reactants	No effect
Temperature Forward reaction is endothermic	Increase	Reactants	Decrease

Variable	Change	Side of reaction favoured	Effect on the value of K
Concentration of reactants	Increase		
Concentration of products	Decrease		
Pressure	Decrease		
Pressure	Increase		
Temperature Forward reaction is exothermic	Increase		
Temperature Forward reaction is endothermic	Increase		

Bronsted-Lowry

Identify whether each substance can act as an acid (A), a base (B), a conjugate acid (CA) or conjugate base (CB). **Note that some substances can act as more than one type.** The first one has been done for you

HCO_3^- (aq) *CB & A*	NH_4^+ (aq)	NH_3(aq)	$HCOO^-$(aq)
CH_3NH_2(aq)	H_3PO_4(aq)	CO_3^{2-} (aq)	$C_6H_5NH_2$(aq)
OH^-(aq)	H_3O^+(aq)	H_2O(l)	$CH_3NH_3^+$(aq)
$H_2NCH_2NH_3^+$ (aq)	$H_2PO_4^-$ (aq)	HSO_3^- (aq)	H_2CrO_4(aq)

Wordsearch

Complete the wordsearch below using the clues given to identify the correct words(s) that can be found in the wordsearch.

```
U W T U Y Z A L S U T A D Z H
G R O Q R L M M N G M I O I Y
V P U F T S Q U C P C V Z D D
P C R V C N P D M A Z R I N R
C O N J U G A T E B A S E O O
C P C G T K N T Q U S B B I N
R F I D N R A K S O Q Z U T I
Q Q W X F G Z P C N E W F U U
Z Z A A U Y E I R T O I F L M
T F F J Z T A O A O I C E O I
P H N D N T L N U V T U R S O
Z O P S I O O T N U F O L M N
C S Y O R D S P A S C D N K R
C Q N R O T A C I D N I R W S
A C C E P T S F H Q Q N N Z T
```

1. This can maintain the pH even when a small amount of acid or alkali is added. (6,8)

2. This is the positive ion formed when a base dissociates. (9,4)

3. Acids do this to protons. (6)

4. The name of $H_3O^+(aq)$. (9,3)

5. A weak acid with one colour and its conjugate base another colour. (9)

6. Gives an indication how weak a weak acid is. (12,8)

7. All bases do this to protons. (6)

8. This is the negative ion formed when an acid dissociates. (9,4)

9. A hydrogen ion is this. (6)

Salts

Identify whether each salt as going to be acidic (A), basic (B) or neutral (N).

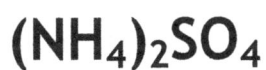

$NaHCO_3$	NH_4Cl	$C_6H_5NH_3Cl$	K_3PO_4
$CH_3NH_3NO_3$	LiH_2PO_4	Na_2CO_3	KNO_3
$(NH_4)_2SO_4$	$CaSO_3$	Na_2SO_4	$C_2H_5NH_3Cl$
$LiCl$	NH_4NO_3	$LiHSO_3$	NaH_2BO_3

pH of Salts Solutions

Fill in the blanks in the explanations given below to explain the pH of different salt solutions.

Weak Acid—Strong Base Salt Solutions:

Sodium ethanoate is formed when _____hydroxide reacts with _____acid. The salt will completely dissociate into sodium and _____ions.

The ethanoate ions, _____(aq) interact with the _____ions, H_3O^+(aq), in the water equilibrium forming ethanoic acid, _____(aq). The water equilibrium shifts to the right forming a greater proportion of hydroxide ions, OH^-(aq). The solution is therefore _____.

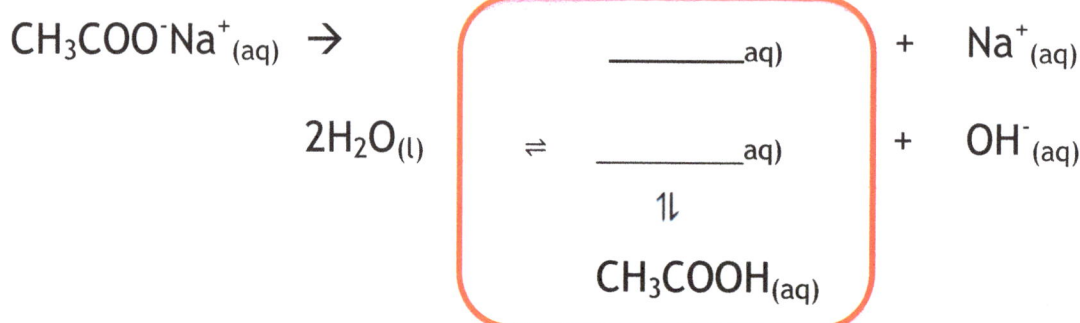

$CH_3COO^-Na^+_{(aq)} \rightarrow$ _____aq) + $Na^+_{(aq)}$

$2H_2O_{(l)}$ $\rightleftharpoons$ _____aq) + $OH^-_{(aq)}$

$\uparrow\downarrow$

$CH_3COOH_{(aq)}$

Strong Acid—Weak Base Salt Solutions:

_____is formed when ammonium hydroxide reacts with hydrochloric acid. The salt will completely dissociate into _____and chloride ions.

The ammonium ions, _____(aq) interact with the _____ions, OH^-(aq), in the water equilibrium forming ammonia & water, _____(aq) & H_2O(l). The water equilibrium shifts to the right forming a greater proportion of hydronium ions, H_3O^+ (aq). The solution is therefore _____.

NH_4Cl(aq)

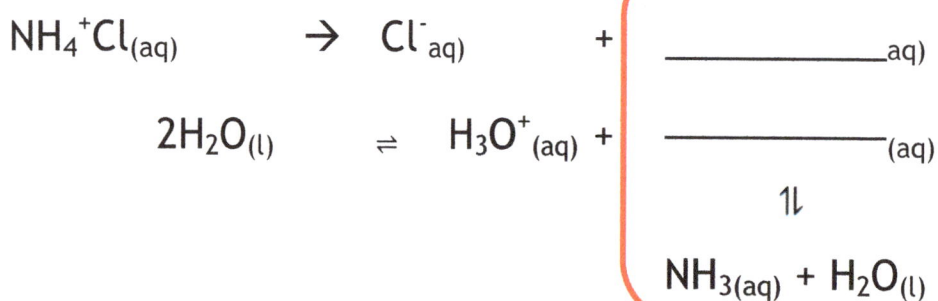

$NH_4^+Cl^-_{(aq)}$ $\rightarrow$ $Cl^-_{aq)}$ + _____aq)

$2H_2O_{(l)}$ $\rightleftharpoons$ $H_3O^+_{(aq)}$ + _____(aq)

$\uparrow\downarrow$

$NH_{3(aq)} + H_2O_{(l)}$

Titration Curves & Indicators

Connect the acid, base and the best indicator(s) for the following titration curves.

0.1 HCl

0.1 HNO$_3$

0.1 HCOOH

0.1 H$_2$SO$_3$

0.1 CH$_3$CO$_2$H

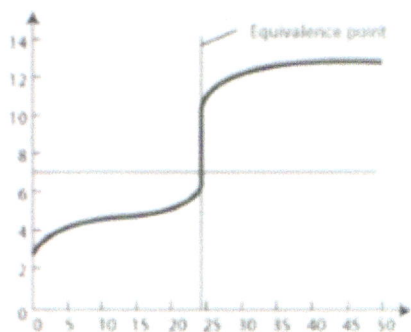

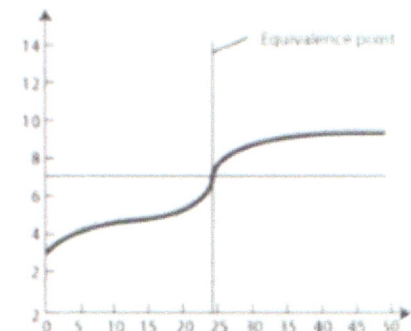

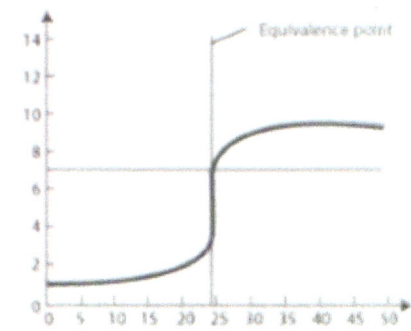

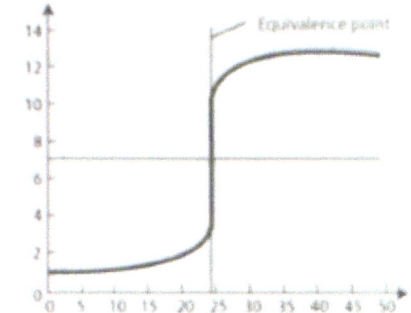

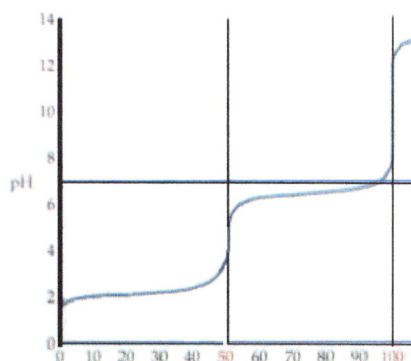

methyl orange
3.2-4.4

phenolphthalein
8.2-10.00

thymol blue
8.0-9.6

methyl red
4.8-6.0

0.1 NH$_4$OH

0.1 CH$_3$NH$_3$OH

bromothymol blue
6.0-7.6

0.1 NaOH

0.1 KOH

0.1 LiOH

Buffer Solutions

Fill in the blanks to complete the note below explaining what a buffer solution is and how they work.

A buffer solution is made up of a weak acid or base and its corresponding _____. A buffer solution maintains its ____ even when a small quantity of _____ or _____ is added.

A buffer solution has an excess of the acid or base molecules and the corresponding conjugate ion.

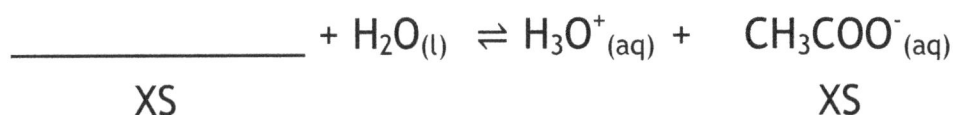

$$\underline{\hspace{3cm}} + H_2O_{(l)} \rightleftharpoons H_3O^+_{(aq)} + CH_3COO^-_{(aq)}$$

$$\text{XS} \qquad\qquad\qquad\qquad\qquad\qquad \text{XS}$$

When more _____ ions are added the equilibrium shifts to the left and mops them up to produce more ethanoic acid molecules. The pH stays the _____.

If OH⁻ ions are added these neutralise the _____ ions but the equilibrium shifts to the _____ producing more of them. The pH stays the same.

Connect the correct acid/base and salt to make the three buffer solutions and work out the pH, using the information given and your data booklet. The first one has been done for you:

0.1 moll⁻¹ HCOOH	**Buffer 1**	0.5 moll⁻¹ CH₃COONa
	pH = 4.45	
	pH = 3.75-log(0.1/0.5)	
2.0 moll⁻¹ CH₃COOH		2.0 moll⁻¹ NaNO₃
	Buffer 2	
2.0 moll⁻¹ HCl	pH =	0.5 moll⁻¹ HCOONa
1.0 moll⁻¹ NH₄OH	**Buffer 3**	1.0 moll⁻¹ CH₃COOK
2.0 moll⁻¹ CH₃COOH	pH =	0.5 moll⁻¹ KCl

Practice Questions

1. The following reaction was allowed to reach equilibrium,

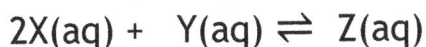

$$2X(aq) + Y(aq) \rightleftharpoons Z(aq)$$

The initial amounts of the reactants present in the 1 litre of solution were 1.00mol of X and 0.75mol of Y. At equilibrium, the amount of X was 0.70mol.

a) Calculate the number of moles of Y and Z present in the equilibrium mixture.

b) Calculate the equilibrium constant, K.

2. For the equilibrium,

$$2NO(g) + O_2(g) \rightleftharpoons 2NO_2(g) \qquad \Delta H = -115 \text{ kJmol}^{-1} \text{ (LEFT TO RIGHT)}$$

Established in a closed vessel at a fixed temperature, the equilibrium constant has a value of 15 lmol^{-1}.

a) Write an expression for the equilibrium constant, K.

b) What does the magnitude of K indicate?

c) What effect will increasing the temperature have on the value of the equilibrium constant K? Explain your answer.

d) Calculate the equilibrium concentration of NO_2 when the equilibrium concentrations of NO and O_2 are both 0.1moll^{-1}

3. Fizzy drinks contain carbon dioxide dissolved in water which dissociates, as shown, to produce carbonic acid.

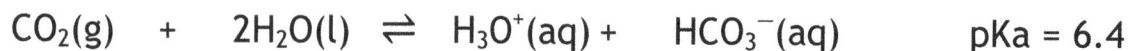

$$CO_2(g) \ + \ 2H_2O(l) \ \rightleftharpoons \ H_3O^+(aq) + \ HCO_3^-(aq) \qquad\qquad pKa = 6.4$$

a) What is the Bronsted-Lowry definition of an acid?

b) Write the formula of the conjugate base in this reaction.

c) Calculate the pH of a 0.1 moll^{-1} solution of carbonic acid.

4. The salt potassium butanoate $C_3H_7COO^-K^+$, is produced when potassium hydroxide reacts with butanoic acid. When potassium butanoate is dissolved in water an alkaline solution is formed.

ai) Write the formula for the conjugate base of butanoic acid.

ii) Explain why potassium butanoate is alkaline.

b) A titration curve for the reaction of 40cm^3 butanoic acid and 0.2moll^{-1} potassium hydroxide is shown.

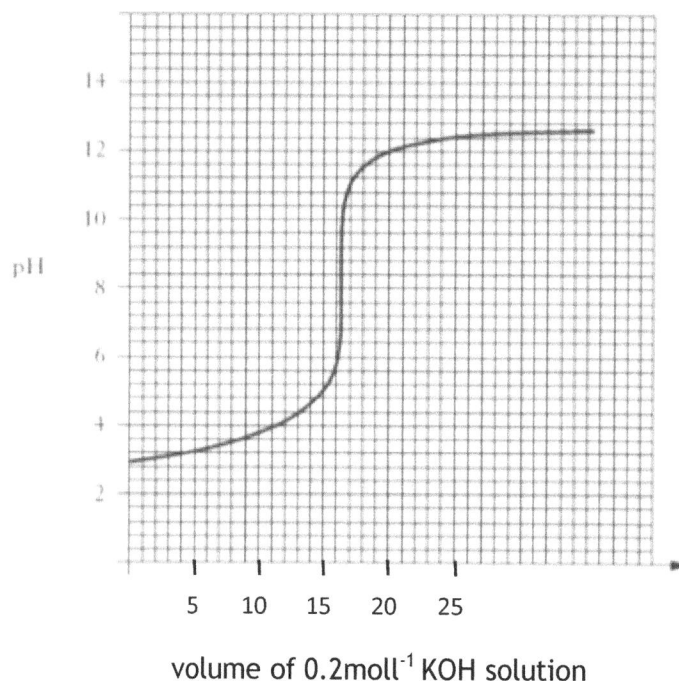

volume of 0.2moll^{-1} KOH solution

i) Calculate the initial concentration of butanoic acid.

ii) Using p20 in your data booklet identify a suitable indicator and explain your choice.

Enthalpy H

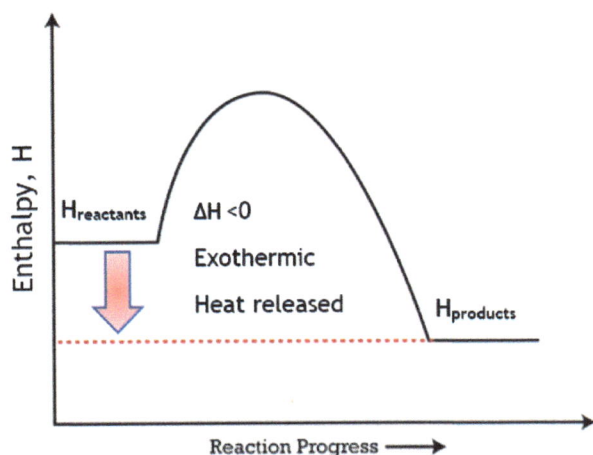

Exothermic reactions always have a negative change in enthalpy, ΔH. The products are more stable than the reactants.

$$\Delta H = H_{products} - H_{reactants}$$
$$\Delta H = -ve$$

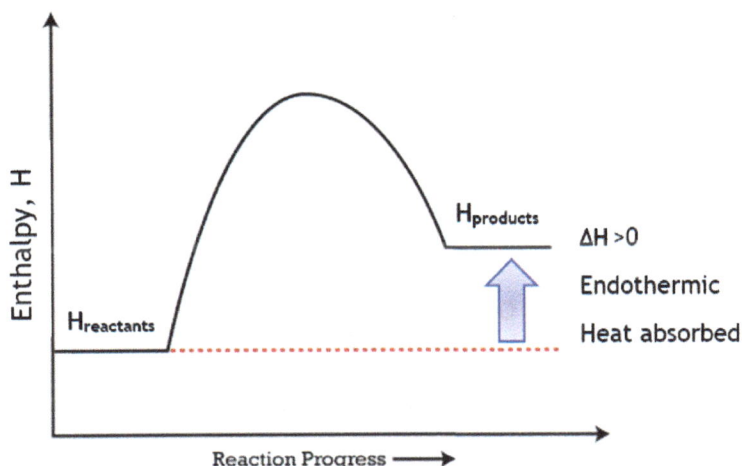

Endothermic reactions always have a positive change in enthalpy, ΔH. The products are less stable than the reactants.

$$\Delta H = H_{products} - H_{reactants}$$
$$\Delta H = +ve$$

The enthalpy change for any reaction can be calculated using enthalpies of formation, where:

Enthalpy of formation, ΔH$_f$ = enthalpy change when 1 mole of a substance is formed from its constituent elements in their natural state. If standard conditions of temperature (298K) & pressure (1atm) are used the symbol ΔH$^{\circ}_f$ is used.

ΔH = Σ ΔH$_f$(products) - Σ ΔH$_f$(reactants) Σ **= sum all**

e.g.

$$2NH_3\ (g) +\ H_2SO_4(l)\ \rightleftharpoons\ 2NH_4SO_4(s)$$

ΔH$_f$ -460   -814   -1181

ΔH = -**2**(1181) –[**2**(-460 + (-814)]   **note: 2 times the value for NH$_4$SO$_4$ & NH$_3$**

    = **-628 kJmol^{-1}**

Entropy (S)

Entropy is a measure of the disorder or randomness of substances. The greater the disorder the greater the value, so gaseous molecules have greater entropy values than ionic crystal lattices. If standard conditions of temperature (298K) & pressure (1atm) are used the symbol S° is used.

Entropy is affected by temperature, the higher the temperature the greater the disorder.

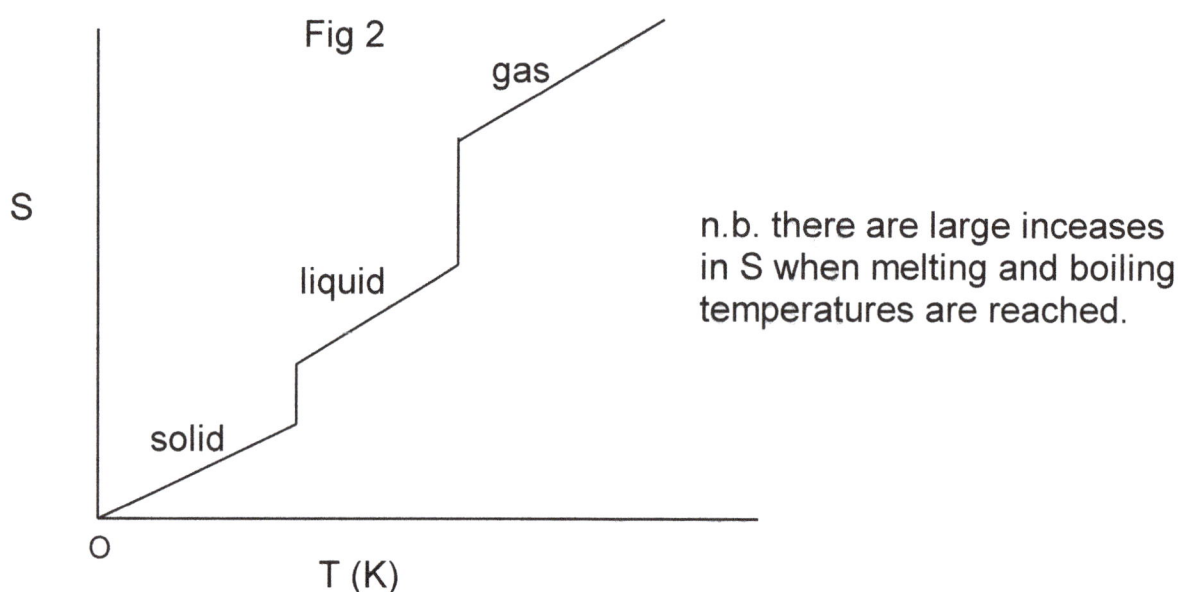

n.b. there are large inceases in S when melting and boiling temperatures are reached.

The Second Law of Thermodynamics states that for any process to be feasible there must be an increase in the total entropy.

Total entropy = entropy of substances + entropy of the surroundings

$$S_{total} = S_{substances} + S_{surroundings}$$

The change in entropy for a reaction, ΔS can be calculated from the standard entropies of the individual components of the reaction:

$\Delta S^0 = \Sigma\, S^\circ$(products) - $\Sigma\, S^0$(reactants)

e.g.

$$N_2(g) \quad + \quad 3H_2(g) \quad \rightleftharpoons \quad 2NH_3(g)$$

S^0 192   131   193

ΔS^0 = 2(193) – [192 + 3(131)]   note: 3 times value for H_2 & 2 times the value for NH_3

       = **-199 JK^{-1}mol^{-1}**   note: units include J (joules) not kJ (kilojoules)

Gibbs Free Energy (ΔG)

For a reaction to be feasible there must be free energy available. The value for ΔG must be negative. If standard conditions of temperature (298K) & pressure (1atm) are used the symbol ΔG^{o} is used.

$$\Delta G^{o} = \Delta H^{o} - T\Delta S^{o}$$

where ΔG^{o} = standard Gibbs free energy ($kJ\,mol^{-1}$)

ΔH^{o} = standard enthalpy change ($kJ\,mol^{-1}$)

T = Temperature (K)

ΔS^{o} = standard entropy change ($JK^{-1}mol^{-1}$)

Note that the units of ΔS^{o} are in $JK^{-1}mol^{-1}$ so need to divide the value by 1000 to get it into $kJK^{-1}mol^{-1}$.

e.g. Is the following reaction feasible at 298K?

	$MgCO_{3(s)}$	$\rightleftharpoons$	$MgO_{(s)}$	+	$CO_{2(g)}$
ΔH^{o}_{f} ($kJ\,mol^{-1}$)	- 1113		- 602		- 394
S^{o} ($J\,K^{-1}mol^{-1}$)	66		27		214

ΔH^{o} = [(-602 x 1) + (-394 x 1)] - [(-1113 x 1)] = **+117 kJ mol^{-1}**

ΔS^{o} = [(27) + (214)] - [(66)] = **+175 J K^{-1}mol^{-1}**

ΔG^{o} = ΔH^{o} - $T\Delta S^{o}$

= 117 - (298 x 0.175)

= **+65 kJ mol^{-1}**   so reaction is not feasible at this temperature

The theoretical temperature that it will be feasible is given by:

$$T = \frac{\Delta H^{o}}{\Delta S^{o}}$$

T = 117 ÷ 0.175

= **668 K**   (395°C)

ΔG^{o} can also be calculated if the standard free energies of formation of both the reactants and products are known:

$$\Delta G^{o} = \Sigma \Delta G^{o}_{f}(products) - \Sigma \Delta G^{o}_{f}(reactants)$$

Quiz Word

Answer the following questions to complete the quiz word and then try to work out what the key phrase in the **bold** boxes should be.

1. ΔG must be this for a reaction to happen. (8)

2. Entropy is a measure of this. (8)

3. Describes a reaction that can occur at a given temperature. (8)

4. The Law of Thermodynamics that states that the total entropy must increase for a reaction to occur. (6)

5. Gives a measure of how stable a substance is. (8)

6. This is defined as been the enthalpy change when one mole of a substance is formed from its constituent elements in their natural state. (9)

Quiz Word Clue: The full name represented by ΔG

Potential Energy Diagrams

Draw lines connecting the energy value given to the correct potential energy diagram it refers to. There are two values required for each diagram.

The following symbols are being used:

$E_{a\ forward}$ = activation energy for the forward reaction

$E_{a\ reverse}$ = activation energy for the reverse reaction

$\Delta H_{forward}$ = enthalpy change for the forward reaction

$\Delta H_{reverse}$ = enthalpy change for the reverse reaction

The first one has been done for you.

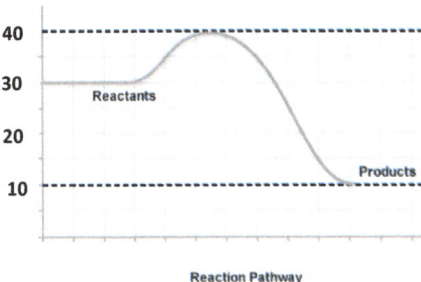

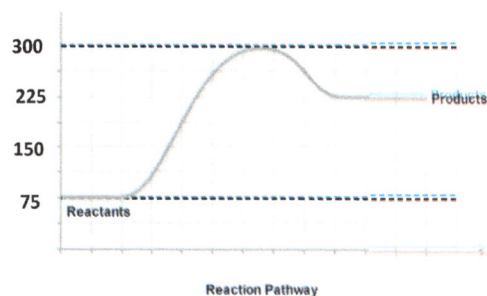

$E_{a\ reverse}$ = +15kJ

$\Delta H_{forward}$ = +150kJ

$\Delta H_{forward}$ = -10kJ

$\Delta H_{reverse}$ = -40kJ

$\Delta H_{reverse}$ = -10kJ

$E_{a\ reverse}$ = +75kJ

$E_{a\ forward}$ = +15kJ

$\Delta H_{forward}$ = -100kJ

$\Delta H_{reverse}$ = +20kJ

$E_{a\ reverse}$ = +60kJ

$E_{a\ forward}$ = +60kJ

$E_{a\ reverse}$ = +150kJ

$E_{a\ forward}$ = +10kJ

$\Delta H_{forward}$ = -40kJ

$\Delta H_{reverse}$ = -100kJ

$E_{a\ forward}$ = +150kJ

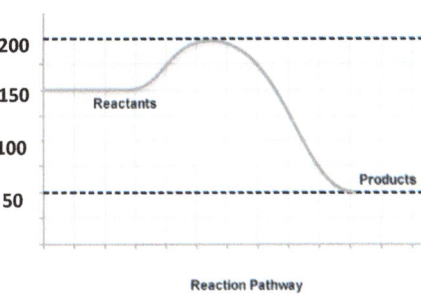

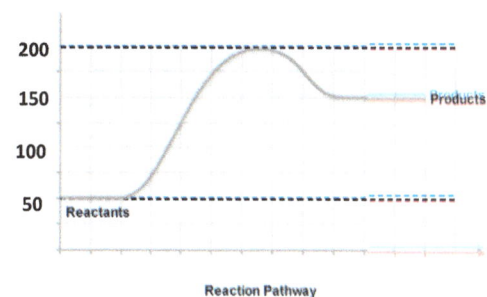

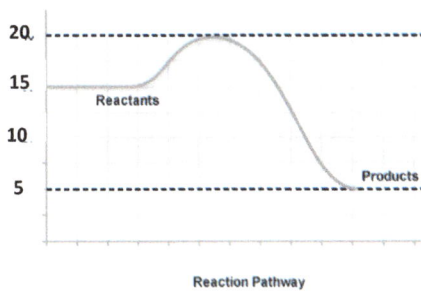

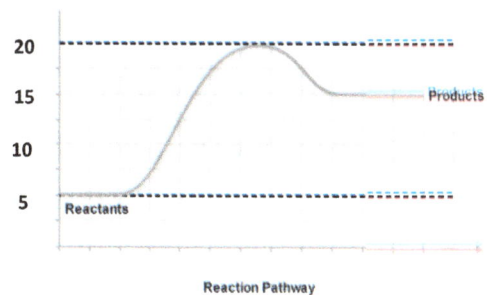

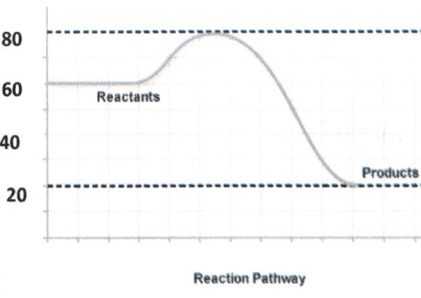

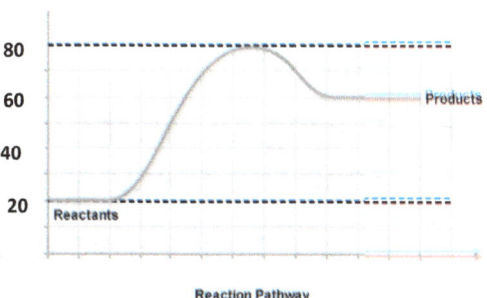

Wordsearch

Complete the wordsearch below using the clues given to identify the correct words(s) that can be found in the wordsearch.

```
S E W F K U E S D E Y P Y U K
B U G D O D R C L Z L P L R A
B V G N J R W I V B O B T K R
I N Q H A K M M K R C X A A K
G Q V T U H C A T X G I O T I
Y G R E N E C N T G F U N N S
R F E J J U E Y S I B S C U F
T C O X A L S D P K O R L H E
J G P E A Y K O K L E N O C A
B O E T G W N M G A A C U O S
N R O B V F U R S Z B H O X I
F T I E D S S E X G M H T W B
T Z U L A O I H E A M E D N L
T E M P E R A T U R E W Q S E
Y Q J X L A R V H U P N G F U
```

1. The change in this must always be negative if a reaction is to happen. (5,4,6)

2. The second law of this says that the total entropy must increase for a reaction to occur. (14)

3. Increasing this always increases the entropy. (11)

4. The enthalpy of this is the energy change when one mole of a substance is formed from its constituent elements. (9)

5. The disorder of a system does this greatly when a solid turns into a gas. (8)

6. During an exothermic reaction the products are more _____ than the reactants. (6)

7. If ΔG^0 is negative a reaction becomes this. (8)

Entropy Changes

The 2nd Law of Thermodynamics states that in order for a reaction or process to be feasible there must be an overall increase in entropy. For each of the following reactions explain how this is the case.

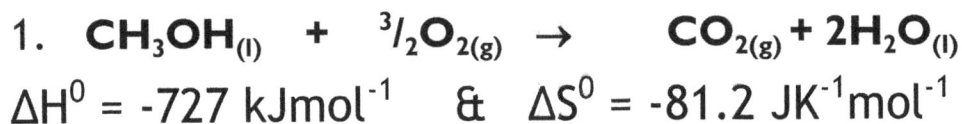

1. $CH_3OH_{(l)}$ + $^3/_2O_{2(g)}$ → $CO_{2(g)}$ + $2H_2O_{(l)}$

ΔH^0 = -727 kJmol^{-1} & ΔS^0 = -81.2 JK^{-1}mol^{-1}

Explanation of why feasible at 298K:

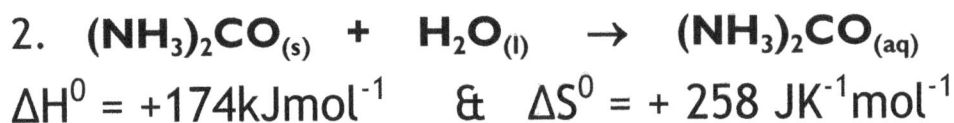

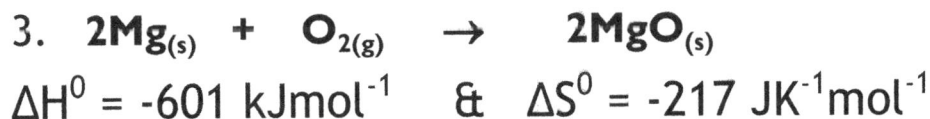

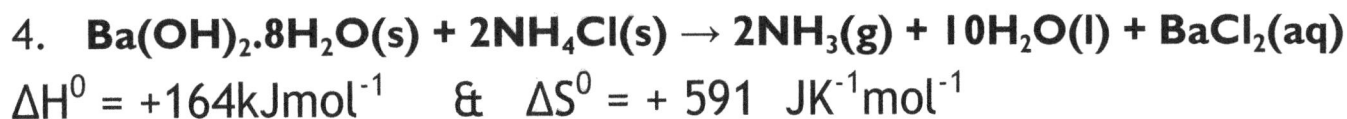

2. $(NH_3)_2CO_{(s)}$ + $H_2O_{(l)}$ → $(NH_3)_2CO_{(aq)}$

ΔH^0 = +174kJmol^{-1} & ΔS^0 = + 258 JK^{-1}mol^{-1}

Explanation of why feasible at 298K:

3. $2Mg_{(s)}$ + $O_{2(g)}$ → $2MgO_{(s)}$

ΔH^0 = -601 kJmol^{-1} & ΔS^0 = -217 JK^{-1}mol^{-1}

Explanation of why feasible at 298K:

4. $Ba(OH)_2.8H_2O(s)$ + $2NH_4Cl(s)$ → $2NH_3(g)$ + $10H_2O(l)$ + $BaCl_2(aq)$

ΔH^0 = +164kJmol^{-1} & ΔS^0 = + 591 JK^{-1}mol^{-1}

Explanation of why feasible at 298K:

Chemical Misconceptions

A student has worked out the values for ΔG at 25⁰C (298K) for the following reactions but has made an error in all of them. Look through their calculation, __identify and circle__ the mistake and then work out what the correct answer should be.

$$FeO_{(s)} \quad + \quad H_{2(g)} \quad \rightarrow \quad Fe_{(s)} \quad + \quad H_2O_{(l)}$$

$\Delta H°_f$ (kJmol^{-1})	-266	0	0	-286
$S°$ (J K^{-1} mol^{-1})	54.0	131.0	27.2	69.9

$\Delta H^0_r = -286 -(-266) = -20$
$\Delta S^0 = (69.9 + 27.2) - (131 + 54) = -87.9$
$\Delta G^0 = -20 - 298(-87.9) = +26174$ kJmol^{-1}

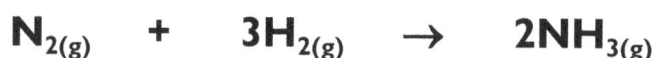

$$N_{2(g)} \quad + \quad 3H_{2(g)} \quad \rightarrow \quad 2NH_{3(g)}$$

$\Delta H°_f$ (kJmol^{-1})	0	0	-46.2
$S°$ (J K^{-1} mol^{-1})	192	131	193

$\Delta H^0_r = -46.2 = -46.2$
$\Delta S^0 = (193) - (131 + 192) = -130$
$\Delta G^0 = -46 - 298(-0.130) = -7.46$ kJmol^{-1}

$$C_2H_5OH_{(l)} \quad + \quad 3O_{2(g)} \quad \rightarrow \quad 2CO_{2(g)} \quad + \quad 3H_2O_{(l)}$$

$\Delta H°_f$ (kJmol^{-1})	-278	0	-394	-286
$S°$ (J K^{-1} mol^{-1})	161	205	214	69.9

$\Delta H^0_r = -278 -[2(-394) + 3(-286)] = 1368$
$\Delta S^0 = [3(69.9) + 2(214)] - [161 + 3(205)] = -138.3$
$\Delta G^0 = 1368 - 298(-0.1383) = +1409$ kJmol^{-1}

$$4NH_{3(g)} \quad + \quad 5O_{2(g)} \quad \rightarrow \quad 6H_2O_{(l)} \quad + \quad 4NO_{(g)}$$

$\Delta H°_f$ (kJmol^{-1})	294	0	-286	90.4
$S°$ (J K^{-1} mol^{-1})	237	205	69.9	211

$\Delta H^0_r = [6(-286) + 4(90.4)] -4(294) = -2530.4$
$\Delta S^0 = [6(69.9) + 4(211)] - [4(237) + 5(205)] = -1192$
$\Delta G^0 = -2530.4 - 25(-0.1192) = -2527.4$ kJmol^{-1}

Practice Questions

1. The Thermite process can be used to extract iron from iron(III) oxide.

$$2Al(s) \quad + \quad Fe_2O_3(s) \quad \rightarrow \quad 2Fe(s) \quad + \quad Al_2O_3(s)$$

Substance	Standard enthalpy of formation $kJmol^{-1}$	Standard entropy $JK^{-1}mol^{-1}$
$Fe_2O_3(s)$	-824	87.0
$Al(s)$	0	28.0
$Al_2O_3(s)$	-1676	51.0
$Fe(s)$	0	27.0

a) Calculate the standard enthalpy change, ΔH^0 in $kJmol^{-1}$ for the Thermite process.

b) Calculate the standard entropy change, ΔS^0 in $JK^{-1}mol^{-1}$ for the Thermite process.

c) Calculate the standard free energy, ΔG^0 in $kJmol^{-1}$ for the Thermite process.

2. Information about the decomposition of silver(I) nitrate is given below.

$$AgNO_3(s) \quad \rightarrow \quad Ag(s) + \tfrac{1}{2} O_2(g) + NO_2(g)$$

Substance	$\Delta H^{\circ}_f / kJmol^{-1}$	$S^{\circ} / JK^{-1}mol^{-1}$
$AgNO_3$	-123.6	141.5
Ag	0	42.6
O_2	0	205.2
NO_2	34.0	241.4

For the decomposition of $AgNO_3$, calculate

a) The standard enthalpy of reaction, ΔH^0 in $kJmol^{-1}$

b) The standard entropy change, ΔS^0 in $JK^{-1}mol^{-1}$

c) The theoretical temperature at which the temperature first becomes feasible.

3. Ethene can be hydrated to produce ethanol.

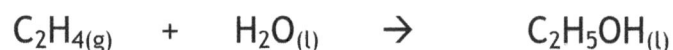

$$C_2H_{4(g)} \quad + \quad H_2O_{(l)} \quad \rightarrow \quad C_2H_5OH_{(l)}$$

Compound	Standard free energy of formation, ΔG^0 (kJmol^{-1})	Standard enthalpy of formation, ΔH^0 (kJmol^{-1})
Ethene	68	52
Water	-237	-286
ethanol	-175	-278

(a) For the hydration of ethene, use the data in the table to calculate:

(i) the standard enthalpy change, ΔH°, in kJ mol^{-1};

(ii) the standard entropy change, ΔS°, in J K^{-1} mol^{-1}.

(b) Calculate the temperature, in K, at which this reaction just becomes feasible.

4. Zinc oxide can be reduced to zinc in a blast furnace.

One of the reactions taking place in the furnace is shown.

$$ZnO(s) \quad + \quad CO(g) \quad \rightarrow \quad Zn(g) \quad + \quad CO_2(g)$$

Compound	Standard free energy of formation, ΔG^0 (kJmol^{-1})	Standard entropy, S° (JK^{-1}mol^{-1})
ZnO(s)	-348	44
CO(g)	-110	198
Zn(g)	+130	161
CO$_2$(g)	-394	214

For the reduction of zinc oxide with carbon monoxide, use the data in the table to calculate:

(a) the standard enthalpy change, ΔH°, in kJ mol^{-1};

(b) the standard entropy change, ΔS°, in J K^{-1} mol^{-1};

(c) the theoretical temperature above which the reaction becomes feasible.

Unit 2   Kinetics

For a given reaction the rate can be expressed quantitively as:

$2A + B + C \rightarrow D + E$

Rate = $k[A]^x [B]^y [C]^z$ Where k = rate constant

[ ]   = concentration

x, y & z = order of reaction for a reactant

The order of a reaction is given by the number of species/molecules/ particles/ions/ moles of reactant(s) involved in the rate determining step/ slowest step.

The orders of reaction can **only** be ascertained by experiments. They are derived from the effect on the initial reaction rate of doubling the concentration of each reactant.

Experiment	[A] moll^{-1}	[B] moll^{-1}	[C] moll^{-1}	Rate (moll^{-1}s^{-1})
1	2.0	2.0	2.0	2×10^{-2}
2	4.0	2.0	2.0	8×10^{-2}
3	2.0	4.0	2.0	4×10^{-2}
4	2.0	2.0	4.0	2×10^{-2}

You can see that:

doubling the concentration of A quadruples the rate = second order $[A]^2$

doubling the concentration of B doubles the rate = first order $[B]^1$

doubling the concentration of C no effect on the rate = zero order $[C]^0$

The rate expression is therefore found to be:

Rate = $k [A]^2 [B]$ as C is zero order it is not in the equation

The value of K can be calculated by substituting the values from any of the experiments, its often convenient to use the first, into the equation:

$$k = \frac{rate}{[A]^2 [B]} \quad k = \frac{2 \times 10^{-2}}{2.0^2 \times 2.0} \quad k = 2.5 \times 10^{-3} \ l^2 mol^{-2}s^{-1}$$

The units of k are derived from the units in the calculation:

$$k = \frac{\cancel{moll^{+}} s^{-1}}{(moll^{-1})^2 \ \cancel{moll^{+}}}$$

The overall order of the reaction is simply found by adding up all the individual orders. So for the above reaction the overall order is 3rd order.

Rate Determining Step (RDS) also known as Slow Step

The rate equation can be used to hypothesise a reaction mechanism. The reaction may involve several steps, one of which will be the slow step and be responsible for controlling the rate of reaction.

The rate determining step must include the same number of moles of reactant as given in the rate equation.

For example the following reaction has the rate equation shown:

2A + B + C → D + E

Rate = $k[A]^2 [B]$

Possible mechanism:

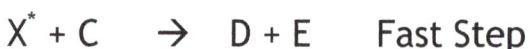

2A + B   →   X*   **Slow Step**   **where X* is an intermediate**

X* + C   →   D + E   Fast Step

The rate determining step is the slow step and involves 2 moles of A and 1 mole of B. This is why the order of reaction for A and B are 2nd and 1st respectively. C is not involved in the RDS and so is zero order and not part of the rate equation.

The following graphs show how the different orders of reaction affect the rate as concentration changes and concentration as the reaction proceeds.

Rate v Concentration graphs

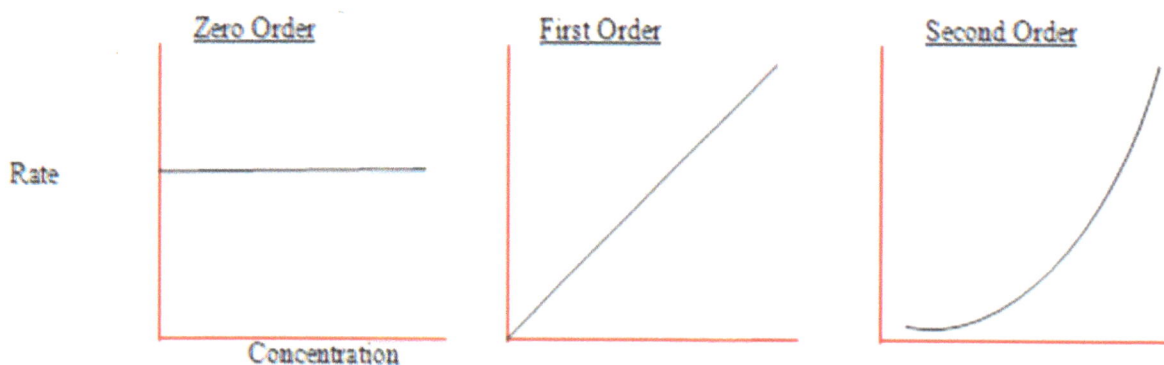

Concentration v Time graphs

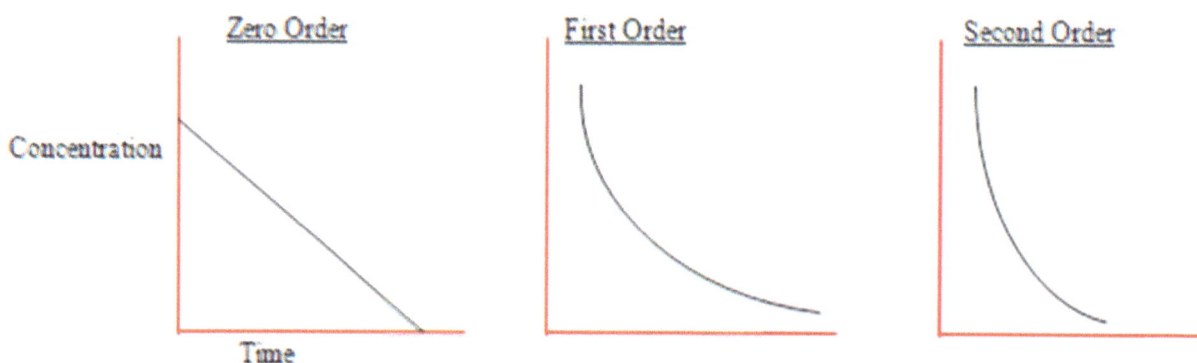

Orders of Reaction

Looking at the following graphs and tables work out the order of reaction for each reactant and the overall order of reaction.

1. $2H_2(g)$ + $2NO(g)$ → $2H_2O(l)$ + $N_2(g)$

Experiment	$[H_2]$ moll^{-1}	$[NO]$ moll^{-1}	Rate (moll^{-1}s^{-1})
1	2.0	2.0	2×10^{-2}
2	4.0	2.0	4×10^{-2}
3	2.0	4.0	8×10^{-2}

Order with respect to H_2 =   Order with respect to NO =

Overall order =

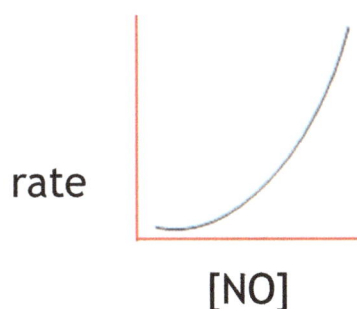

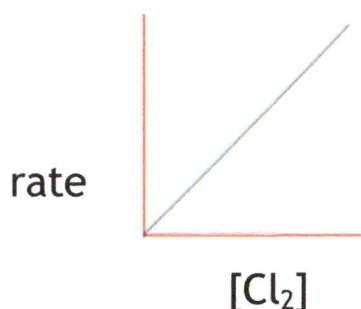

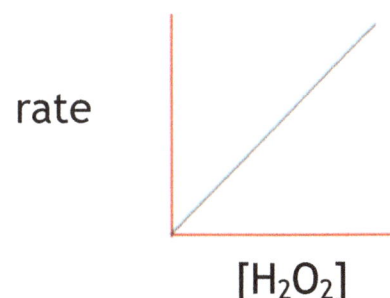

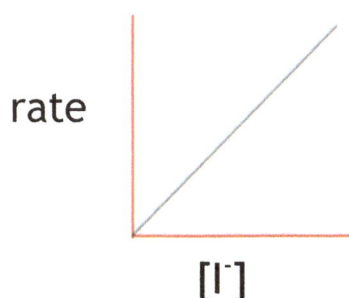

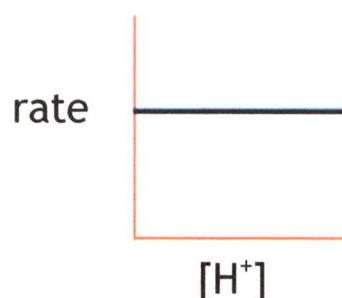

2.   2NO   + Cl_2 →   2NOCl

rate   rate

          [NO] $[Cl_2]$

Order with respect to NO =   Order with respect to Cl_2 =

Overall order =

3. $C(CH_3)_3Br$ +   NaOH   → $C(CH_3)_3OH$ +   NaBr

Experiment	$[C(CH_3)_3Br]$ moll^{-1}	$[NaOH]$ moll^{-1}	Rate (moll^{-1}s^{-1})
1	2.0×10^{-3}	2.0	2×10^{-4}
2	4.0×10^{-3}	2.0	4×10^{-4}
3	2.0×10^{-3}	4.0	2×10^{-4}

Order with respect to $C(CH_3)_3Br$ =   Order with respect to NaOH=

Overall order =

4. $H_2O_2(aq) + 3I^-(aq) + 2H^+(aq)$ → $I_3^-(aq) + 2H_2O(l)$

rate   rate   rate

          $[H_2O_2]$ $[I^-]$ $[H^+]$

Order with respect to H_2O_2 =   Order with respect to I^- =

Order with respect to H^+ =   Overall order =

Quiz Word

Answer the following questions to complete the quiz word and then try to work out what the key phrase in the **bold** boxes should be.

1. The reactants in this step have no effect on the rate. (4)
2. Another name for the reaction that controls the rate of reaction. (4,11,4)
3. The study of rates of reaction. (8)
4. Order of reaction which doubles the rate when the concentration is doubled. (5)
5. The overall order of reaction with units of $l^2 mol^{-2} s^{-1}$. (5)

Rate Equations

Looking at the following information write out the rate equation and work out the units for k. The first one has been done for you:

1. $2H_2(g) + 2NO(g) \rightarrow 2H_2O(l) + N_2(g)$

1st order with respect to H_2 2nd order with respect to NO

Rate equation: units:

Rate = $k[H_2][NO]^2$ $k = rate/[H_2][NO]^2$

$k = \cancel{moll^{-1}}s^{-1}/\cancel{moll^{-1}} \times (moll^{-1})^2$

$k = l^2mol^{-2}s^{-1}$

2. $2NO + Cl_2 \rightarrow 2NOCl$

2nd order with respect to NO   1st order with respect to Cl_2

3. $C(CH_3)_3Br + NaOH \rightarrow C(CH_3)_3OH + NaBr$

1st order with respect to $C(CH_3)_3Br$ 0 order with respect to NaOH

4. $H_2O_2(aq) + 3I^-(aq) + 2H^+(aq) \rightarrow I_3^-(aq) + 2H_2O(l)$

1st order with respect to H_2O_2 1st order with respect to I^-

0 order with respect to H^+

Wordsearch

Complete the wordsearch below using the clues given to identify the correct words(s) that can be found in the wordsearch.

```
R E D R O D N O C E S R I S R
X G T Y A R P O Y T A R E X E
D G N K B A S E E T Y L U M D
Y O M I U T Y P E O P Y W X R
Q F U S N E K C A U O H E R O
A W Y B F I O Q R F L R L J T
T C O R L N M D M E Q U B Z S
X F Q L S E A R B P P Y S Z R
O D D T S U S Y E I H Q V W I
F K A H Q J J N L T N F D F F
Q N U Z E R O O R D E R W A P
T H O O T S A F D F G D E N R
I Z I T Y T M K W N R L H B W
S D Z E S J O X L W N W C G G
B S F D H L V G O K H E A Q Z
```

1. If a reactant is second order, this happens to the rate when you double its concentration. (10)

2. This has the symbol k. (4,8)

3. This is the reaction that controls the rate. (4,11,4)

4. This is a step that doesn't affect the rate. (4)

5. This step controls the speed of reaction. (4)

6. If a reactant is first order, this happens to the rate when you double its concentration. (7)

7. If a reaction is this overall, k will have units of $lmol^{-1}s^{-1}$. (6,5)

8. If a reactant is this then changing its concentration will have no effect on the rate. (4,5)

9. If a reaction is this overall, k will have units of s^{-1}. (5,5)

Rate Determining Step

Looking at the following information either identify the rate determining step or suggest a rate determining step involving an intermediate compound X.

1. step 1 $Cu^{2+}(aq)$ + $V^{3+}(aq)$ → $Cu^+(aq)$ + $V^{4+}(aq)$

    step 2 $Cu^+(aq)$ + $Fe^{3+}(aq)$ → $Cu^{2+}(aq)$ + $Fe^{2+}(aq)$

    Rate = $k[Fe^{3+}(aq)]$

2.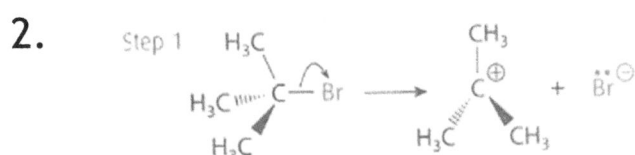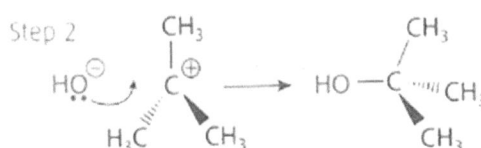

    Rate = $k[OH^-]^0[C(CH_3)_3Br]^1$

3.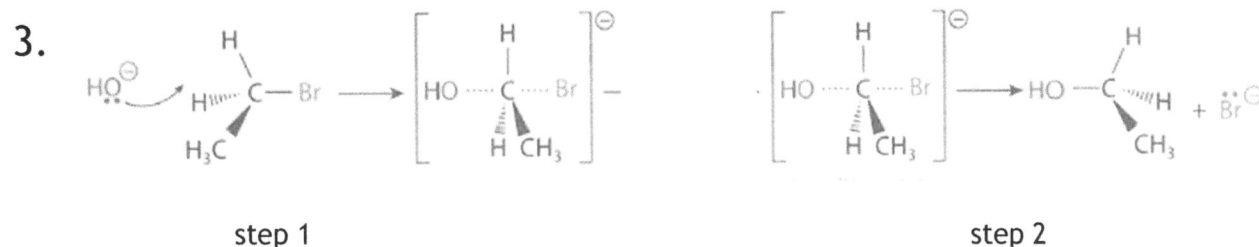

    step 1   step 2

    Rate = $k[OH^-]^1[CH_3CH_2Br]^1$

4. $CH_3COCH_3(aq)$ + $Br_2(aq)$ → $CH_3COCH_2Br(aq)$ + $HBr(aq)$

    Rate = $k[Br_2(aq)][H^+(aq)]$

5. $HC(CH_3)_2Cl$ + $NaOH$ → $C(CH_3)_2OH$ + $NaCl$

    Rate = $[HC(CH_3)_2Cl]$

Practice Questions

1. For the reaction:
$$2H_2(g) \quad + \quad 2NO(g) \quad \rightarrow \quad 2H_2O(l) \quad + \quad N_2(g)$$

the following initial rates were determined:

Initial [NO] /x10-3 mol l-1	Initial [H₂] /x10-3 mol l-1	Initial rate /x10-3 mol l-1 s-1
6	1	3
6	2	6
6	3	9
1	6	0.5
2	6	2
3	6	4.5

a)   What is the order of the reaction :

   (i)   with respect to NO;

   (ii) with respect to H_2;

   (iii) overall ?

 Explain your reasoning for each answer.

b)   Write the rate expression for the reaction.

c)   Using values from the table above, determine the rate constant, with appropriate units.

2.   The reaction between iron(III) ions and vanadium(III) ions is first order with respect to both species.

   $$Fe^{3+}(aq) \quad + \quad V^{3+}(aq) \quad \rightarrow \quad Fe^{2+}(aq) \quad + \quad V^{4+}(aq)$$

In the presence of copper(II) ions the reaction proceeds much more rapidly and there is evidence to suggest the following mechanism:

step 1 $Cu^{2+}(aq) \ + \ V^{3+}(aq) \ \rightarrow \quad Cu^+(aq) \ + \ V^{4+}(aq)$ Fast

step 2 $Cu^+(aq) \ + \ Fe^{3+}(aq) \ \rightarrow \quad Cu^{2+}(aq) \ + \ Fe^{2+}(aq)$ Slow

a)   Write the rate expression for the reaction between iron(III) ions and vanadium(III) ions.

b)   What is the order of reaction with respect to iron(III) ions when copper(II) ions are   present. Explain your answer.

3. The results of experiments on the alkaline hydrolysis of 2-iodobutane, $CH_3CHIC_2H_5$, are shown in the table below.

The equation for the hydrolysis is

$CH_3CHIC_2H_5(l) + OH^-(aq) \rightarrow CH_3CH(OH)C_2H_5(l) + I^-(aq)$

Experiment	$[CH_3CHIC_2H_5]$/mol l^{-1}	$[OH^-]$/mol l^{-1}	Initial Rate/mol l^{-1}s^{-1}
1	0·10	0·10	$1·4 \times 10^{-4}$
2	0·20	0·20	$2·9 \times 10^{-4}$
3	0·30	0·10	$4·1 \times 10^{-4}$

a) Determine the order of reaction with respect to

i) $CH_3CHIC_2H_5$

ii) OH^-.

b) Using your answers to part (a):

i) write the rate equation for the reaction;

ii) calculate a value for the rate constant, k, including the appropriate units.

4. Reaction kinetics can be used to determine the order and mechanism of chemical reactions.

A proposed mechanism for the reaction between hydrogen peroxide, $H_2O_2(aq)$, and iodide ions, $I^-(aq)$, is shown below.

Step 1 $H_2O_2(aq) + I^-(aq) \rightarrow IO^-(aq) + H_2O(\ell)$ slow

Step 2 $IO^-(aq) + H_3O^+(aq) \rightarrow HIO(aq) + H_2O(\ell)$ fast

Step 3 $HIO(aq) + H_3O^+(aq) + I^-(aq) \rightarrow I_2(aq) + 2H_2O(\ell)$ fast

a) State what is meant by the order of a reaction.

bi) Write the rate equation for this reaction.

ii) Determine the overall order of reaction for the mechanism above.

c) Write a balanced equation for the overall reaction.

Unit 3   Molecular Orbitals

Organic molecules are always covalently bonded. A covalent bond occurs when two atomic orbitals overlap. We can represent molecules in a number of ways:

E.g. 2-methyl propan-1-ol

Full structural formula – shows all atoms and all bonds

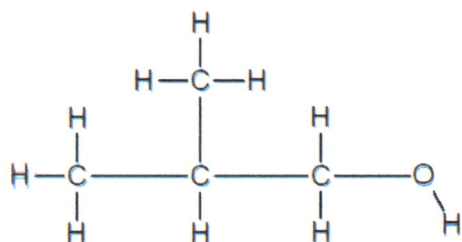

Shortened structural formula – shows groups of atoms and some bonds

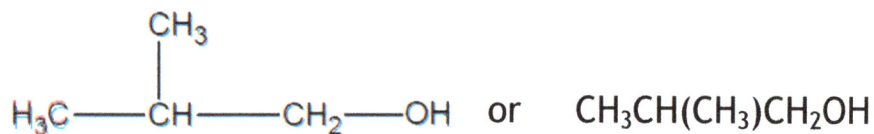

or $CH_3CH(CH_3)CH_2OH$

Molecular formula – Shows the number of each type of atom and some functional groups.

C_4H_9OH or $C_4H_{10}O$

Skeletal structural formula – shows only bonds between carbon atoms and functional groups, H atoms are not shown unless they are part of a functional group. Skeletal formula make drawing complex organic molecules much easier.

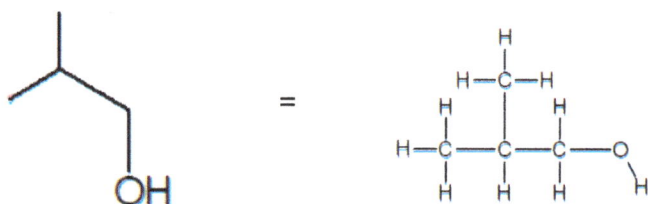

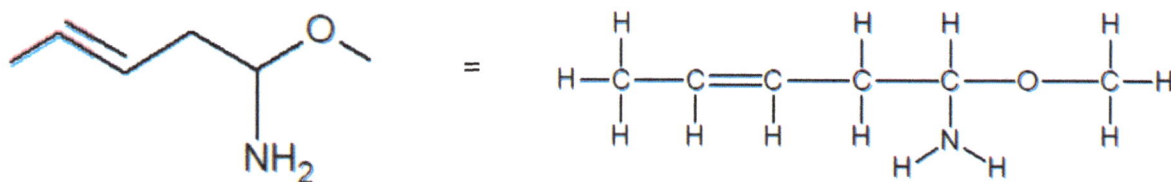

=

=

When a covalent bond forms, the two atomic orbitals combine to form two **molecular orbitals, one bonding orbital of lower energy and a higher anti bonding orbital**. Normally the bonding electrons reside in the lower energy bonding orbital.

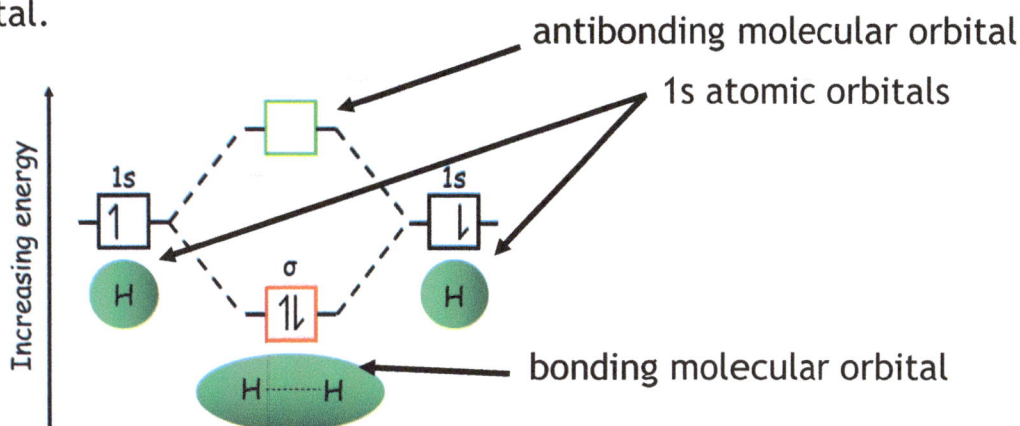

When atomic orbitals overlap end-on they form a sigma bond, σ

When atomic orbitals overlap side-on they form a pi bond, π

Bonding in alkanes

Carbon has 6 electrons and the electron arrangement $1s^2\ 2s^2\ 2p^2$.

When a carbon atoms starts to bond the one 2s and three 2p orbitals undergo sp^3 hybridisation where 4 identical orbitals form, its these orbitals that overlap to form the molecular orbitals.

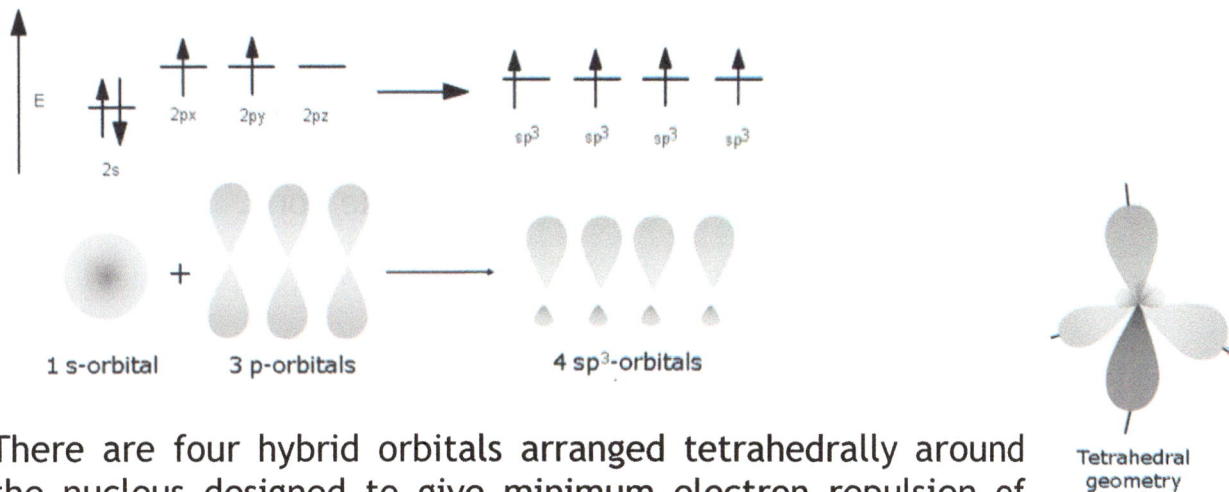

There are four hybrid orbitals arranged tetrahedrally around the nucleus designed to give minimum electron repulsion of the bonding electrons.

Tetrahedral geometry

All the covalent bonds in the alkanes are formed by end – on overlap of the hybridised orbitals, each carbon atoms forming 4 sigma (σ) bonds.

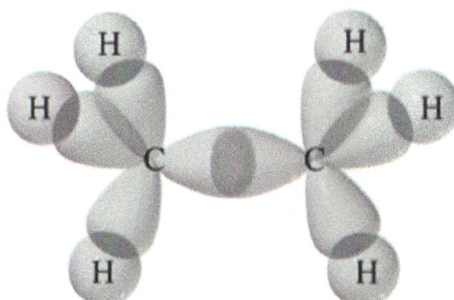

Bonding in Alkenes:

If only 2 of the 2p orbitals hybridise with the 2s orbital you get sp^2 hybridisation:

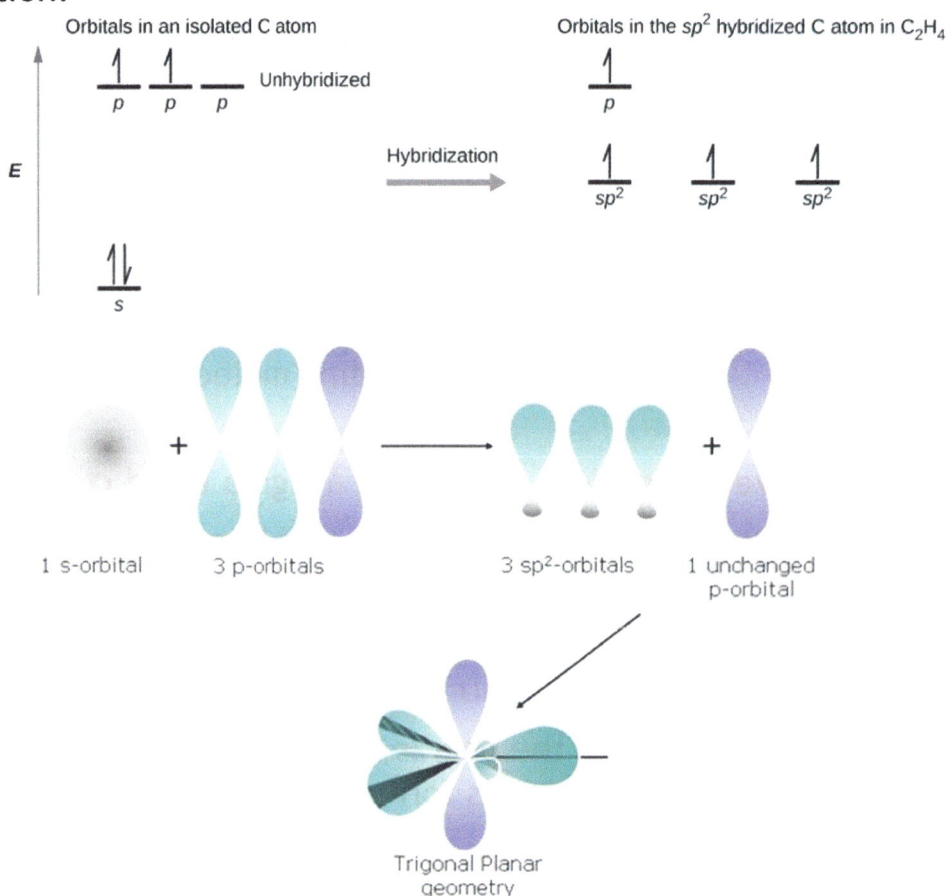

Orbitals in an isolated C atom

Orbitals in the sp^2 hybridized C atom in C_2H_4

Unhybridized

Hybridization

E

1 s-orbital   3 p-orbitals   3 sp²-orbitals   1 unchanged p-orbital

Trigonal Planar geometry

When two carbon atoms bond with sp^2 hybridisation bond they form 3 sigma bonds with end-on overlap of the sp^2 orbitals but also side-on overlap with the unhybridized p orbitals. Thus forming both a sigma and pi bond between the two carbon atoms, this is known as a carbon-carbon double bond.

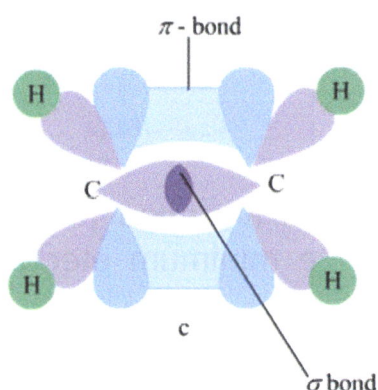

π - bond

H   H

C   C

H   H

c

σ bond

When carbon atoms undergo sp hybridization one s and just one 1 p orbital hybridise giving two sp hydrid orbitals that can undergo end-on overlap. This leaves two unhybridized p orbitals which can both undergo side-on overlap.

This leads to the formation of the carbon-carbon triple bond found in alkynes.

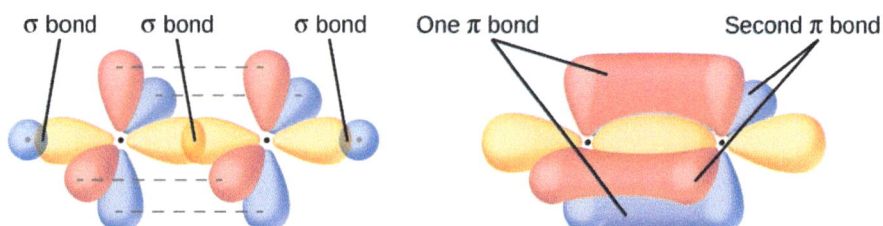

σ bond σ bond σ bond   One π bond   Second π bond

Bond type	Bonding orbitals present	Bond length	Mean bond enthalpy
Single	1 σ	154 pm	370 kJ mol^{-1}
Double	1 σ + 1 π	134 pm	602 kJ mol^{-1}
Triple	1 σ + 2 π	121 pm	835 kJ mol^{-1}

You can see that the strength of a π bond is much less than a σ bond. This is due to the side-on overlap of the p orbitals.

A common question is to ask how many of each bond type is present in a compound.

e.g. How many σ bonds and how many π bonds are present in the following structure:

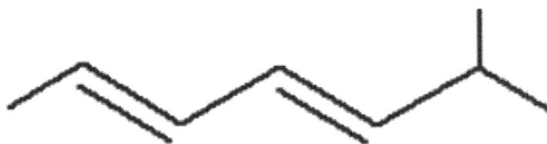

The best thing to do is to redraw the molecule as a full structural formula so that you remember to count all the C-H bonds:

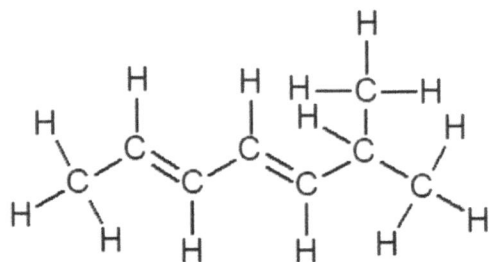

Remember each single bond is a σ bond and each double is a σ and a π bond.
σ = 21
π = 2

Bonding in benzene :

Originally benzene, C_6H_6 was thought to have the following structure:

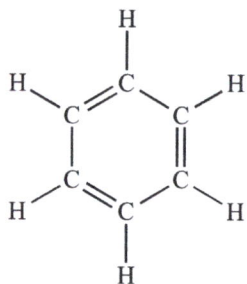

However it was not found to undergo addition reactions and its molecular shape was found to be planar and with 6 equal bond lengths between the 6 carbon atoms in the ring.

This led to the idea that carbon atoms all had sp^2 hybridisation and that the π bonds form a delocalised ring above and below the ring of 6 σ bonded carbon atoms.

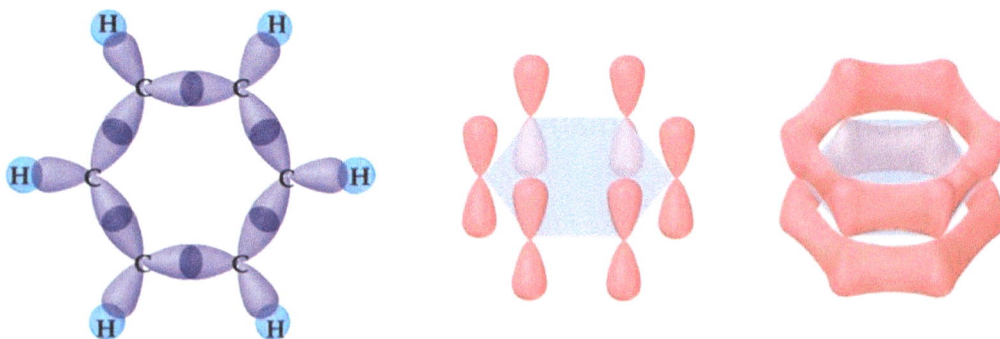

The skeletal structure of benzene is now drawn as a hexagon with a ring in the middle representing the ring of delocalised electrons:

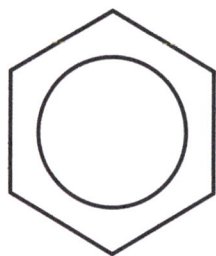

A substituted benzene ring is called a phenyl group (C_6H_5) and can be represented as below where R is the rest of the molecule:

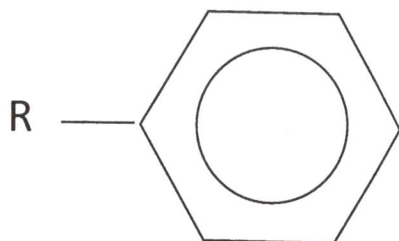

Colour in organic compounds:

Organic molecules that are coloured contain delocalised electrons spread over a number of atoms called **conjugated systems**. This is sometimes called a conjugated pi system due to the presence of a pi bond attached to each carbon atom. Benzene is an example of a conjugated system. They occur when you get alternating single and double bonds, this part of the compound is called the **chromophore**.

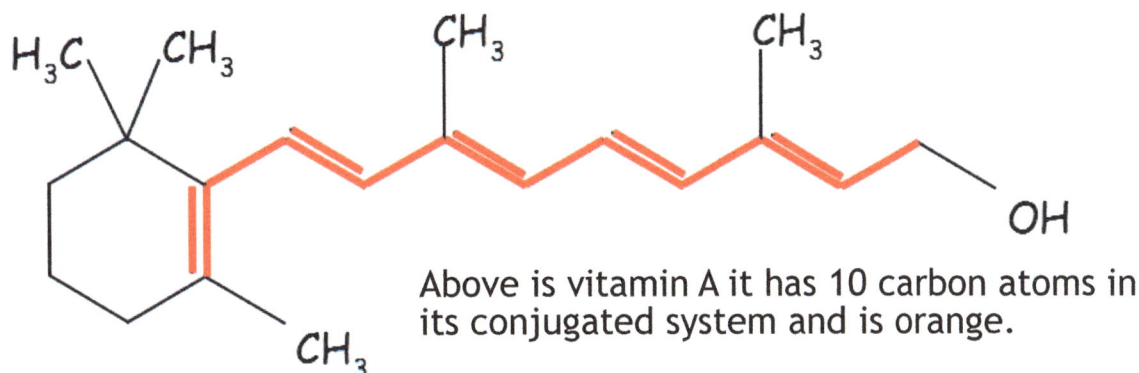

Above is vitamin A it has 10 carbon atoms in its conjugated system and is orange.

In a conjugated system you have the following molecular orbitals available:

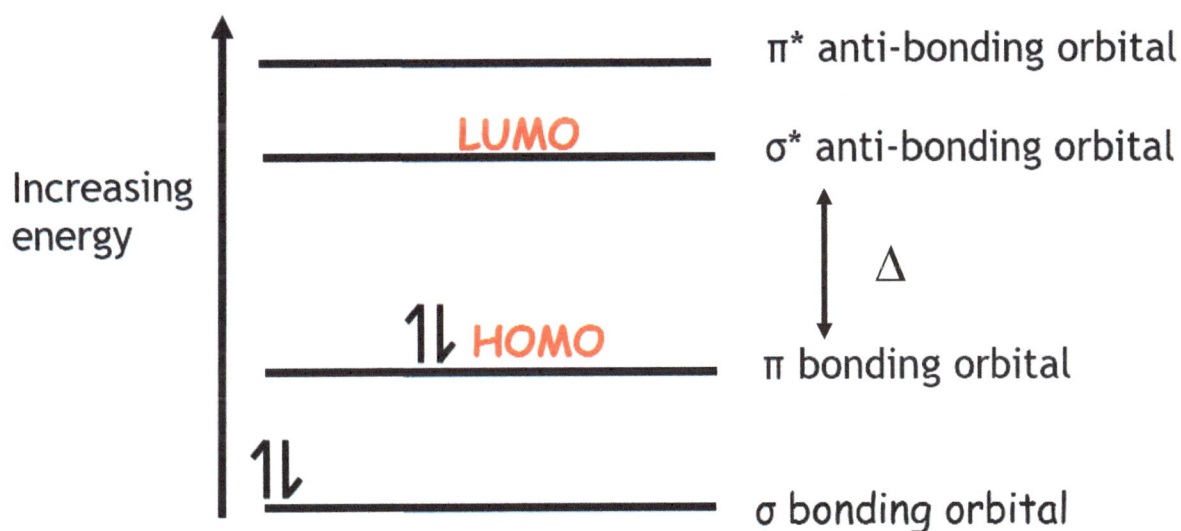

The electrons in the highest occupied molecular orbital (**HOMO**) can be promoted to the lowest unoccupied molecular orbital (**LUMO**) by the absorption of a photon of light with wavelength corresponding to the energy gap, Δ.

In conjugated systems the energy gap falls within the visible spectrum and so these compounds appear coloured. Remember the colour seen will be the opposite colour to the wavelength of light absorbed (see Transition metals topic p33-34).

The greater the length of conjugation the closer the HOMO and LUMO are and so a longer wavelength of light gets absorbed as the energy gap is smaller.

Structural Formulae

Connect the skeletal structure to the correct structural formulae shown.

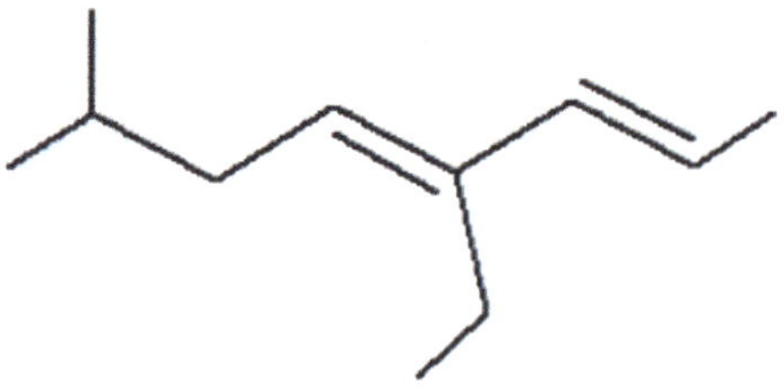

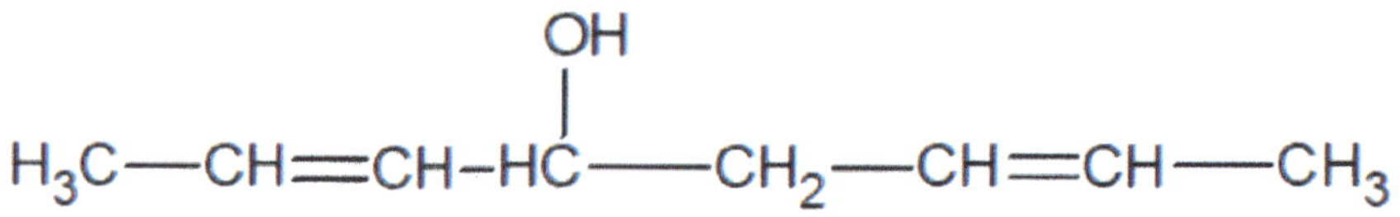

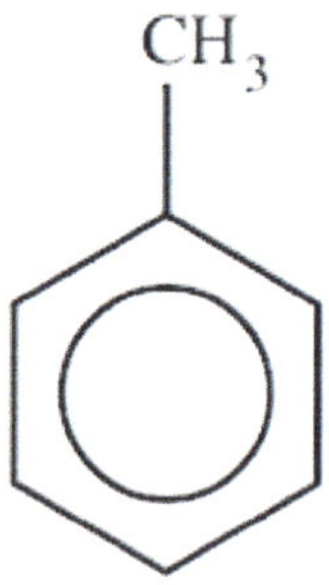

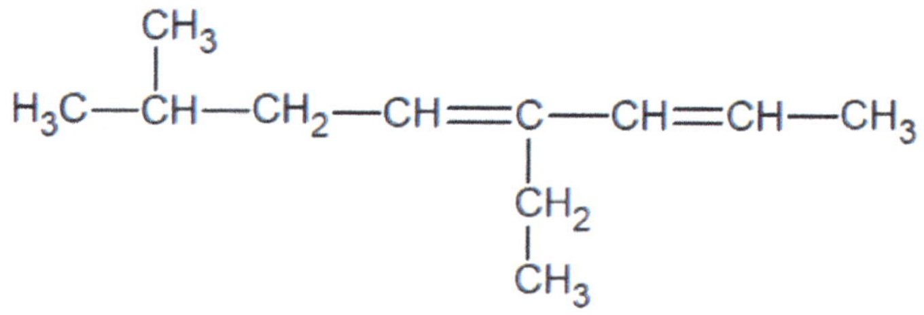

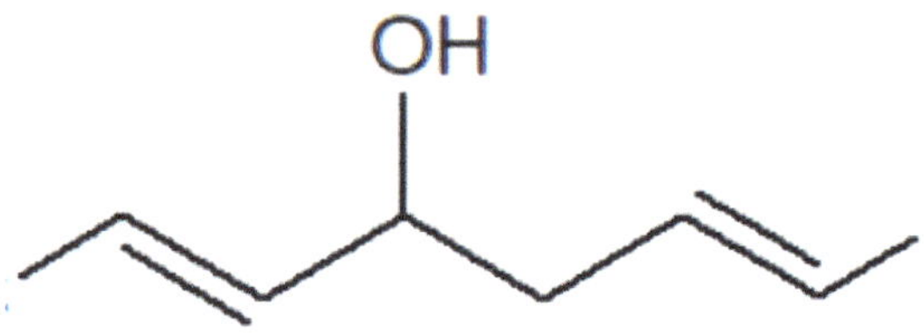

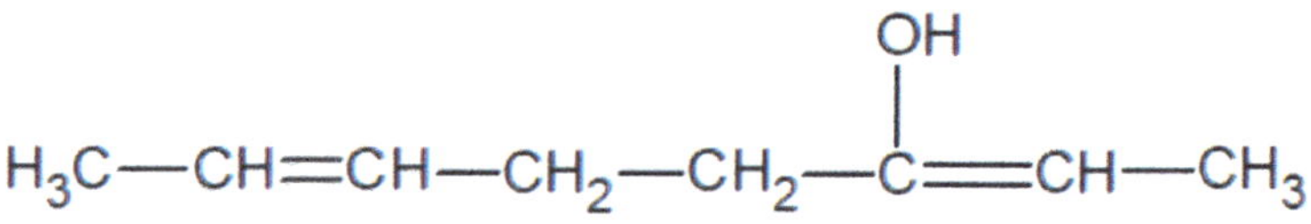

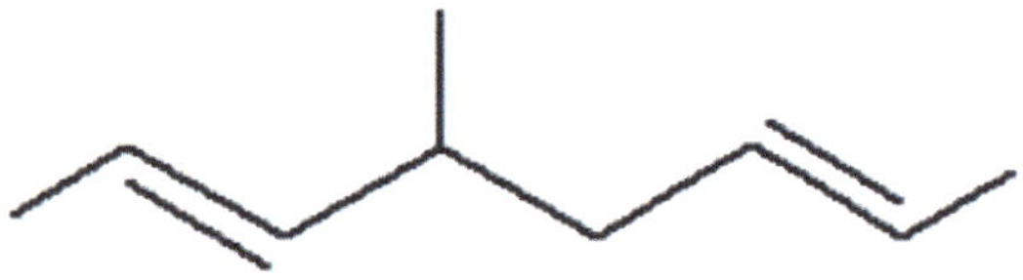

$H_3C-CH=CH-HC \overset{\underset{|}{OH}}{}-CH_2-CH=CH-CH_3$

$H_3C-\overset{\underset{|}{CH_3}}{CH}-CH_2-CH=\overset{\underset{|}{\underset{CH_3}{CH_2}}}{C}-CH=CH-CH_3$

$H_3C-CH=CH-CH_2-CH_2-\overset{\underset{|}{OH}}{C}=CH-CH_3$

C_7H_8

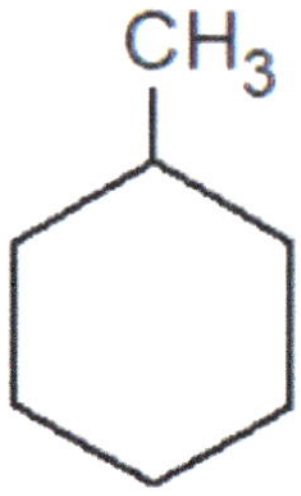

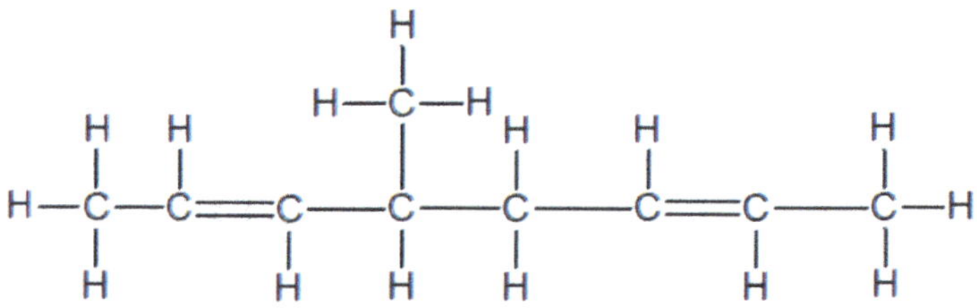

C_7H_{14}

© P & L Johnson 2021

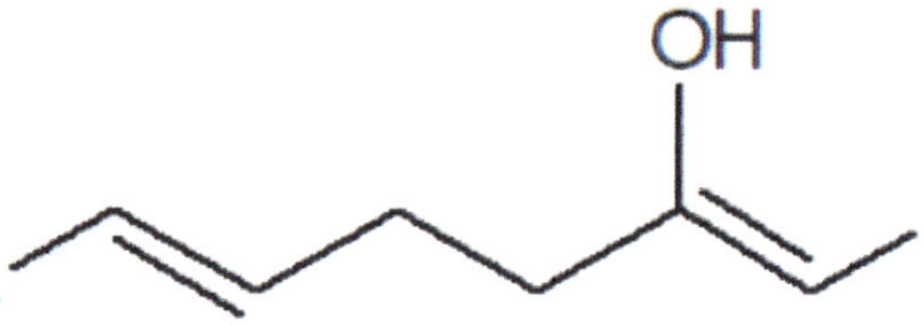

Sigma & Pi Bonds

Look at the following structures and complete the table showing the number of sigma & pi bonds in each.

1

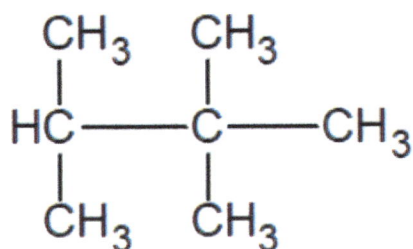

2

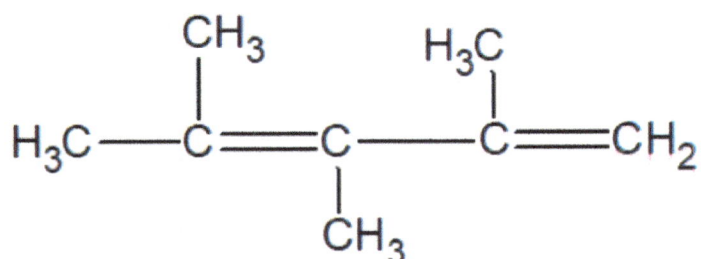

3

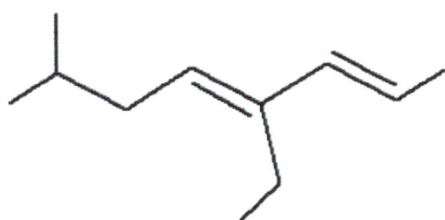

4

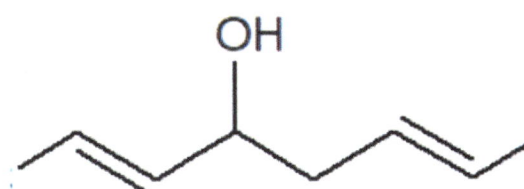

5

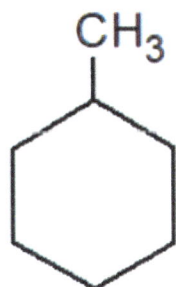

6

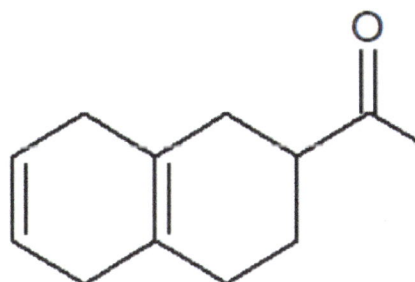

Structure	Sigma bonds	Pi bonds
1		
2		
3		
4		
5		
6		

Quiz Word

Answer the following questions to complete the quiz word and then try to work out what the key phrase in the **bold** boxes should be.

1. A double bond contains one of these and a triple two. (2,4)
2. sp hybridisation is found in this group of hydrocarbons. (7)
3. This substance has a ring shaped conjugated π system. (7)
4. Sigma bonds are formed by this type of orbital overlap. (3-2)
5. sp^3, sp^2 and sp are names of orbitals that are this. (10)
6. π bonds are formed by this type of orbital overlap. (4-2)

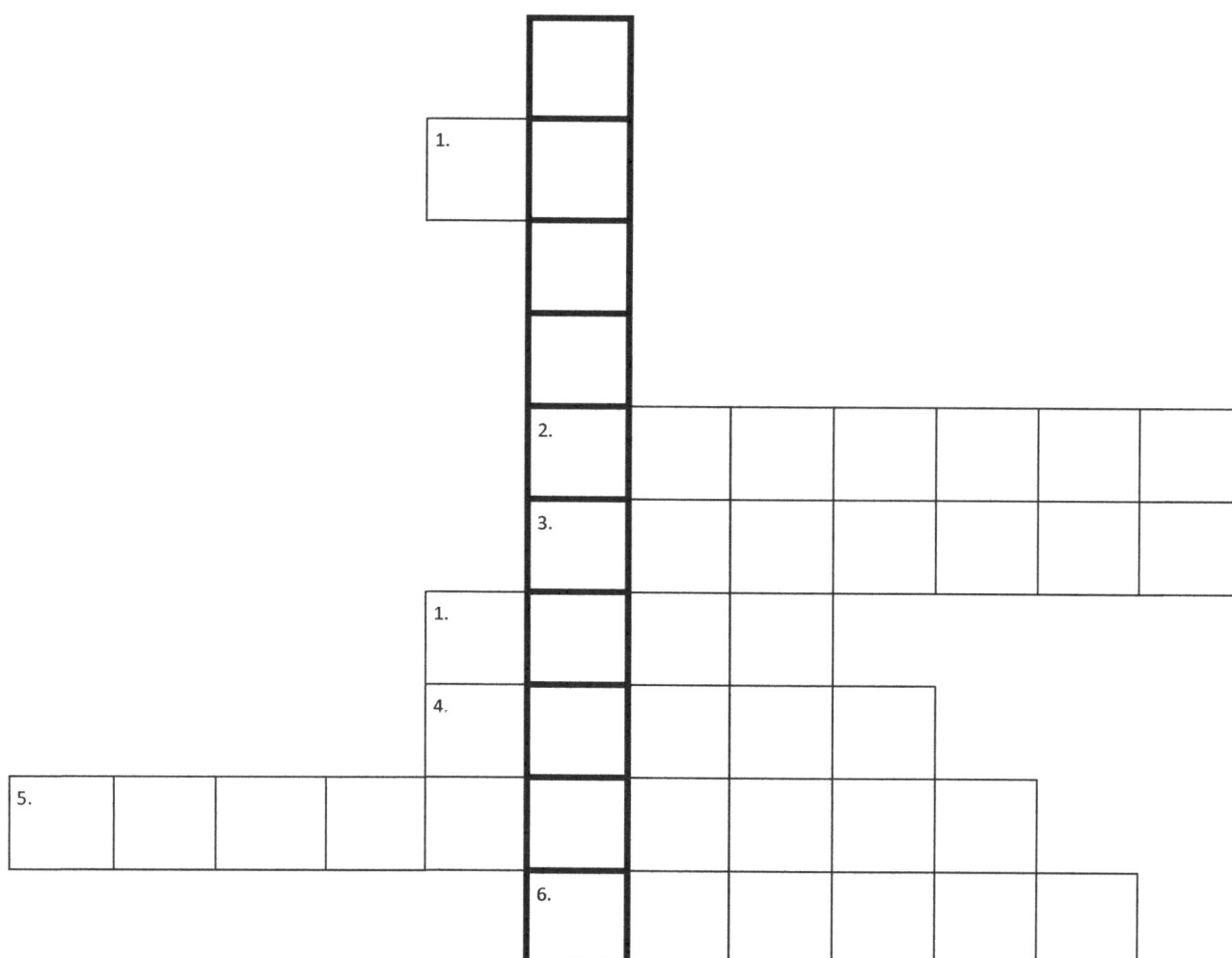

Chemical Misconceptions

A student has written some notes on different types of hybridisation. They have made a number of mistakes that have been highlighted. Using the space below make the corrections.

sp³ hybridisation

In carbon, three s and one p orbitals merge to form 3 sp³ hybrid orbitals. These can undergo side-on overlap to form 4 sigma bonds as shown in the ethene molecule below:

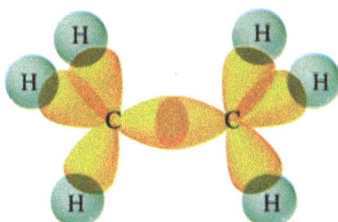

sp hybridisation

In carbon, one s and two p orbitals merge to form 4 sp² hybrid orbitals and an unhybridized p orbital. Three of these overlap side-on forming 3 sigma bonds and the other two can undergo side-on overlap to form two double bonds as shown in the ethane molecule below:

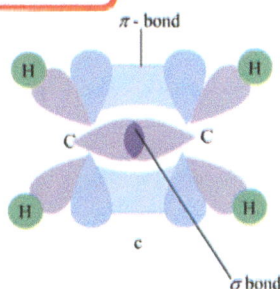

Coloured Organic Compounds

Highlight or circle the conjugated π systems and therefore identify which of the following organic molecules are likely to be coloured.

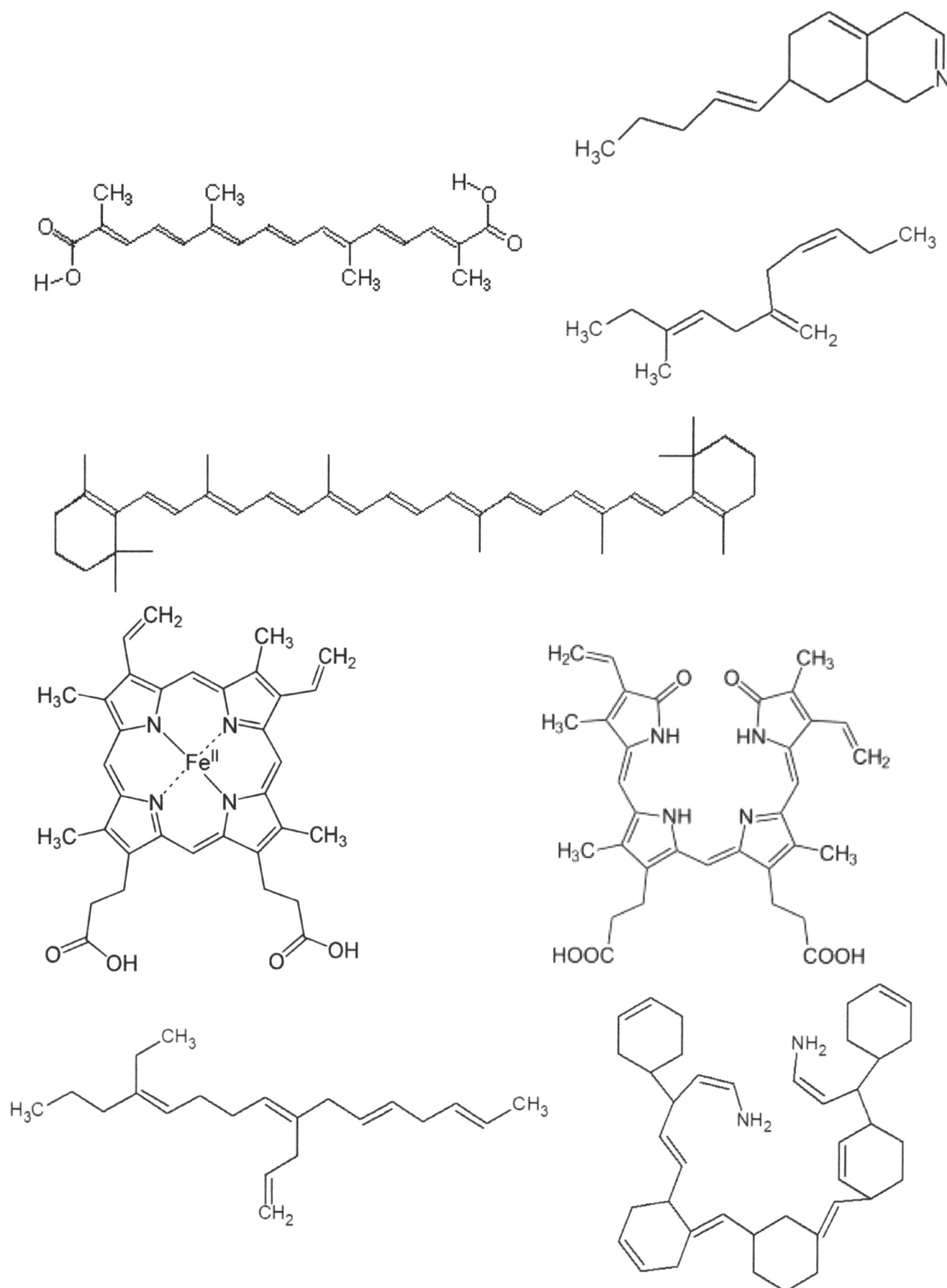

Wordsearch

Complete the wordsearch below using the clues given to identify the correct words(s) that can be found in the wordsearch.

```
G W I I V S U D U K M N R W D
D P I J M P M O I I S S O N E
F B R O T H C Z R R Y U O G Z
I Y L O R Y N U X S B B J O L
C T V S I B I S T L A Y U O A
Z V E W E R I E D M U Q H M B
H W T P H I M T G H G T V U S
N W C U I D Q I A E S M W L O
O U L Y X I S V Z L G J O O R
D R B P D S O R B Z S J O T B
N P X J O A F V Q T Q N S O E
E I P D E T A G U J N O C M D
H N O E D I S B S G T T J O Z
J N L E M O L E C U L A R H C
U K Y B O N Q C G Z N G P S D
```

1. A coloured organic compound will do this to certain wavelengths of light. (6)

2. All coloured organic compounds contain this. (10,2,6)

3. This type of overlap results in σ bonds. (3-2)

4. This explains the electron jump that results in some organic compounds being coloured. (4,2,4)

5. sp^3, sp^2 and sp are examples of these. (6,8)

6. When two unhybridized p orbitals overlap in this way a pi bond forms. (4-2)

7. A molecule of hydrogen, H_2 will have just one of these. (5,4)

8. The carbon atoms in alkynes undergo this. (1,1,13)

Practice Questions

1. Propyl paraben is used as a preservative in cosmetics. It has the following structure.

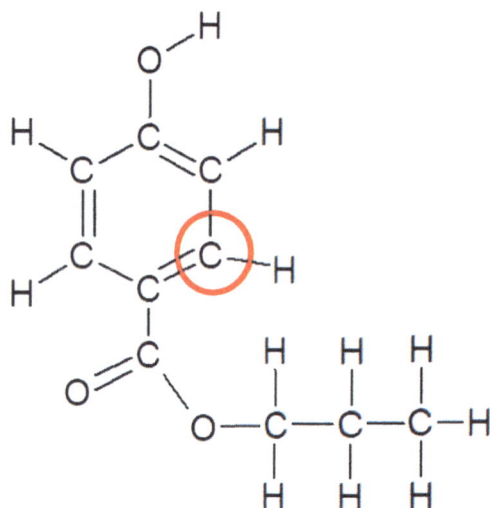

a) Draw a skeletal structure for this molecule.

b) What type of hybridisation does the circled carbon atom have in the above structure.

c) Describe how sigma bonds form.

2. The structure of two common dyes are shown below:

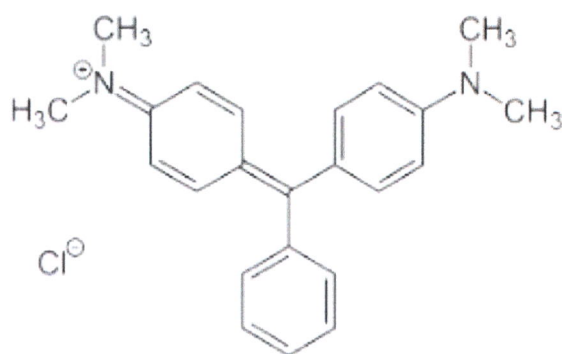

Malachite green (MG)

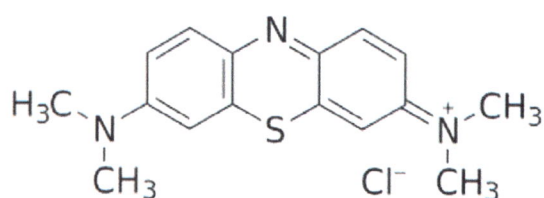

Methylene blue (MB)

a. What structural feature is present in both molecules that is responsible for the colours seen?

b. Clearly explain how colours arise in these types of molecules.

3. Indigo is the dye used to make jeans blue:

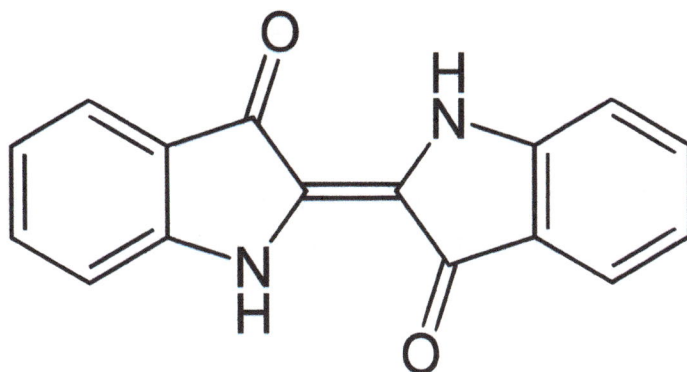

a. What structural features causes the colour.

b. Explain clearly how colour arises in these types of compounds.

c. How many sigma bonds are there in this molecule?

d. Circle a carbon atom with sp^2 hybridisation.

4. Paracetamol is a widely used analgesic, it has the following structure:

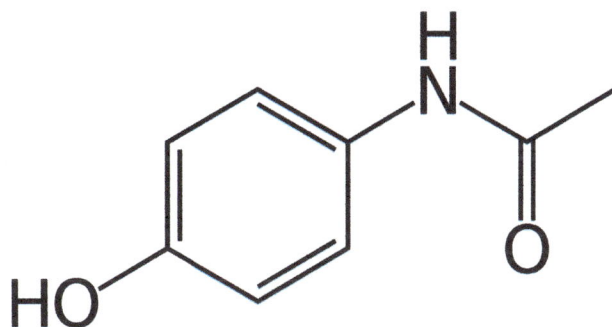

a. Draw the full structural formula for this molecule.

b. The molecule contains a number of sigma and pi bonds, explain clearly the difference between the two types of bonds describing how both occur.

c. Circle the carbon atom in the structure with sp^3 hybridisation.

d. Explain clearly how sp^3 hybridisation occurs.

Unit 3 Organic Synthesis - Bonding

Curly Arrows

The movement of electrons can be shown by single or double headed arrows. Using curly arrows helps to show the reaction mechanisms.

Homolytic Fission:

Halogens can undergo homolytic fission when struck by ultraviolet light.

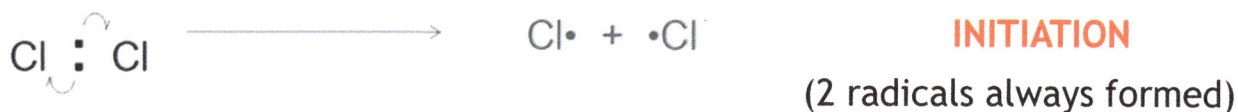

$$Cl : Cl \longrightarrow Cl\bullet + \bullet Cl \qquad \textbf{INITIATION}$$

(2 radicals always formed)

The single headed arrow shows the movement of one of the shared bonding electrons to each atom producing two very reactive free radicals.

Free radicals are atoms with an unpaired outer electron.

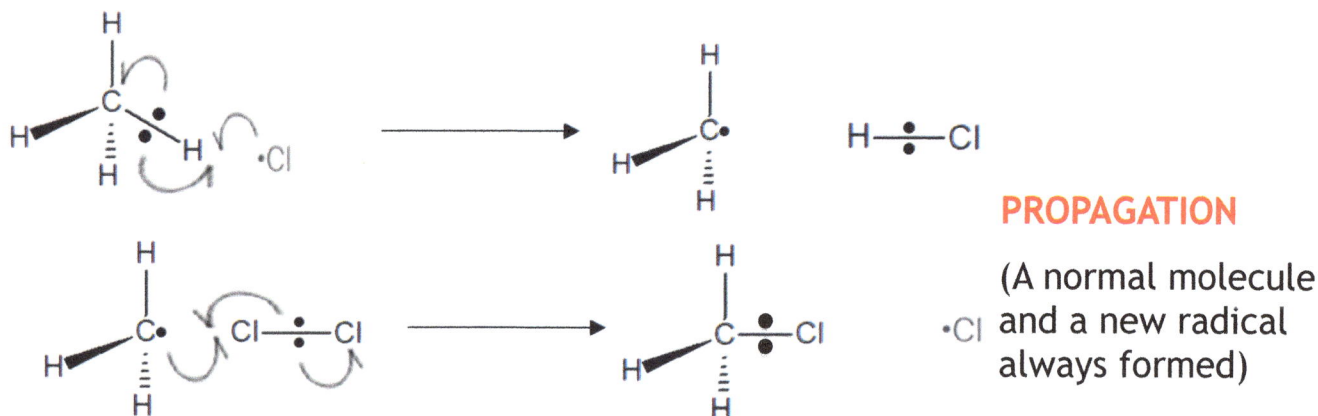

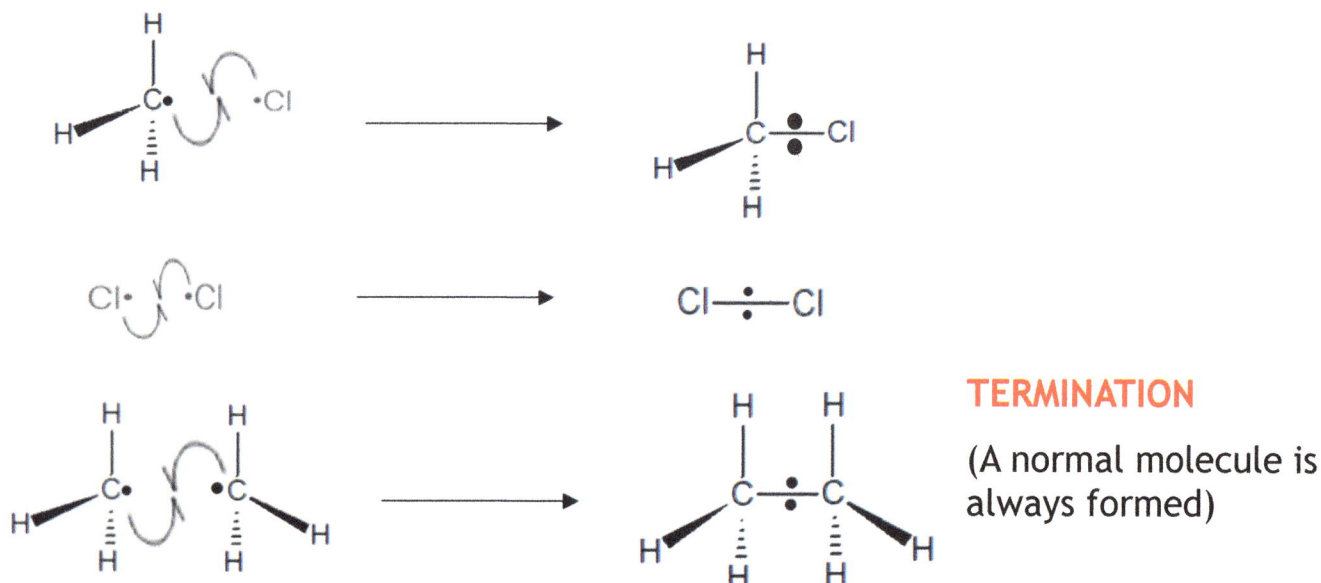

PROPAGATION

(A normal molecule and a new radical always formed)

TERMINATION

(A normal molecule is always formed)

© P & L Johnson 2021

Heterolytic Fission:

When a bond is polar the atom with the higher electronegativity will take both electrons, causing the formation of two oppositely charged ions. In organic chemistry a positively charge hydrocarbon is called a carbocation or carbonium ion and a negatively charged hydrocarbon is called a carbanion.

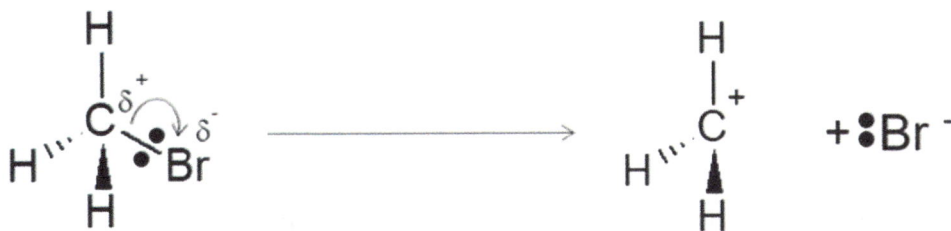

The double headed arrow shows the movement of both electrons to the bromine atom.

The charged ions can be described as being nucleophiles (nucleus or positive charge loving) or electrophiles (electron or negative charge loving).

Nucleophiles are negative charged ions such OH^-, Cl^-, Br^-, CN^- or molecules with lone pairs of electrons such as H_2O and NH_3.

Electrophiles are positive charged ions such as H^+, Cl^+, NO_2^+, or carbocations like CH_3^+.

Formation of stable carbocations

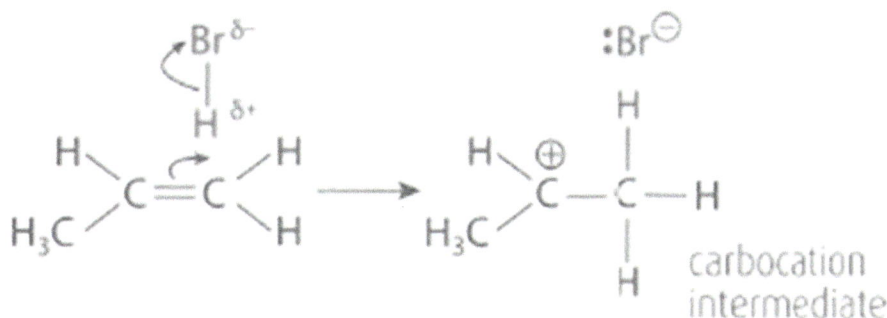

The double headed arrows show the H—Br bond being broken and a new bond being made between the carbon atom and the hydrogen.

Stable carbocations are preferred and will readily form when the positive charge can be stabilised by the inductive effect of branches, or halogens. Tertiary halogenoalkanes readily form these when they undergo nucleophilic substitution reactions.

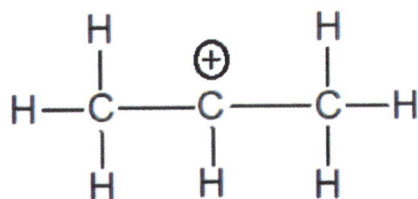

Stable cation

readily forms

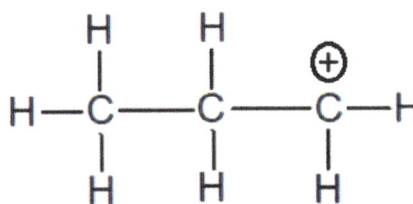

Unstable cation

doesn't readily form

Free Radical Reactions

Free radical reactions follow three stages; initiation, propagation and termination. Label the following equations using the codes below:

1 Initiation

2 Propagation

3 Termination

Then draw the electrons as dots and use single headed arrows to show the movement of the electrons in each process.

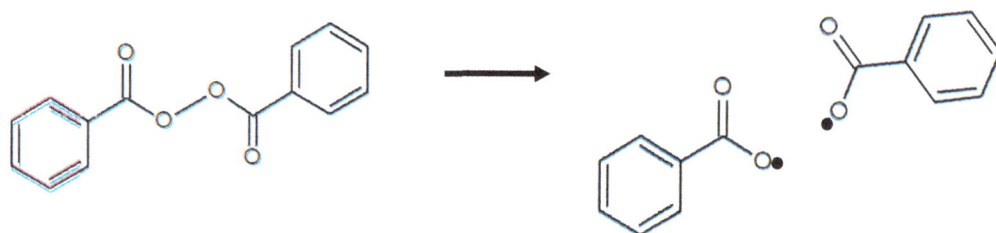

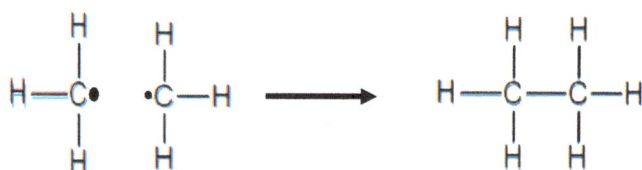

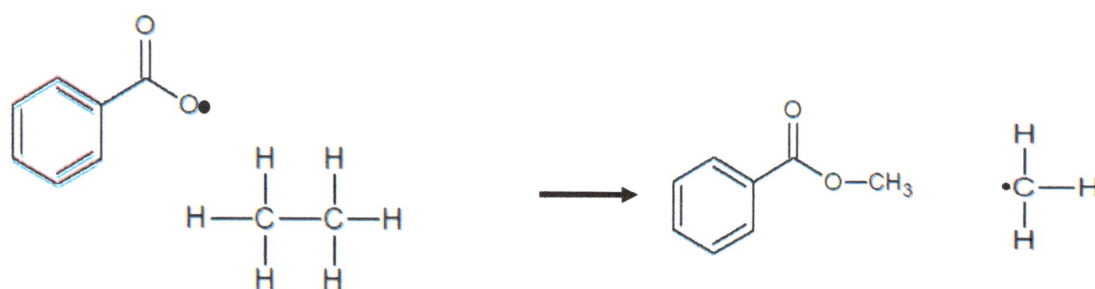

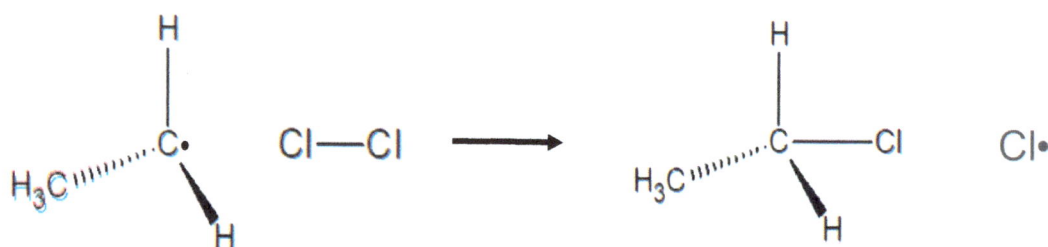

$Cl\bullet \quad + \quad Cl\bullet \quad \longrightarrow \quad Cl-Cl$

$Br-Br \quad \longrightarrow \quad Br\bullet \quad \bullet Br$

Quiz Word

Answer the following questions to complete the quiz word and then try to work out what the key phrase in the **bold** boxes should be.

1. These are used to show the movement of electrons in reaction mechanisims. (5,6)

2. This is the positively charged hydrocarbon that can be formed during heterolytic fission. (11)

3. Process usually occurring when UV light is supplied. (10)

4. These are atoms or molecules with an unpaired outer electron present. (8)

5. These help to stabilise carbocations. (8)

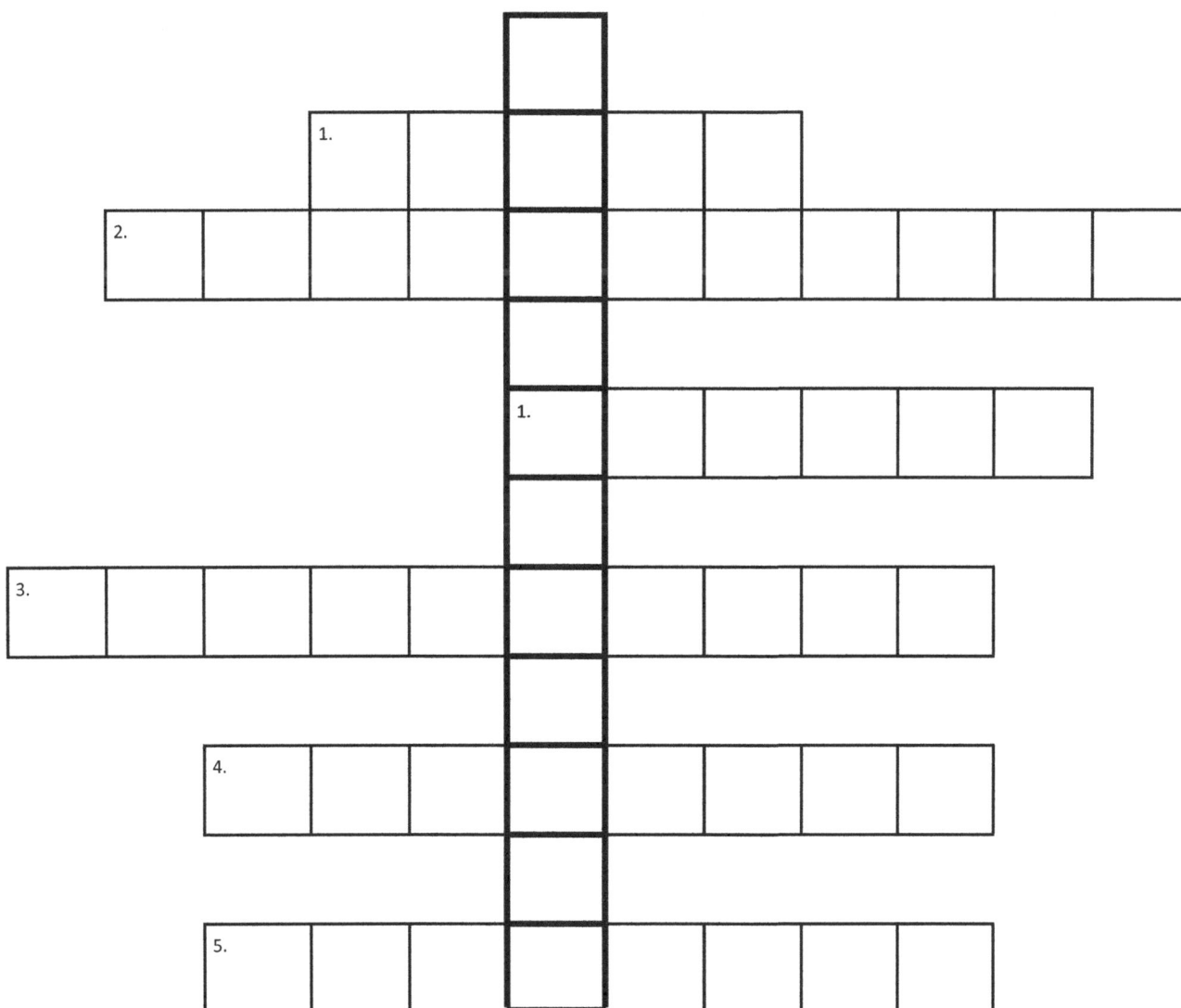

Quiz Word Clue: A radical is always reformed during this process.

© P & L Johnson 2021   95

Stable Carbocations

Look at the following pairs of carbocations and identify which is the more stable and therefore more likely to form.

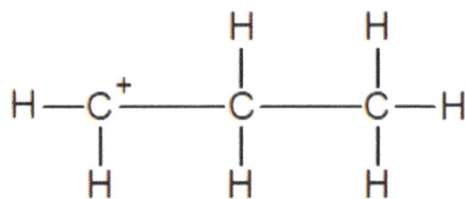

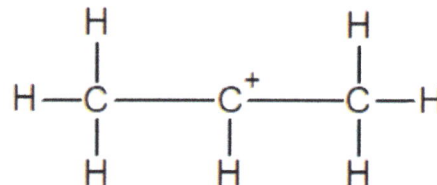

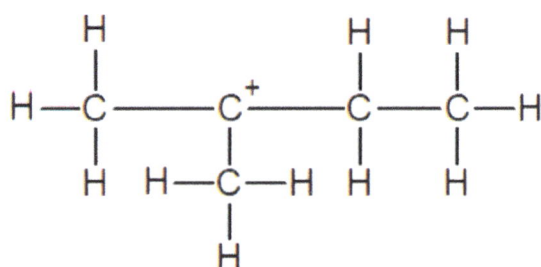

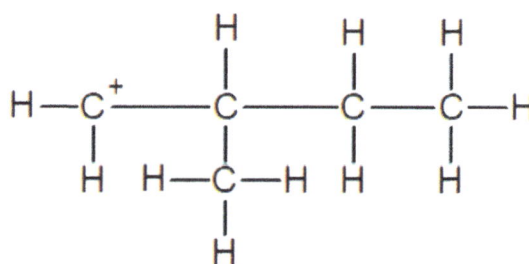

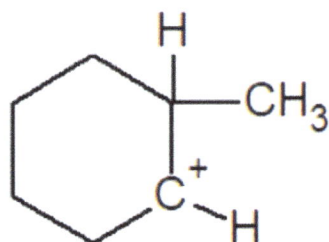

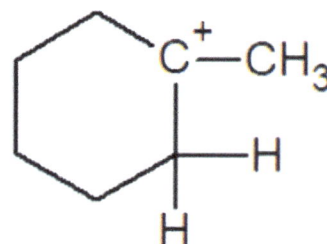

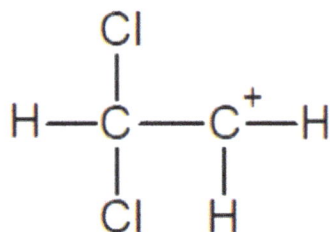

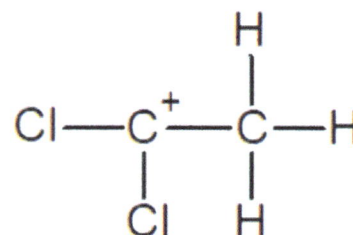

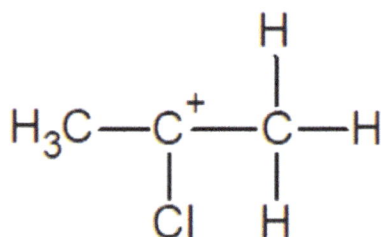

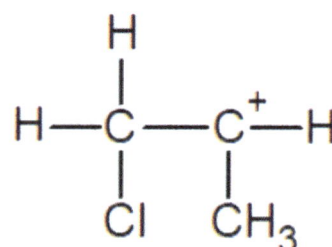

Wordsearch

Complete the wordsearch below using the clues given to identify the correct words(s) that can be found in the wordsearch.

```
C L E G H D C O R K U F S N G
A A L V G E E U O D Q B S D B
R C E H I R T N N W V W E I P
B I C I Y M U E Q P O L N U N
O D T M N X R H R R A T F U B
C A R G E O P U R O I I B G I
A R O C X N I A F T L Q R Z J
T E N P P X Y T I U I Y Y E O
I E S X H L I A A Z M R T H D
O R H P R Q T S I N O R D I O
N F S U Z I F H D D I A J J C
H G C Y O Z W N L X D M U M P
U Z U N O I T A G A P O R P F
H O M O L Y T I C I H K B E B
Q C C B M B X R Z W X H E K T
```

1. A positively charge hydrocarbon ion. (11)
2. The very reactive particle formed when bonding electrons are shared equally between the two atoms. (4,7)
3. This type of fission occurs when one atom has a higher electronegativity than the other atom in the bond. (11)
4. UV light often causes this form of fission. (9)
5. This stage occurs when two radicals react together. (11)
6. All radicals contain one of these. (8,8)
7. Used to show the movement of electrons during reactions. (5,6)
8. The stage when radicals react with a molecule forming a stable molecule and another radical. (11)

Reactions Involving Heterolytic Fission

Look at the following processes and complete them by either drawing the structure of the product or drawing curly arrows to show the movement of the electron pair(s).

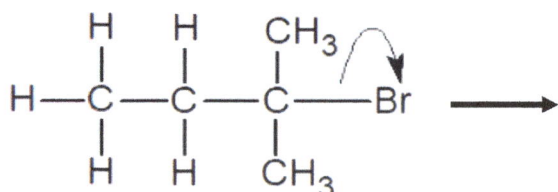

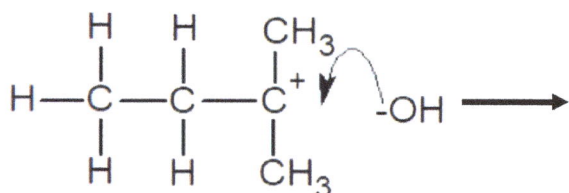

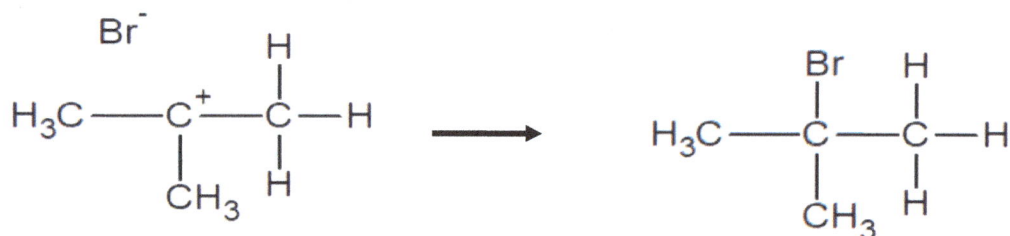

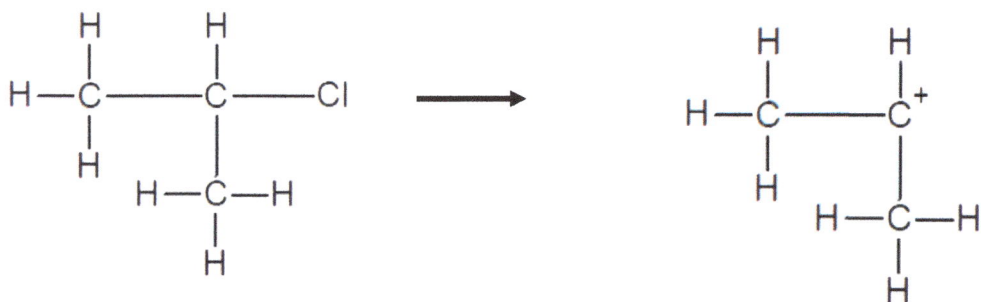

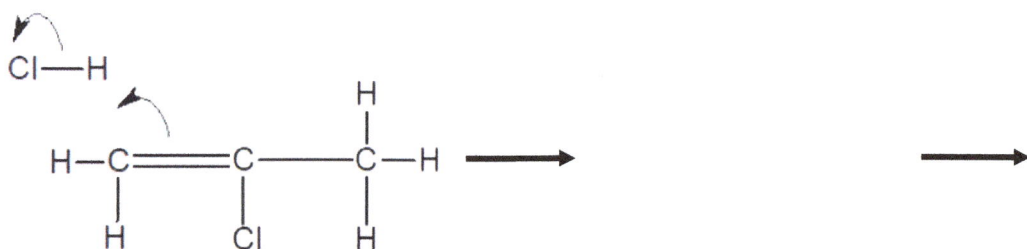

Practice Questions

1. Aldehydes and ketones can exist in two forms, a keto form and an enol form.

    A possible mechanism for acid-catalysed enolization of 3-methylbutan-2-one is shown below:

    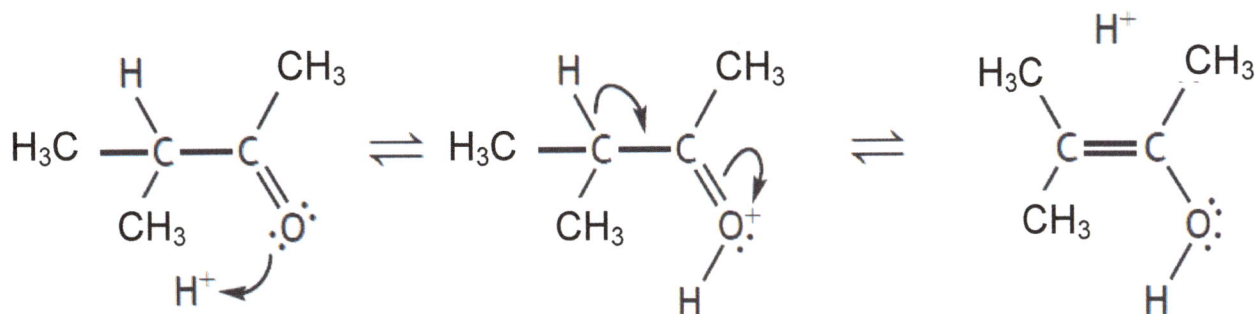

    Using structural formulae and curly arrow notation, show a possible mechanism for the acid-catalysed enolisation of 2-methylpentan-3-one.

2. 1-methycyclohexene can undergo addition reactions and the subsequent product reacted with an alkali to form 1-methylcyclohexan-1-ol, as shown in the reaction sequence below:

    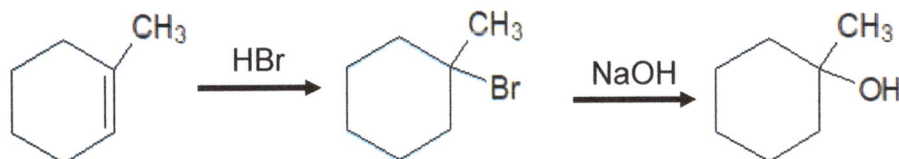

    a. Explain why the carbocation A is formed rather than carbocation B in the first reaction.

    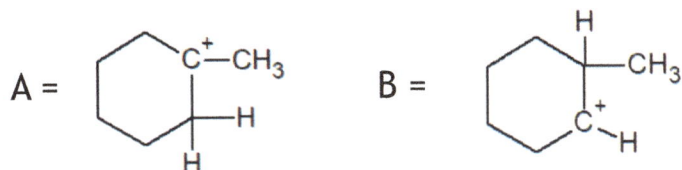

    b. The reaction mechanism for the second reaction is shown below, using curly arrows show the movement of electron pairs for each stage.

    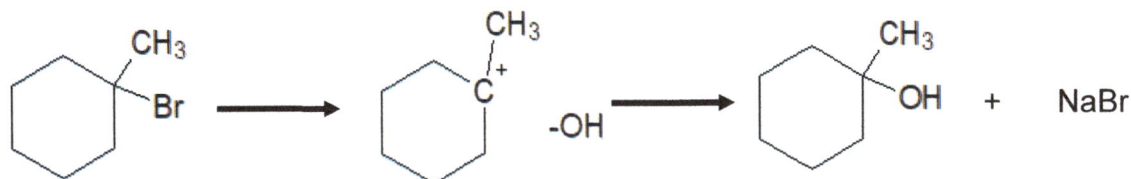

Unit 3   Organic Synthesis - Alkenes

Alkenes

Unsaturated hydrocarbons with a C=C bond.

In industry catalytic cracking of hydrocarbons is used.

In the laboratory there are two ways.

Catalytic dehydration of an alcohol:

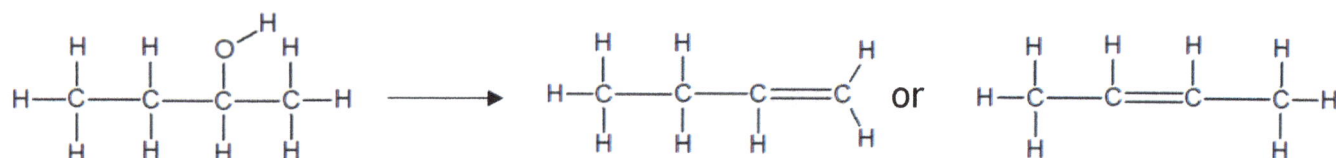

or base induced elimination of a monohalogenoalkane:

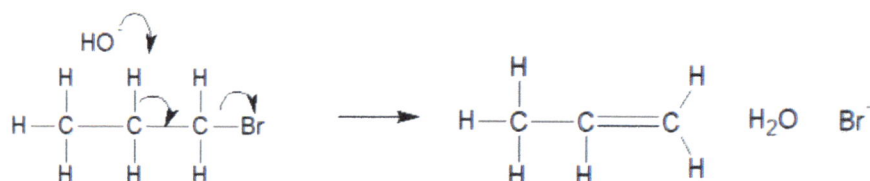

Reactions of alkenes:

Addition of halogens

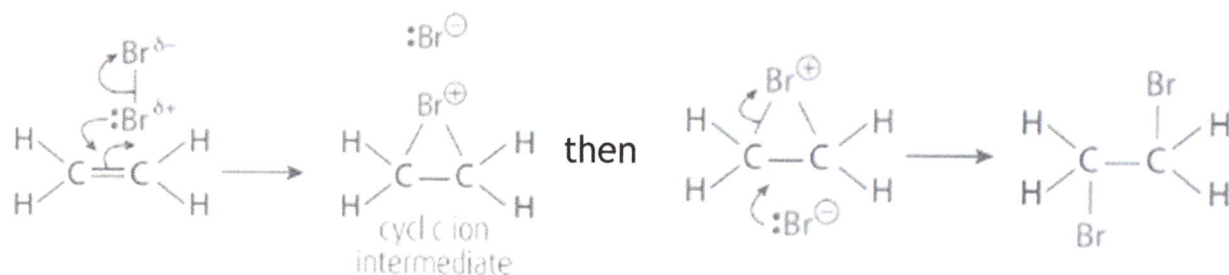

cyclic ion
intermediate

then

Addition of hydrogen halides

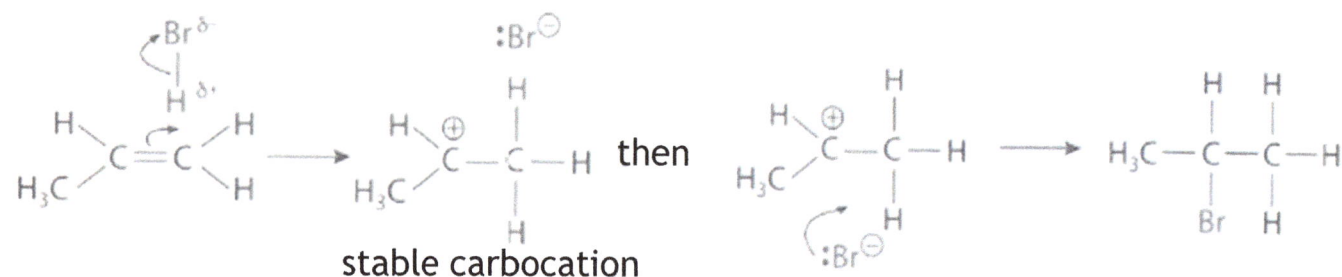

stable carbocation

then

Acid catalysed addition of water

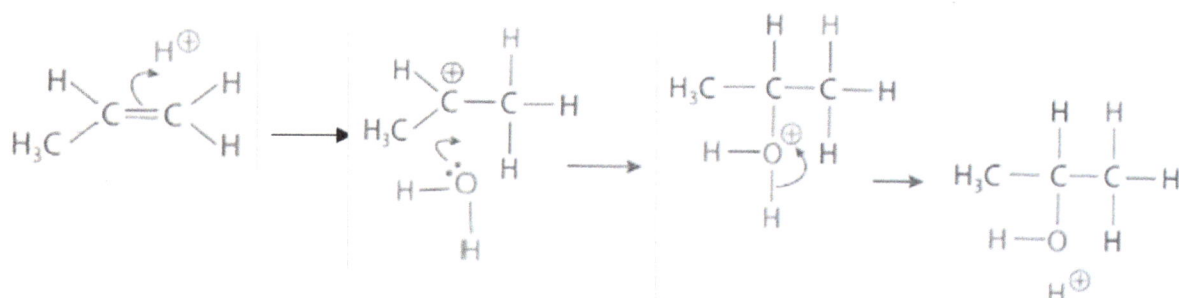

Markovnikov's Rule

This states that with addition reactions of an alkene if there is a **hydrogen atom it will always add to the carbon atom with the greatest number of hydrogen atoms already attached to it**. This is due to the greater stability of the carbocation when there is another group attached to the carbon rather than a hydrogen atom.

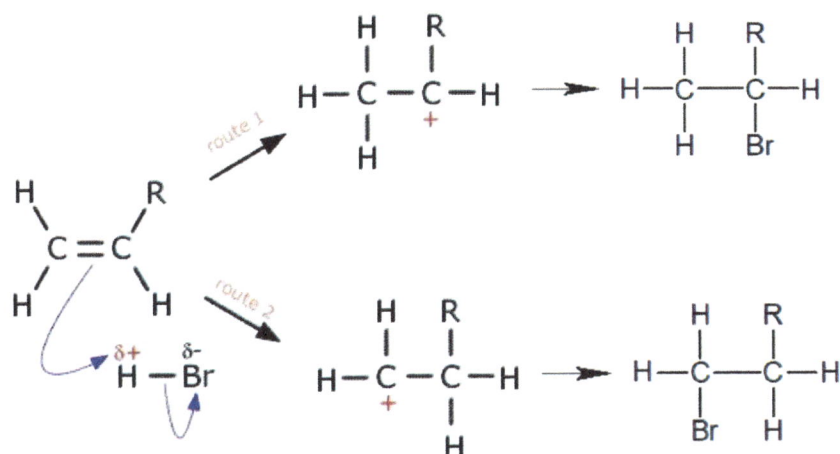

Major Product

The carbocation is stabilised by the inductive effect of the R-branch, R could be an alkyl group or another halogen like Cl or Br.

Minor Product

The carbocation is not stabilised by the hydrogens as they have a weak inductive effect.

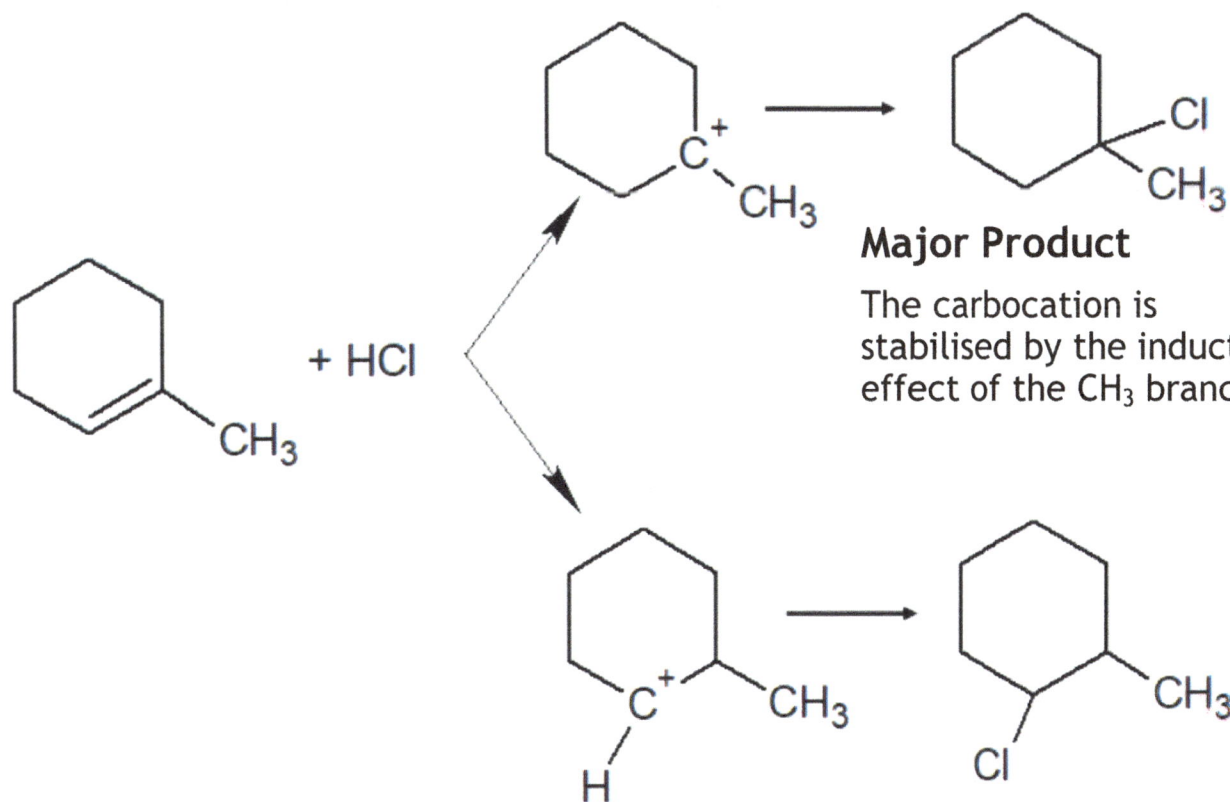

Major Product

The carbocation is stabilised by the inductive effect of the CH_3 branch.

Minor Product

The carbocation is not stabilised by the hydrogen as they have a weak inductive effect.

Addition Reactions

Connect the alkene to the correct reagent and product they form. The first one has been done for you:

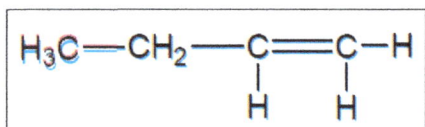

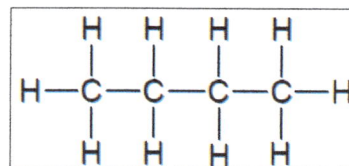

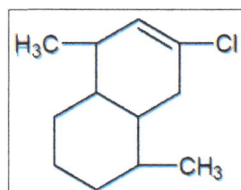

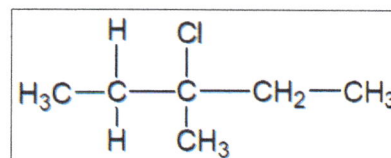

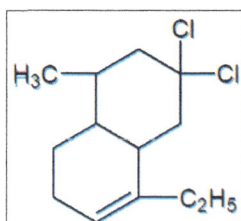

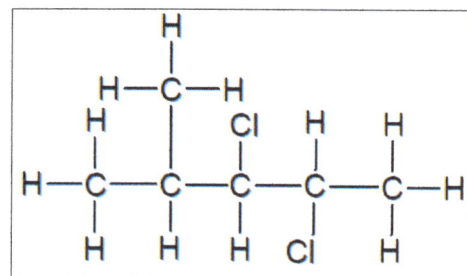

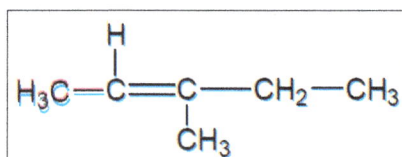

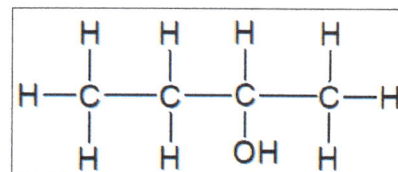

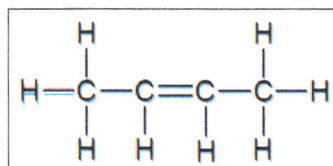

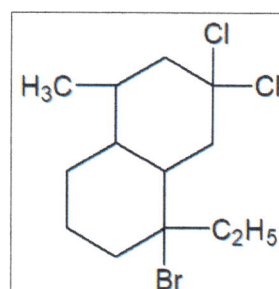

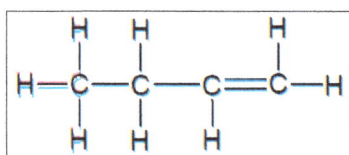

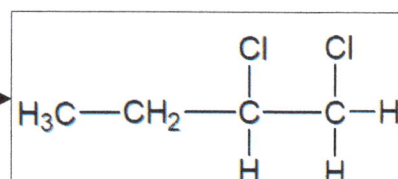

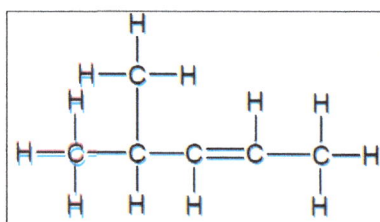

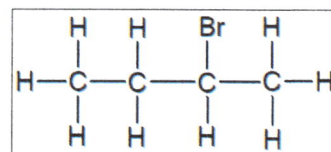

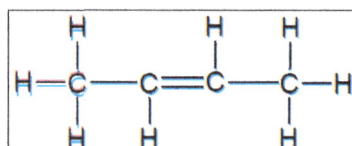

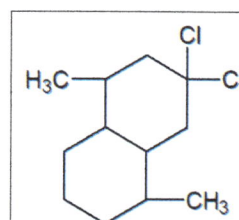

Quiz Word

Answer the following questions to complete the quiz word and then try to work out what the key phrase in the **bold** boxes should be.

1. Product that is more likely to form. (5)
2. This is formed when the positive carbon atom has a methyl attached to it. (6,11)
3. Reaction creating alkenes from alcohols. (11)
4. Product that is less likely to form. (5)
5. Monohalogenoalkanes and alkalis undergo this to form alkenes. (11)
6. Formed by the catalytic hydration of an alkene. (7)

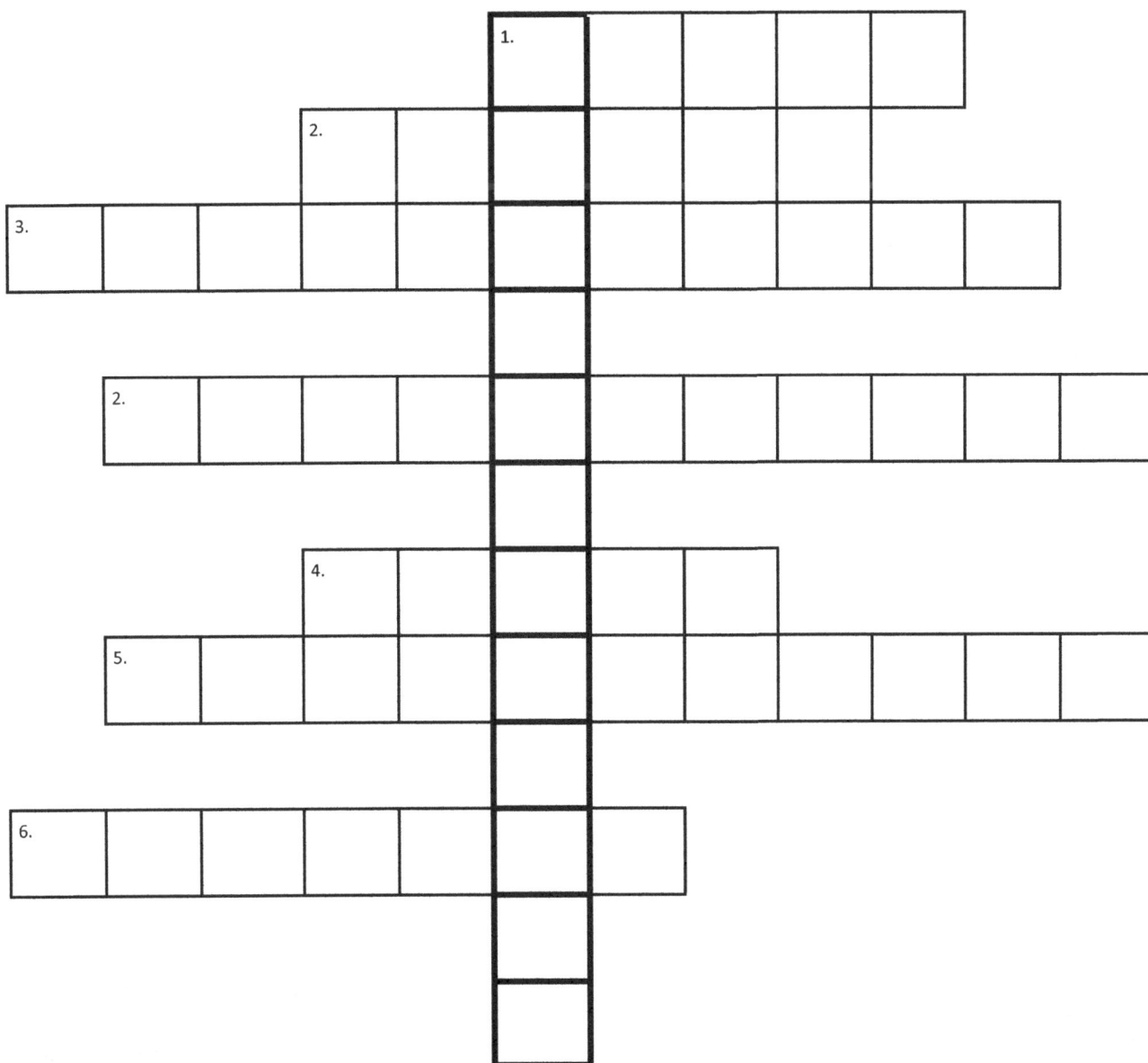

Quiz Word Clue: Rule that identifies the major product in an addition reaction.

Cyclic Intermediates

Look at the following reactions, draw the cyclic intermediate and movement of electron pairs using curly arrows to form the product given:

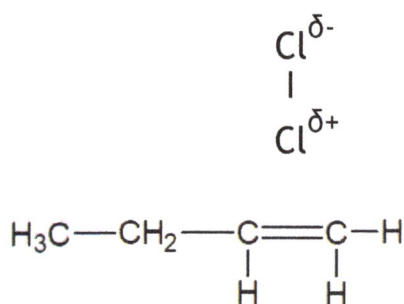

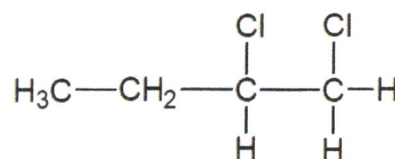

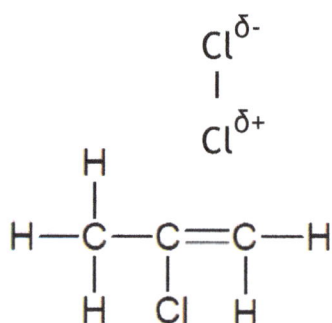

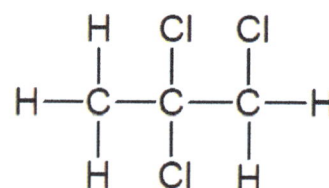

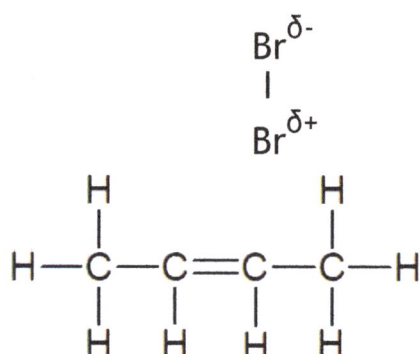

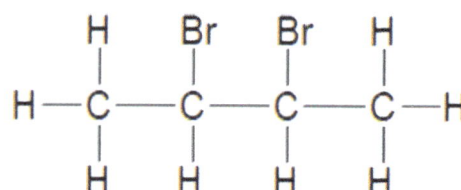

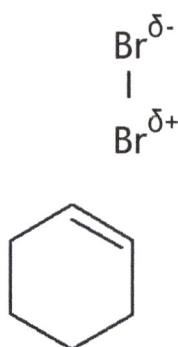

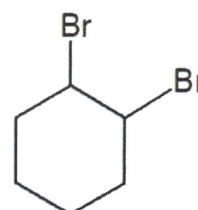

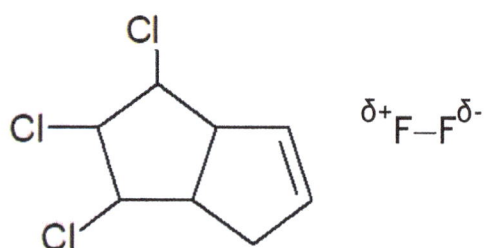

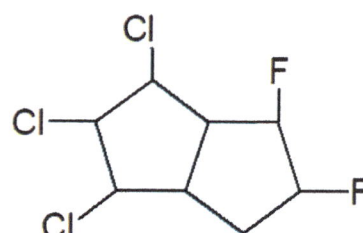

$Cl^{\delta-}$
|
$Cl^{\delta+}$

$H_3C-CH_2-C{=}C-H$ with H and H below the double bond carbons

$H_3C-CH_2-\overset{Cl}{\underset{H}{C}}-\overset{Cl}{\underset{H}{C}}-H$

$Cl^{\delta-}$
|
$Cl^{\delta+}$

$H-\overset{H}{\underset{H}{C}}-\overset{}{\underset{Cl}{C}}{=}C-H$ with H below

$H-\overset{H}{\underset{H}{C}}-\overset{Cl}{\underset{Cl}{C}}-\overset{Cl}{\underset{H}{C}}-H$

$Br^{\delta-}$
|
$Br^{\delta+}$

$H-\overset{H}{\underset{H}{C}}-\overset{}{\underset{H}{C}}{=}C-\overset{H}{\underset{H}{C}}-H$

$H-\overset{H}{\underset{H}{C}}-\overset{Br}{\underset{H}{C}}-\overset{Br}{\underset{H}{C}}-\overset{H}{\underset{H}{C}}-H$

$Br^{\delta-}$
|
$Br^{\delta+}$

(cyclohexene ring)

(cyclohexane ring with Br and Br)

(bicyclic ring with three Cl substituents and a double bond) $^{\delta+}F-F^{\delta-}$

(bicyclic ring with three Cl substituents, and F, F)

Markovnikov's Rule

Look at the following reactions and identify which product will be the **major** product based on Markovnikov's rule:

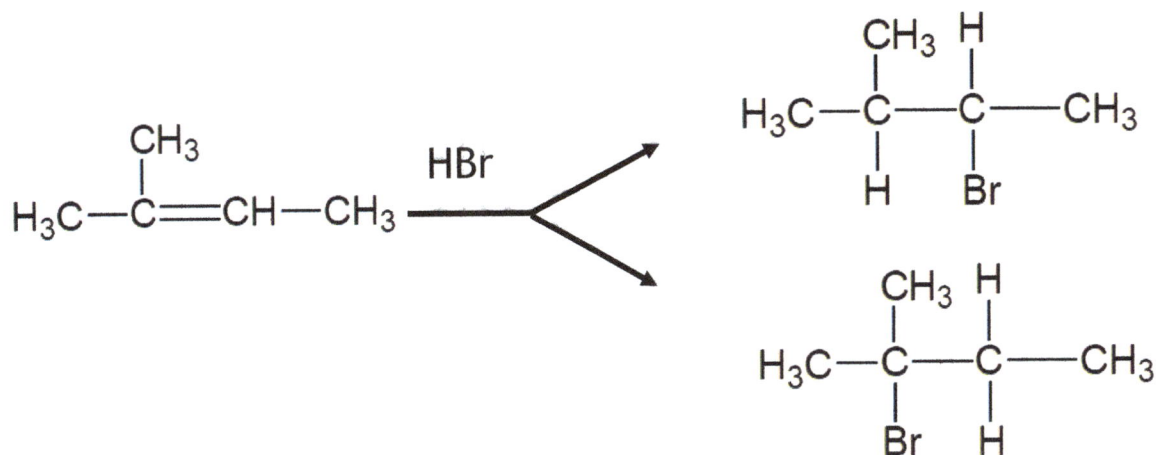

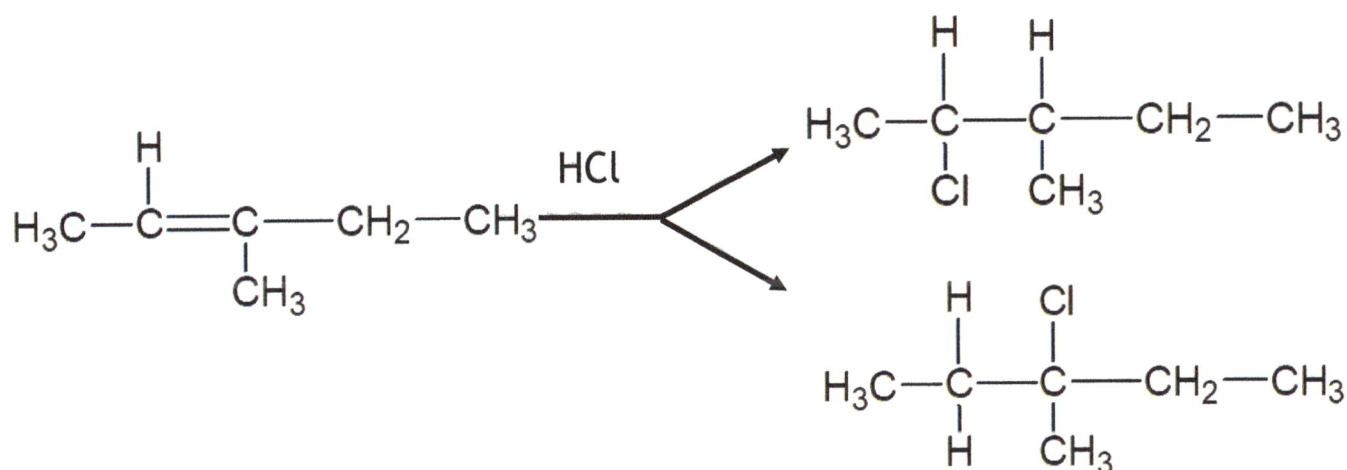

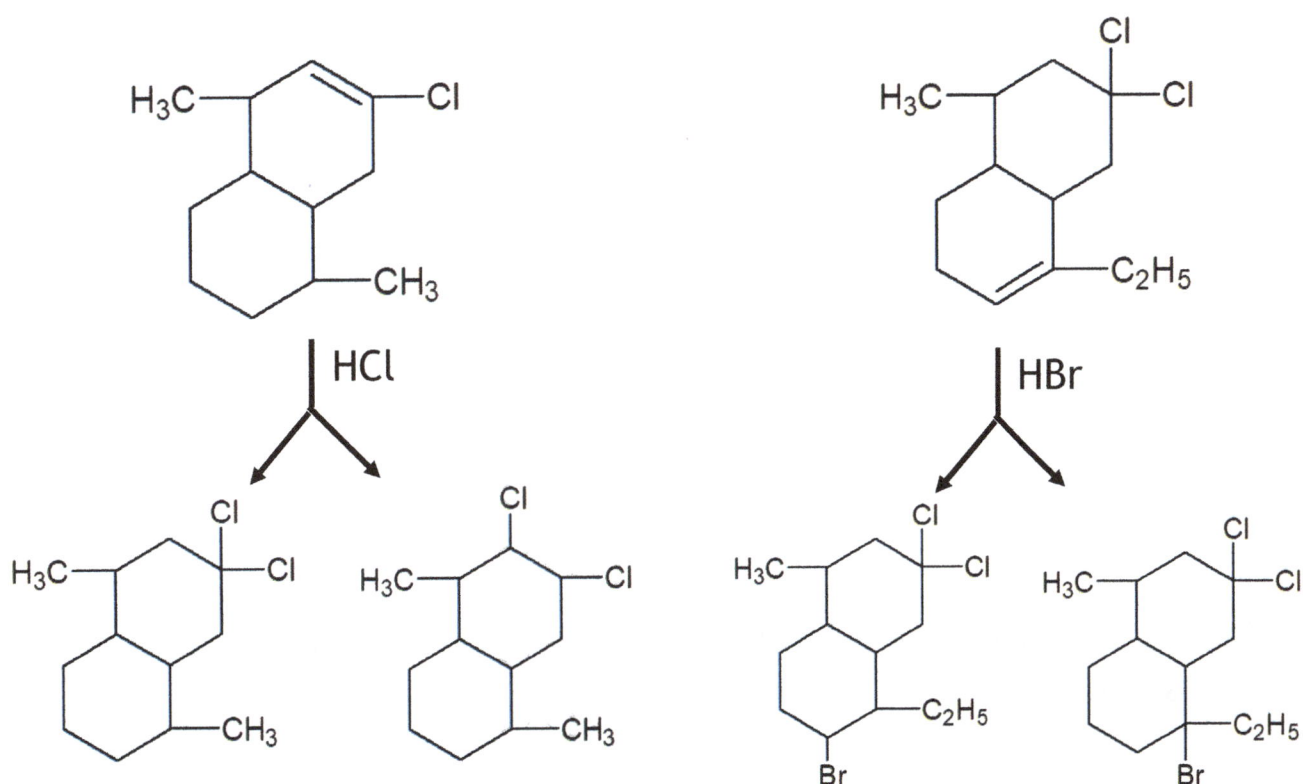

Wordsearch

Complete the wordsearch below using the clues given to identify the correct words(s) that can be found in the wordsearch.

```
N O I T A N I M I L E M S I T
V E S W S C L E K O E T V C B
Y R Q O E W E F Q T A O E J I
M E P Y O T K O H B Q F C X C
C A Q C V S Q Y L Y F Z H X A
I C J M W T L E P E J N I E R
T T A O E G U E E Y O Y H Q B
Y I M A R K O V N I K O V S O
L O H O B P I Q T R F L F Y C
A N U G E T R A W U G S Q J A
T P D L C S R O N T A T V C T
A E L U R D A D D I T I O N I
C L D S Y W O B M U L M Q R O
W N C H F Z V Q K A C C E G N
I N V J S H L L F Y I T I A L
```

1. Used to predict what the major product will be. (12,4)

2. Can help to stabilise the carbocation. (6,5)

3. How alkenes are turned into alkanes. (8,8)

4. The reaction that creates alkenes from monohalogenoalkane. (4,11)

5. Reaction used to make alcohols from alkenes. (9,9)

6. The positive carbon intermediate is stabilised by the _____ _____ of alkyl groups and chlorine atoms. (9,6)

7. This is formed when reactions follow Markovnikov's rule. (5,7)

8. The positively charged intermediate when the major product forms. (6,11)

Practice Questions

1. Butan-1-ol and butan-2-ol are both formed during the acid catalysed hydration of but-1-ene.

a) Name the major product and using Markovnikov's rule clearly explain why it forms more often than the other product.

b) Using structural formulae and curly arrows show how one of the two products forms.

2. Propene can be made by reacting 1-bromopropane with sodium hydroxide.

a) Name the type of reaction that makes alkenes from monohalogenoalkanes.

b) 1,2-dibromopropane can be made by reacting propene with bromine. Using structural formulae and curly arrows show how this occurs.

3. 1-chlorocyclohexene can react with HCl to form two products as shown in the reaction sequence below:

a) Draw a structural formula for the other product.

b) Using structural formulae and curly arrows show how 1,1-dichlorocyclohexane forms.

Monohalogenoalkanes:

Here one of the hydrogens in an alkane has been replaced by a halogen either F, Cl, Br or I.

There are three types:

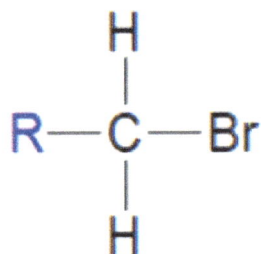

Primary

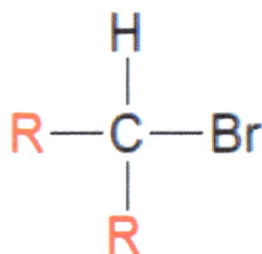

Secondary

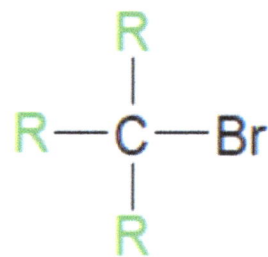

Tertiary

Where R = any alkyl group.

This is the same as for alcohols.

Naming halogenoalkanes:

The halogen is regarded as a branch and named in a similar way with the position, number of, then type of halogen followed by the alkane name.

e.g.

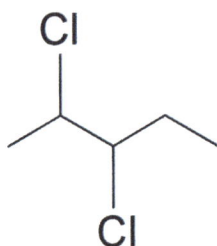

2,3-dichloropentane

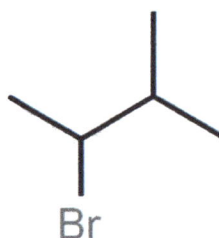

2-bromo-3-methyl-butane

Reactions of halogenoalkanes:

Halogenoalkanes undergo nucleophilic substitution reactions because the halogen is a very good leaving group. This makes them ideal starting materials for the synthesis of a wide range of important hydrocarbon compounds.

The mechanism for the reaction depends upon whether the halogenoalkane is primary, secondary or tertiary and the type of solvent used.

Reactions involving tertiary halogenoalkanes in polar solvents:

Reaction of 2-bromo,2-methylpropane with sodium hydroxide in water.

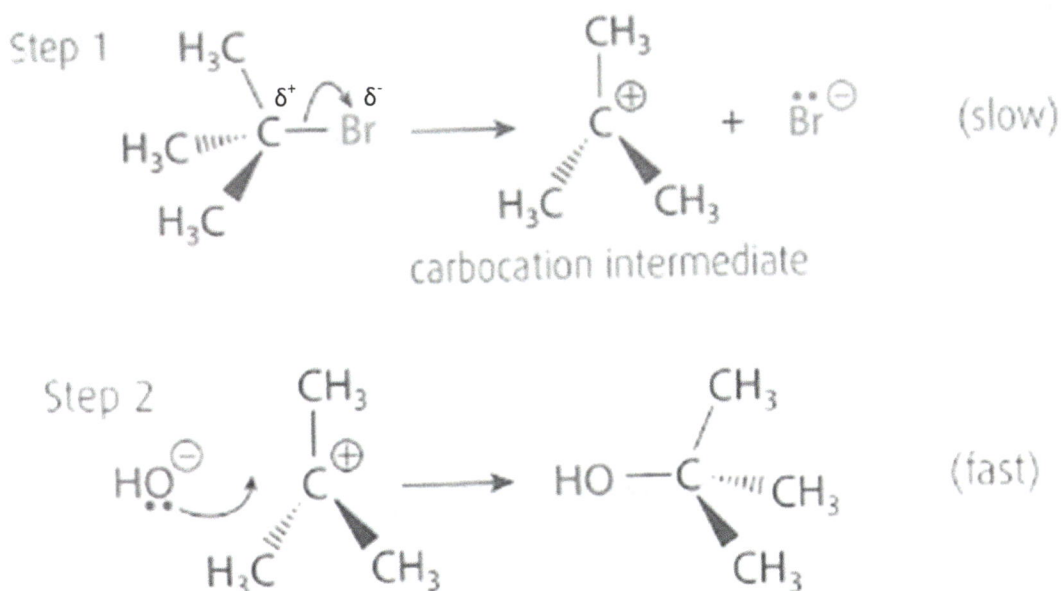

carbocation intermediate

The slow rate determining step involves just one component and so is 1st order overall. As it is a nucleophilic substitution the mechanism is referred to as S_N1.

Reactions involving primary halogenoalkanes in less polar solvents:

Reaction of bromoethane with sodium hydroxide in ethanol.

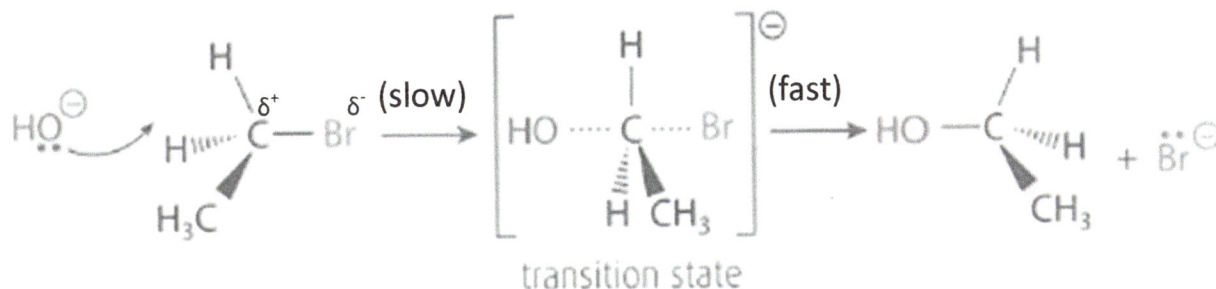

transition state

The slow rate determining step involves two components and so is 2nd order overall. As it is a nucleophilic substitution the mechanism is referred to as S_N2.

Observations	S_N1	S_N2
Reaction rate	Independent of the concentration of the nucleophile.	Dependent of the concentration of the nucleophile.
Favourable halogenoalkanes	tertiary > secondary > primary	primary > secondary > tertiary
Favourable solvent	Polar solvents that stabilise the carbocation e.g. aqueous ethanol or propanone.	Less polar solvents e.g. anhydrous ethanol or propanone.

Summary of Reactions of Halogenoalkanes

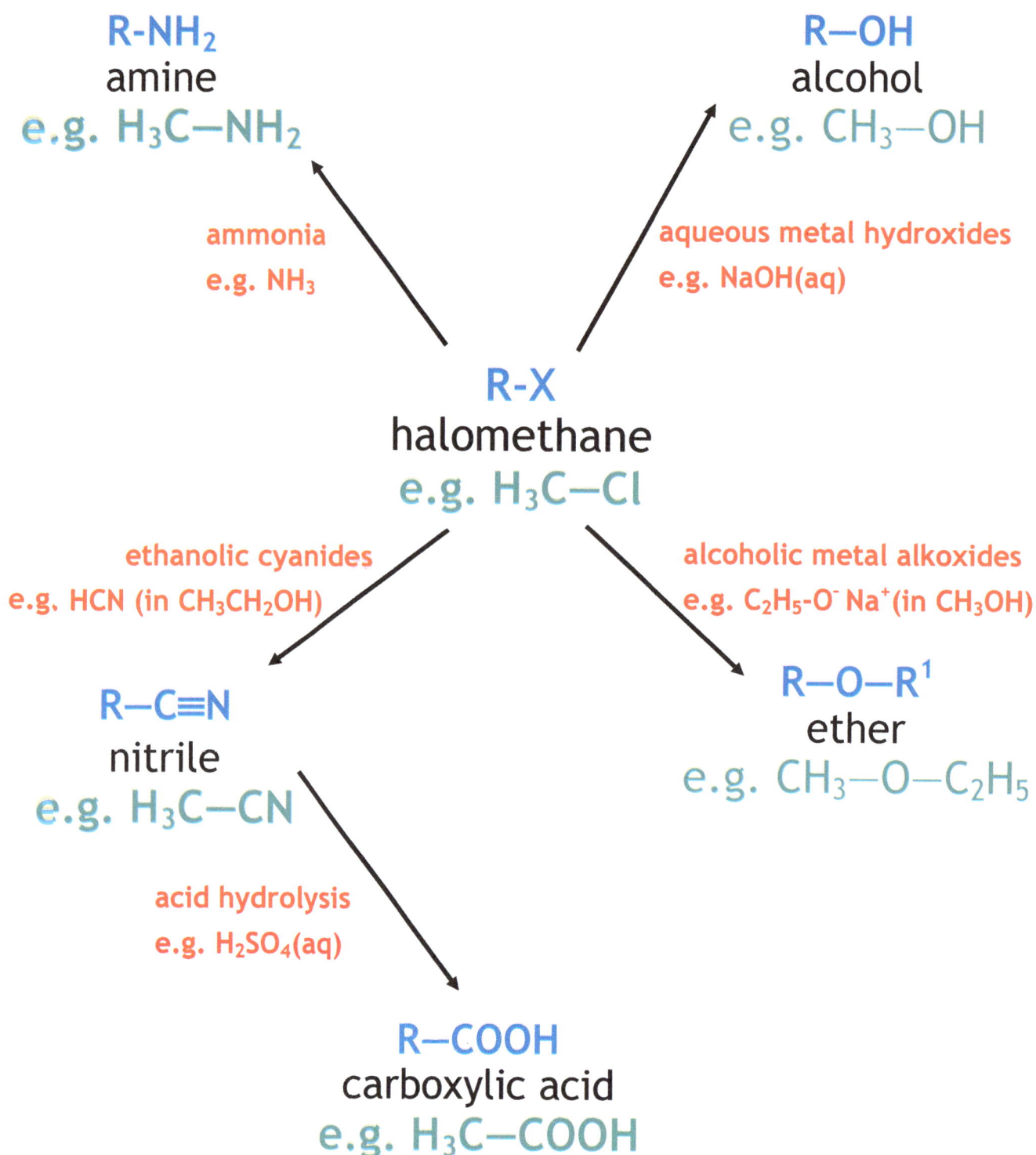

R-NH$_2$
amine
e.g. H$_3$C—NH$_2$

R—OH
alcohol
e.g. CH$_3$—OH

ammonia
e.g. NH$_3$

aqueous metal hydroxides
e.g. NaOH(aq)

R-X
halomethane
e.g. H$_3$C—Cl

ethanolic cyanides
e.g. HCN (in CH$_3$CH$_2$OH)

alcoholic metal alkoxides
e.g. C$_2$H$_5$-O$^-$ Na$^+$(in CH$_3$OH)

R—C≡N
nitrile
e.g. H$_3$C—CN

R—O—R^1
ether
e.g. CH$_3$—O—C$_2$H$_5$

acid hydrolysis
e.g. H$_2$SO$_4$(aq)

R—COOH
carboxylic acid
e.g. H$_3$C—COOH

Where
X = either F, Cl, Br or I
R and R^1 = any alkane chain

Naming Halogenoalkanes

Connect the structure to its correct name.

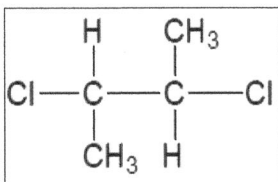

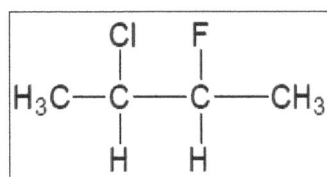

Structure	Name
$Cl-\overset{\displaystyle H}{\underset{\displaystyle CH_3}{C}}-\overset{\displaystyle CH_3}{\underset{\displaystyle H}{C}}-Cl$	1,1-dichloro-2,2-difluoroethane
$H-\overset{\displaystyle H}{\underset{\displaystyle H}{C}}-\overset{\displaystyle CH_3}{\underset{\displaystyle H}{C}}-Cl$	2,2-dibromo-3-methylbutane
$H-\overset{\displaystyle H}{\underset{\displaystyle H}{C}}-\overset{\displaystyle H}{\underset{\displaystyle H}{C}}-Br$	2,3-dichlorobutane
$Cl-\overset{\displaystyle Cl}{\underset{\displaystyle H}{C}}-\overset{\displaystyle F}{\underset{\displaystyle H}{C}}-F$	bromoethane
$H_3C-\overset{\displaystyle Cl}{\underset{\displaystyle H}{C}}-\overset{\displaystyle F}{\underset{\displaystyle H}{C}}-CH_3$	1,2-dichloro-1,2-difluoroethane
$Br-\overset{\displaystyle Br}{\underset{\displaystyle CH_3}{C}}-\overset{\displaystyle CH_3}{\underset{\displaystyle H}{C}}-CH_3$	2-chloropropane
$Cl-\overset{\displaystyle F}{\underset{\displaystyle H}{C}}-\overset{\displaystyle F}{\underset{\displaystyle H}{C}}-Cl$	2-chloro-3-fluorobutane

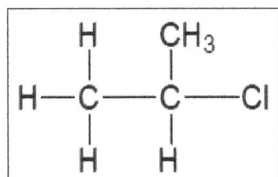

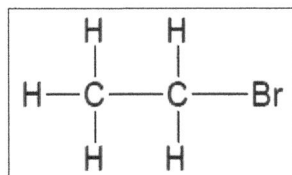

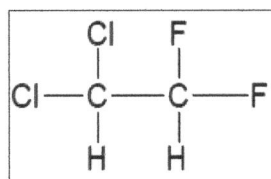

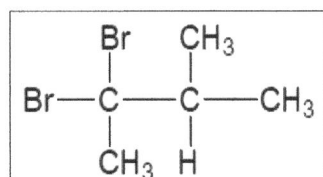

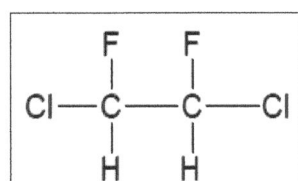

Primary, Secondary or Tertiary Halogenoalkanes

Look at the following halogenoalkanes and decide whether they are primary, secondary or tertiary using the following code:

1 = Primary

2 = Secondary

3 = Tertiary

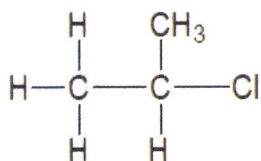

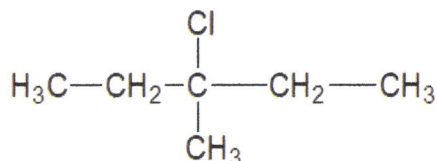

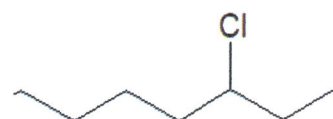

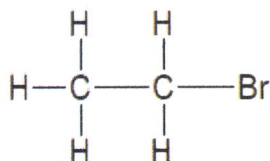

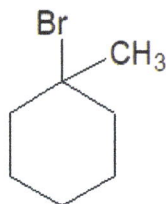

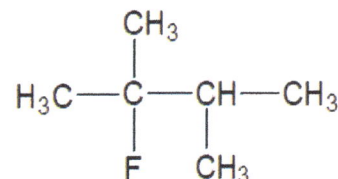

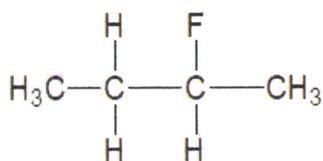

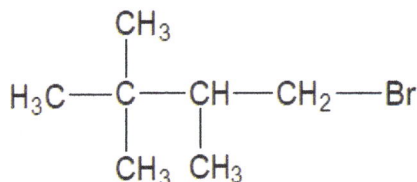

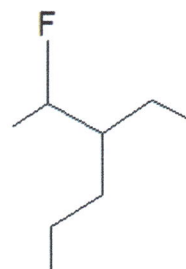

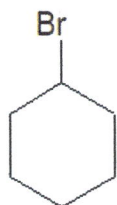

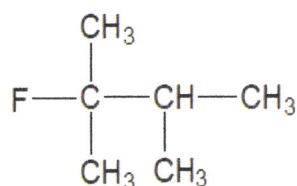

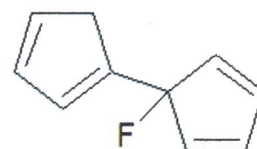

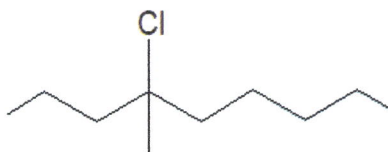

Quiz Word

Answer the following questions to complete the quiz word and then try to work out what the key phrase in the **bold** boxes should be.

1. Produced when ammonia reacts with a halogenoalkane. (5)
2. Can be a nucleophile used to make a nitrile. (6,7)
3. Reaction used to convert a nitrile into a carboxylic acid. (4,10)
4. Name given to substances attracted to positive charges. (11)
5. Reacts with a halogenoalkane to form an ether. (8)
6. Halogenoalkane that follows an S_N2 mechanism. (7)

Nucleophilic Substitution

Connect the correct nucleophile and product to the given halogenoalkane. The first one has been done for you:

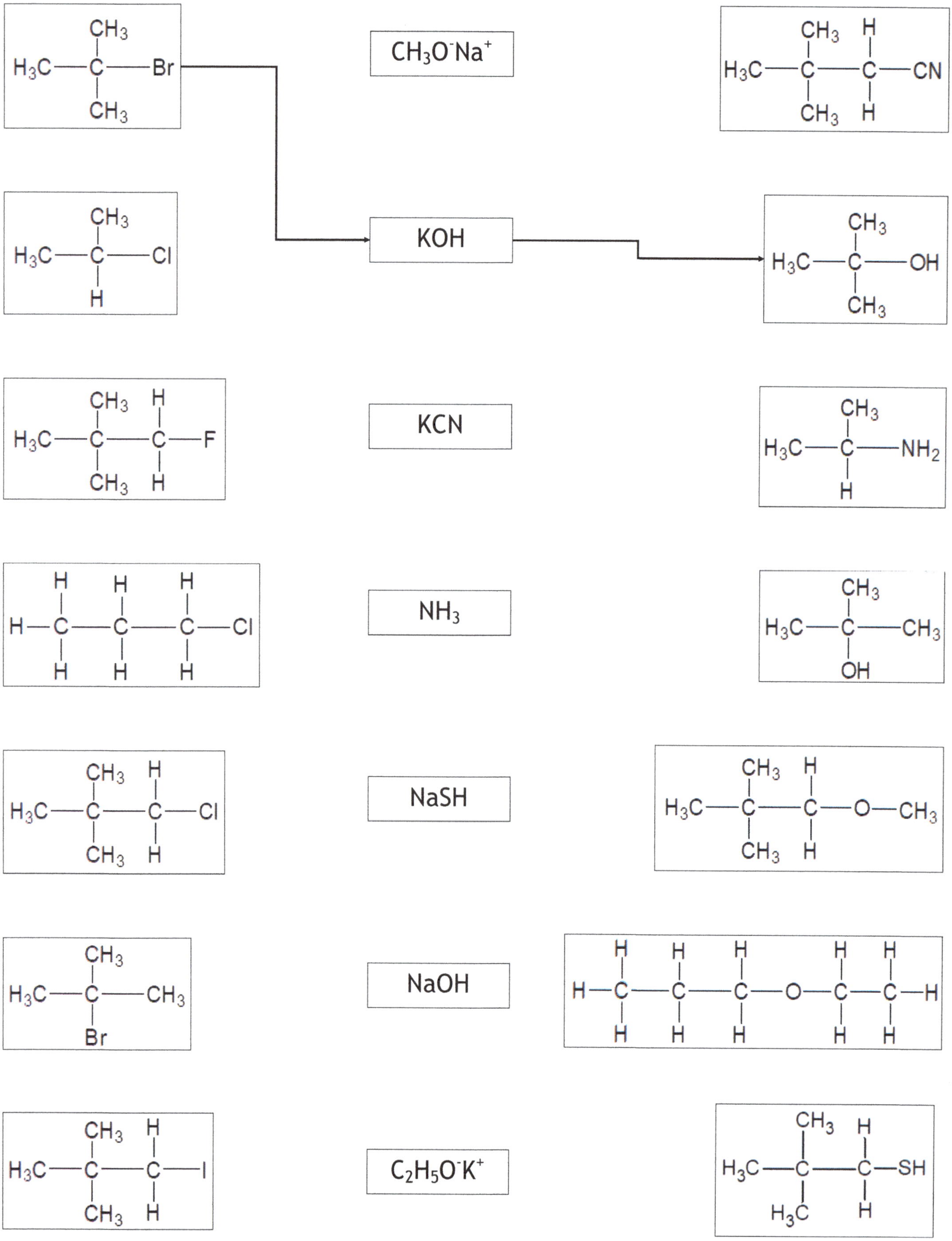

Halogenoalkanes (left column):

- $H_3C-\underset{CH_3}{\overset{CH_3}{C}}-Br$

- $H_3C-\underset{H}{\overset{CH_3}{C}}-Cl$

- $H_3C-\underset{CH_3}{\overset{CH_3}{C}}-\underset{H}{\overset{H}{C}}-F$

- $H-\underset{H}{\overset{H}{C}}-\underset{H}{\overset{H}{C}}-\underset{H}{\overset{H}{C}}-Cl$

- $H_3C-\underset{CH_3}{\overset{CH_3}{C}}-\underset{H}{\overset{H}{C}}-Cl$

- $H_3C-\underset{Br}{\overset{CH_3}{C}}-CH_3$

- $H_3C-\underset{CH_3}{\overset{CH_3}{C}}-\underset{H}{\overset{H}{C}}-I$

Nucleophiles (middle column):

- $CH_3O^-Na^+$
- KOH
- KCN
- NH_3
- NaSH
- NaOH
- $C_2H_5O^-K^+$

Products (right column):

- $H_3C-\underset{CH_3}{\overset{CH_3}{C}}-\underset{H}{\overset{H}{C}}-CN$

- $H_3C-\underset{CH_3}{\overset{CH_3}{C}}-OH$

- $H_3C-\underset{H}{\overset{CH_3}{C}}-NH_2$

- $H_3C-\underset{OH}{\overset{CH_3}{C}}-CH_3$

- $H_3C-\underset{CH_3}{\overset{CH_3}{C}}-\underset{H}{\overset{H}{C}}-O-CH_3$

- $H-\underset{H}{\overset{H}{C}}-\underset{H}{\overset{H}{C}}-\underset{H}{\overset{H}{C}}-O-\underset{H}{\overset{H}{C}}-\underset{H}{\overset{H}{C}}-H$

- $H_3C-\underset{H_3C}{\overset{CH_3}{C}}-\underset{H}{\overset{H}{C}}-SH$

S_N1 and S_N2 Mechanisms

Complete the reaction mechanisms using structural formulae and curly arrows:

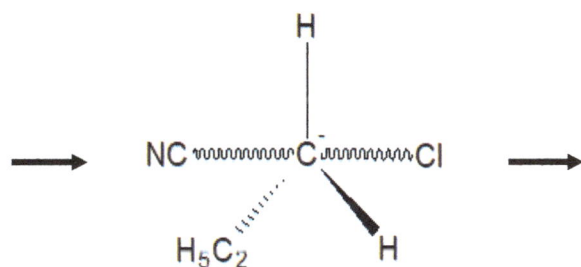

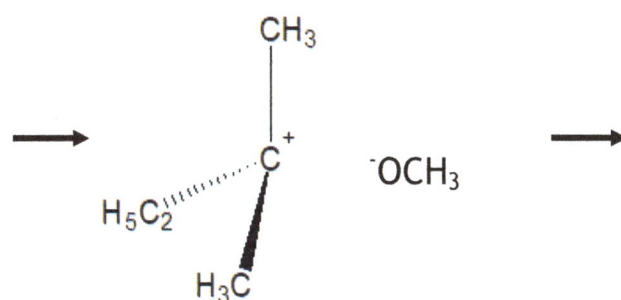

Wordsearch

Complete the wordsearch below using the clues given to identify the correct words(s) that can be found in the wordsearch.

```
A J Y X O T W X L H Y Y G I
J C R N H L Z H A A R S E F
D E I T O Z S A L L A L A H
X T Z D N I P J M O I S B B
P H A L H N T A Z G T J D Q
P E J G D Y I A T E R Z B B
D R U Q I N D L C N E Q B R
D L I E O Y T R D O T H Y U
H T H M N V Q K O A B A Z Q
R M M Y A B U C N L G R R K
V A N I T R I L E K Y T A Q
N W B W K P Y G J A X S G C
R J V T Z K D S Q N W M I M
X J E E E N C F N E E I O S
C I L I H P O E L C U N L U
```

1. Used to convert nitriles into carboxylic acids. (4,10)

2. The nucleophile used to make amines. (7)

3. The intermediate formed during an S_N1 mechanism. (11)

4. Formed when a halogenoalkane reacts with an alkoxide (5)

5. Hydrocarbon that has a halogen instead of a hydrogen. (14)

6. Product formed when a halogenoalkane reacts with potassium cyanide. (7)

7. Type of substitution reaction involving halogenoalkanes. (12)

8. Type of halogenoalkane that always follows an S_N2 mechanism. (7)

9. Type of halogenoalkane that always follows an S_N1 mechanism. (8)

Practice Questions

1. Halogenoalkanes can undergo a number of reactions. The following reaction sequence shows a number of these reactions:

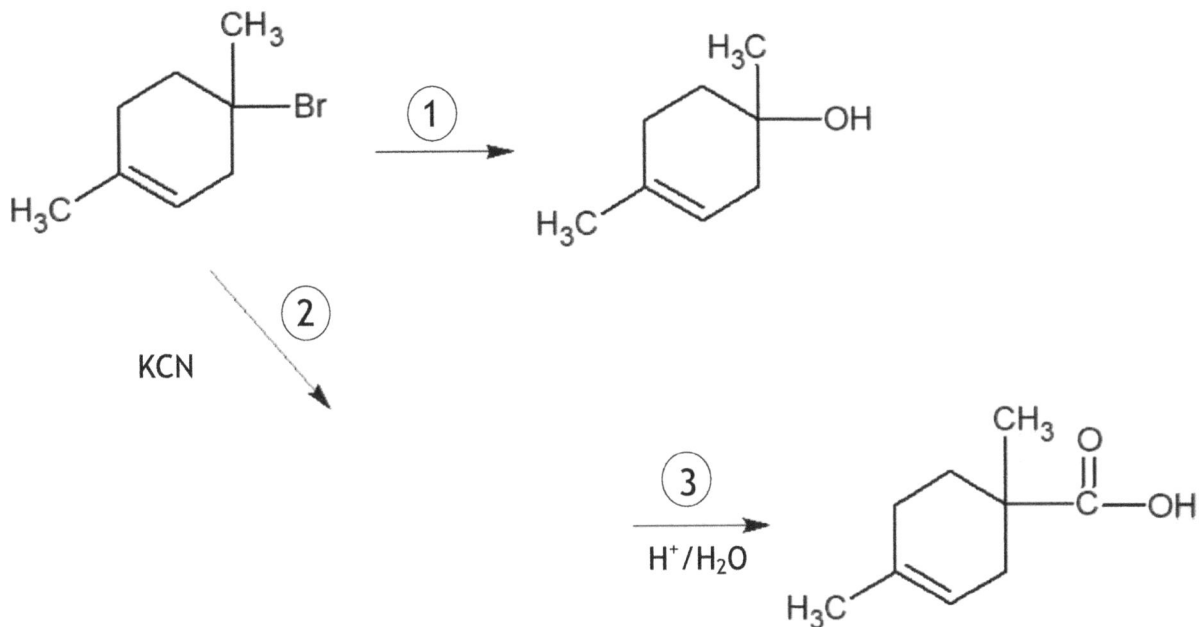

a) In reaction 1 the mechanism is found to be S_N1. Using curly arrows and structural formula show the mechanism.

b) Reaction 2 uses potassium cyanide as the nucleophile. Draw the structural formula of the product.

c) What is the name of reaction 3.

2. Ethers can be made by reacting an alkoxide with a halogenoalkane as shown by the following reaction.

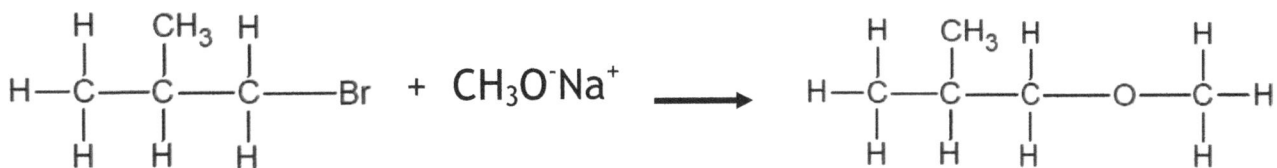

a) Name the halogenolkane shown.

b) Identify what class of halogenoalkane it belongs to.

c) Suggest what mechanism this reaction would follow and explain your choice.

3. Cyclohexane can be converted into cyclohexene via a three-stage synthesis.

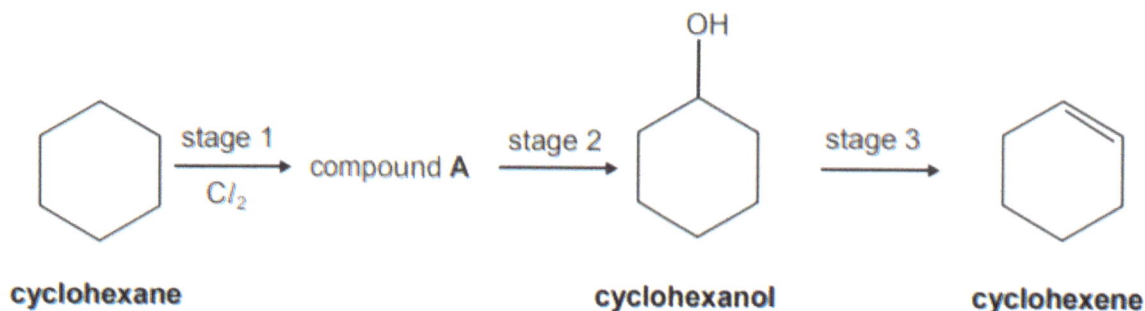

cyclohexane → (stage 1, Cl_2) compound A → (stage 2) cyclohexanol → (stage 3) cyclohexene

a. In stage 1, cyclohexane reacts with chlorine to form the organic product, compound A. Show the structure of compound A.

b. In stage 2 it has been shown using ethanolic KOH that the mechanism is S_N1.
i. What does the term S_N1 mean?

ii. Show using structural formula and curly arrows this mechanism.

b. Stage 3 involves the dehydration of an alcohol. State a suitable reagent for dehydrating an alcohol.

c. The reaction in stage 1 is difficult to control. One other possible chlorinated product is 1,4-dichlorocyclohexane.This is shown below.

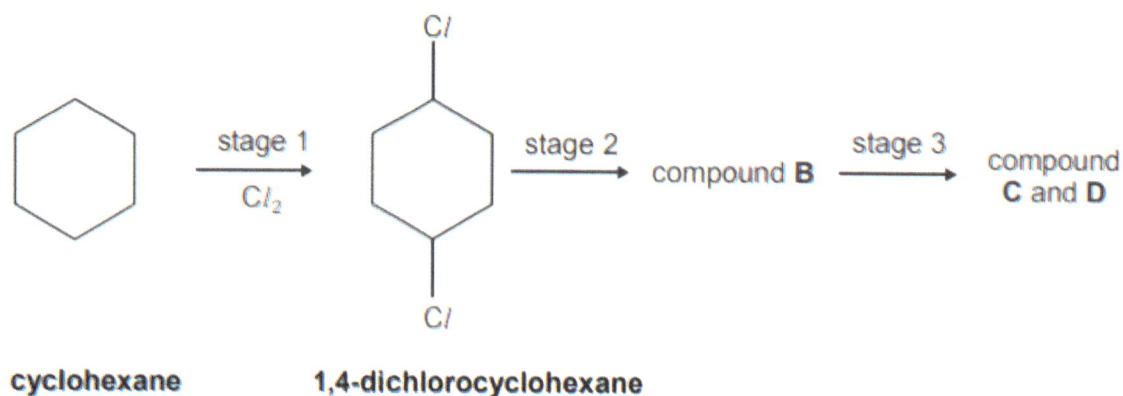

cyclohexane → (stage 1, Cl_2) 1,4-dichlorocyclohexane → (stage 2) compound B → (stage 3) compound C and D

1,4-Dichlorocyclohexane reacts in the same way as compound A in stages 2 and 3.
i. Suggest the structure of compound B.

ii. Two cyclic alkenes, C and D are formed in stage 3. C and D are structural isomers. Suggest the structures of C and D.

Unit 3   Organic Synthesis - Alcohols

Making alcohols:

1.   Fermentation

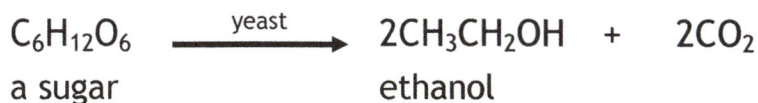

$$C_6H_{12}O_6 \xrightarrow{\text{yeast}} 2CH_3CH_2OH + 2CO_2$$

a sugar   ethanol

2.   Acid catalysed addition of water (usually concentrated phosphoric acid)–

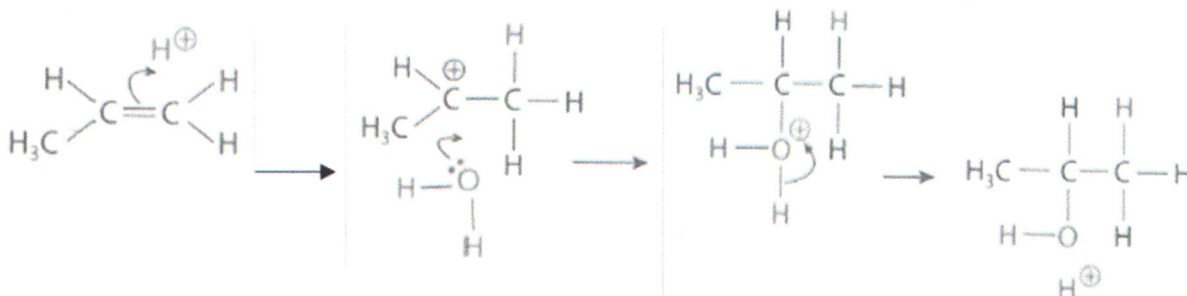

3. Nucleophilic substitution of halogenoalkanes with sodium hydroxide

(See previous section)

4. Reduction of carboxylic acids or carbonyls (aldehydes & ketones)

Use a **strong reducing agent** such as **lithium aluminium hydride ($LiAlH_4$)**.

Carboxylic acids & aldehydes form primary alcohols, ketones form secondary alcohols.

Properties of alcohols:

Need to compare alkanes and alcohols of similar masses, i.e. ethane (molecular mass = 30) with methanol (molecular mass = 32).

Alkane	Boiling Point (K)	Boiling Point (K)	Primary alcohol
Ethane	185	335	Methanol
Propene	228	355	Ethanol
Butane	275	375	Propanol
Pentane	310	390	butanol

The large difference in boiling point is due to strong hydrogen bonds between the alcohol molecules, this becomes less pronounced as the carbon chain increases.

Alcohols are very soluble in water when the carbon chain is small like methanol and ethanol, due to ability to form hydrogen bonds with water molecule but become less soluble as the chain length increases.

At Higher you learnt that alcohols can be classed as primary, secondary or tertiary. Alcohols with two hydroxyl functional groups are called diols and those with three are called triols; both types are more soluble than normal alcohols.

Uses of alcohols:

They are excellent solvents as they can dissolve non-ionic compounds due to lipophilic alkyl group and ionic compounds due to their hydrophilic hydroxyl group. This allows chemist to bring together chemicals in the alcohol solvent to react that would normally not mix (immiscible).

Making Esters

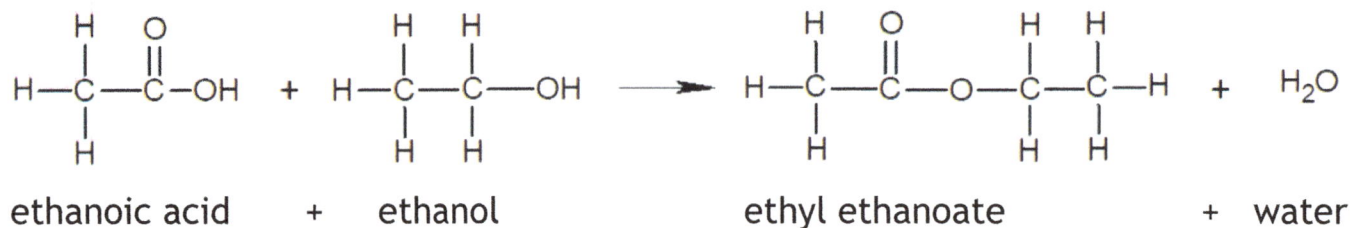

ethanoic acid   +   ethanol   →   ethyl ethanoate   +   water

Reactions with alkali metals

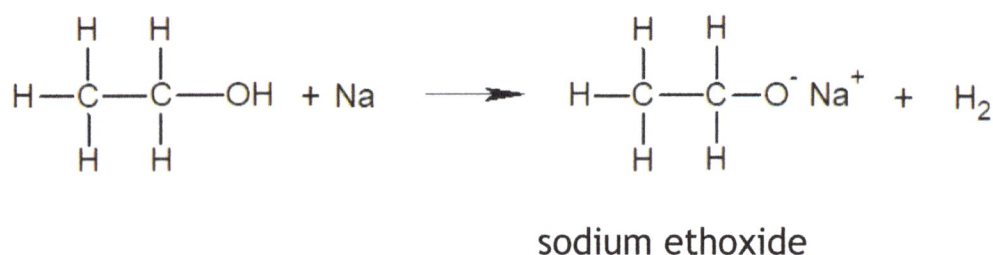

sodium ethoxide

Making Alcohols

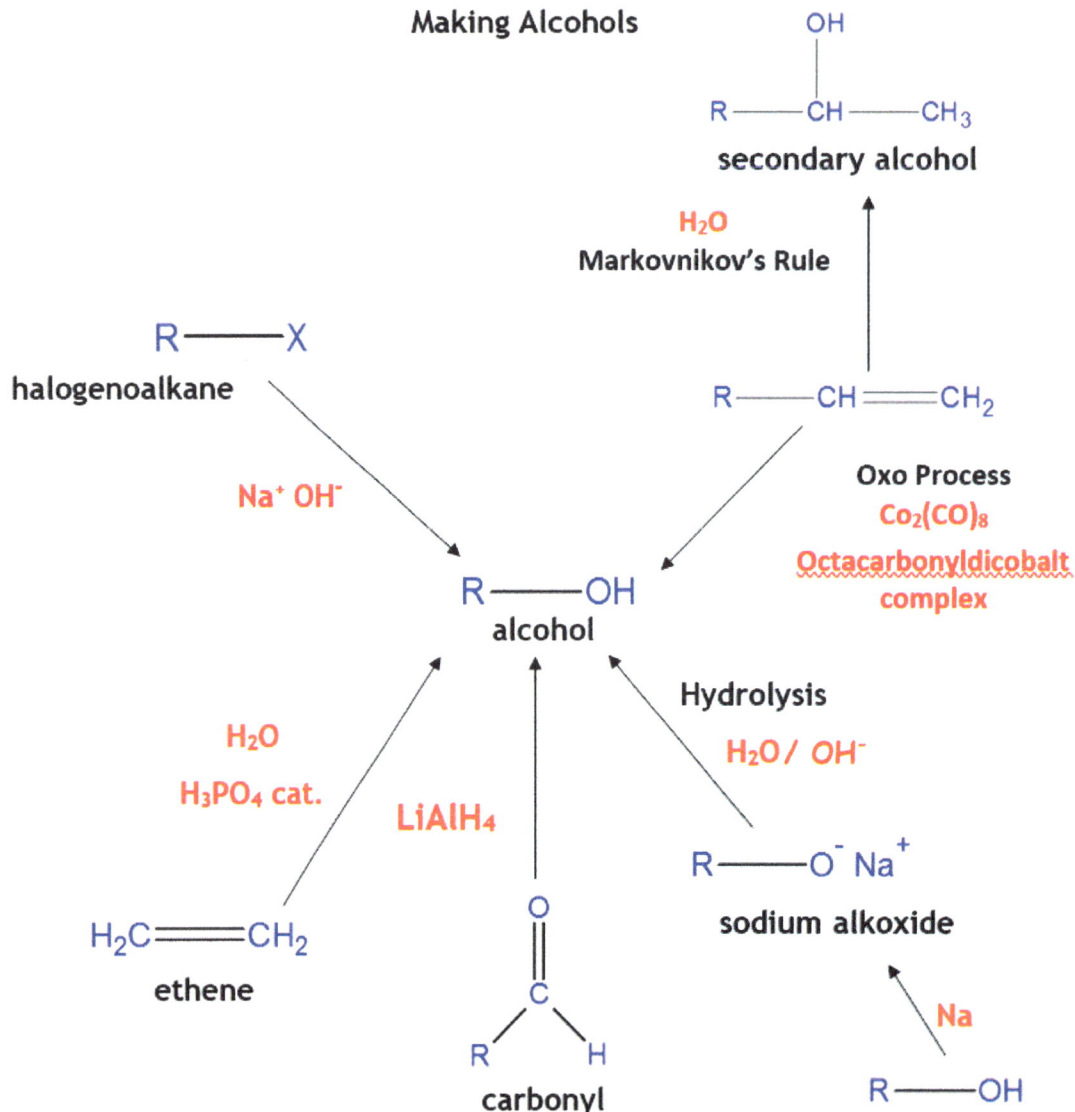

Making Alcohols

Connect the starting material to the correct reagent and alcohol produced. The first has been done for you:

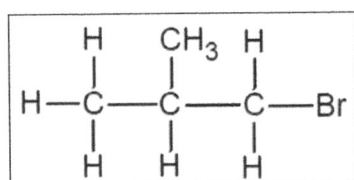

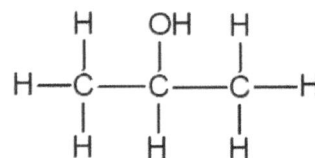

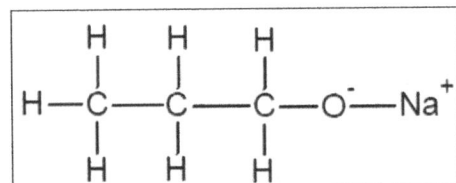

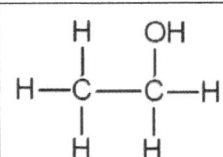

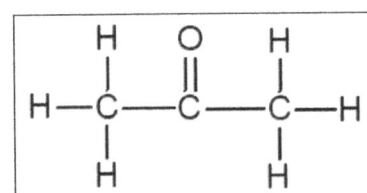

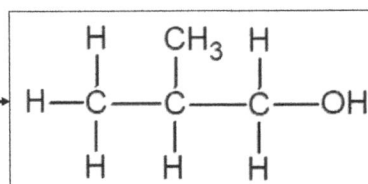

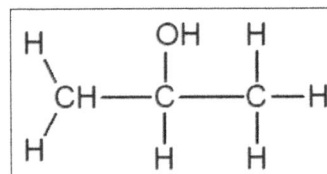

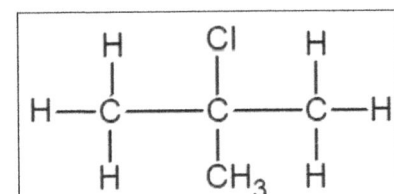

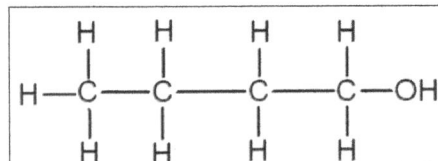

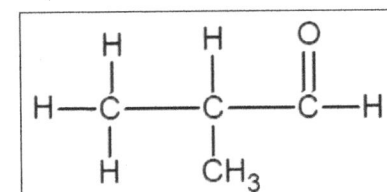

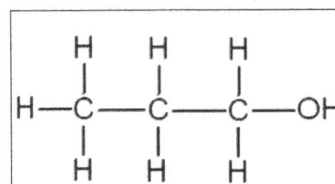

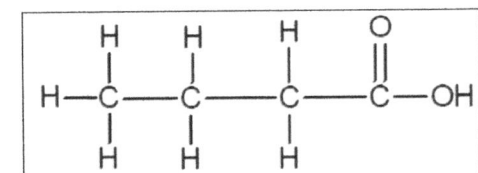

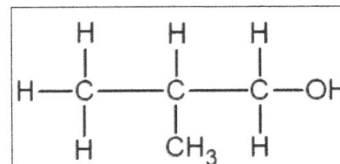

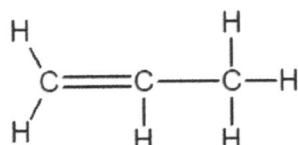

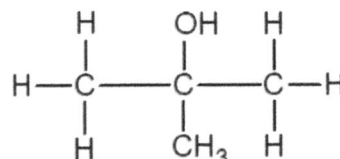

Starting materials (left column):

1. H_3C branched structure: $H-\underset{H}{\overset{H}{C}}-\underset{H}{\overset{CH_3}{C}}-\underset{H}{\overset{H}{C}}-Br$

2. $H-\underset{H}{\overset{H}{C}}-\underset{H}{\overset{H}{C}}-\underset{H}{\overset{H}{C}}-O^-\!-Na^+$

3. $H-\underset{H}{\overset{H}{C}}-\overset{O}{\overset{\|}{C}}-\underset{H}{\overset{H}{C}}-H$

4. $H_2C\!=\!CH_2$

5. $H-\underset{H}{\overset{H}{C}}-\underset{CH_3}{\overset{Cl}{C}}-\underset{H}{\overset{H}{C}}-H$

6. $H-\underset{H}{\overset{H}{C}}-\underset{CH_3}{\overset{H}{C}}-\overset{O}{\overset{\|}{C}}-H$

7. $H-\underset{H}{\overset{H}{C}}-\underset{H}{\overset{H}{C}}-\underset{H}{\overset{H}{C}}-\overset{O}{\overset{\|}{C}}-OH$

8. $\underset{H}{\overset{H}{>}}C\!=\!\underset{H}{\overset{H}{C}}-\underset{H}{\overset{H}{C}}-H$

Reagents (middle column):

- LiAlH₄
- NaOH
- H₂O/H⁺
- LiAlH₄
- H₂O/H₃PO₄
- H₂O/OH⁻
- KOH
- LiAlH₄

Alcohols produced (right column):

1. $H-\underset{H}{\overset{H}{C}}-\underset{H}{\overset{OH}{C}}-\underset{H}{\overset{H}{C}}-H$

2. $H-\underset{H}{\overset{H}{C}}-\underset{H}{\overset{OH}{C}}-H$

3. $H-\underset{H}{\overset{H}{C}}-\underset{H}{\overset{CH_3}{C}}-\underset{H}{\overset{H}{C}}-OH$

4. $\underset{H}{\overset{H}{>}}CH-\underset{H}{\overset{OH}{C}}-\underset{H}{\overset{H}{C}}-H$

5. $H-\underset{H}{\overset{H}{C}}-\underset{H}{\overset{H}{C}}-\underset{H}{\overset{H}{C}}-\underset{H}{\overset{H}{C}}-OH$

6. $H-\underset{H}{\overset{H}{C}}-\underset{H}{\overset{H}{C}}-\underset{H}{\overset{H}{C}}-OH$

7. $H-\underset{H}{\overset{H}{C}}-\underset{CH_3}{\overset{H}{C}}-\underset{H}{\overset{H}{C}}-OH$

8. $H-\underset{H}{\overset{H}{C}}-\underset{CH_3}{\overset{OH}{C}}-\underset{H}{\overset{H}{C}}-H$

Chemical Misconceptions

A student has written a note on the properties of alcohols. They have made **nine** mistakes, can you find them and write the correct note in the space below:

Properties of alcohols

Alcohols are polar with a hydroxyl functional group and so the predominant force of attraction between them is permanent dipole-permanent dipole interactions. In order to compare their boiling points with alkanes you should make sure they have the same number of carbon atoms. Alcohols have lower boiling points than similar sized alkanes.

Alcohols are usually soluble in water and become more soluble the longer the hydrocarbon chain. Increasing the number of hydroxyl groups has no effect on solubility. Alcohols also make good solvents for reactions where you have miscible reactants.

Alcohols react in a variety of ways:

Reduction reactions to form carbonyls and carboxylic acids using acidified potassium dichromate.

Condensation reactions with hydrochloric acid to make esters.

Reactions with reactive metals like sodium to make hydroxides.

Systematic Naming of Alcohols

Match the following alcohol compounds to the correct systematic name.

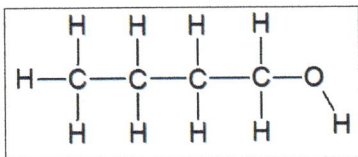

2-methylbutan-2-ol

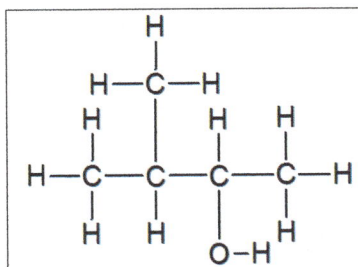

2-methylbutan-1,2-diol

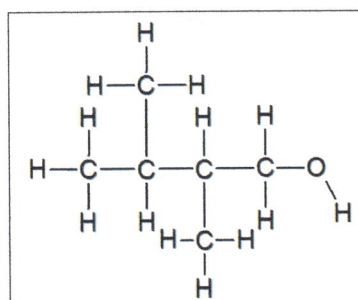

butan-1-ol

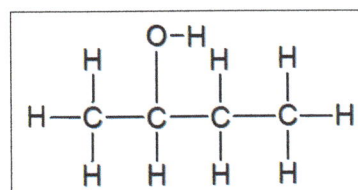

2-methylpropan-1,3-diol

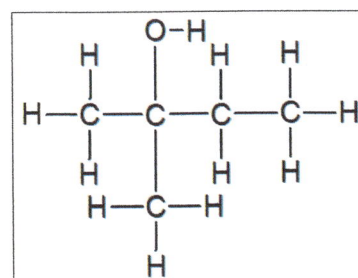

butan-2-ol

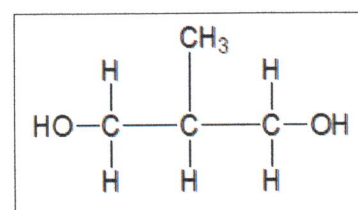

3-methylbutan-2-ol

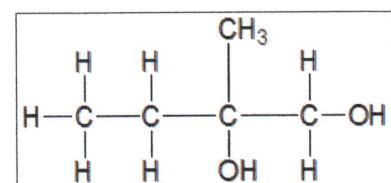

2,3-dimethylbutan-1-ol

Quiz Word

Answer the following questions to complete the quiz word and then try to work out what the key phrase in the **bold** boxes should be.

1. Functional group found in alcohols. (8)
2. Alcohols help reactants come together if they are this with one another. (10)
3. Product of the reaction between alcohols and carboxylic acids. (6)
4. Having more hydroxyl groups does this to their solubility. (9)
5. Made when an alcohol reacts with a metal. (8)
6. Type of reaction that turns a carbonyl into an alcohol. (9)
7. Van der Waal force that gives alcohols a higher boiling point than an equivalent alkane. (8,7)

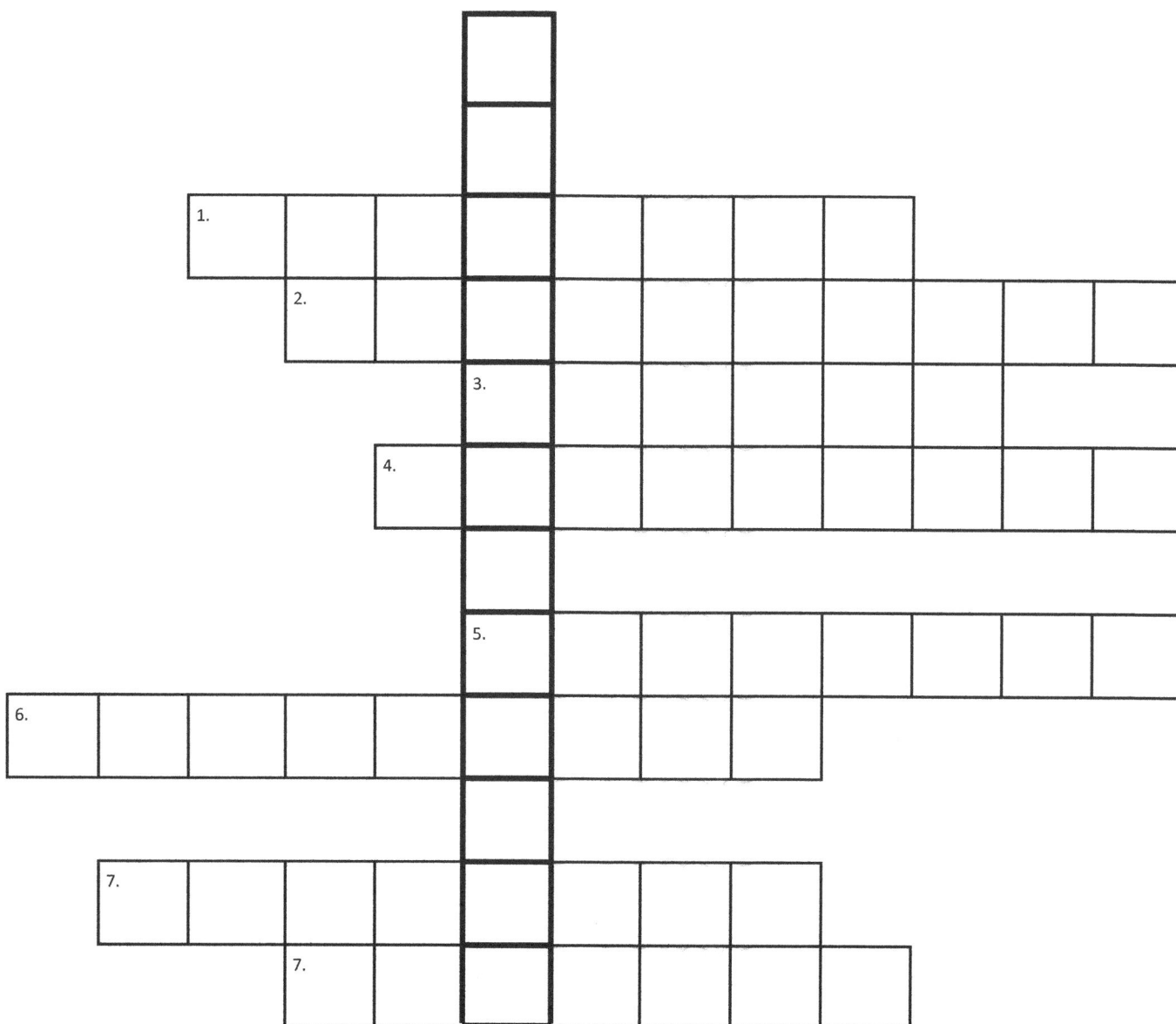

Mechanisms

Look at the following reaction sequences and complete them using structural formulae and curly arrows.

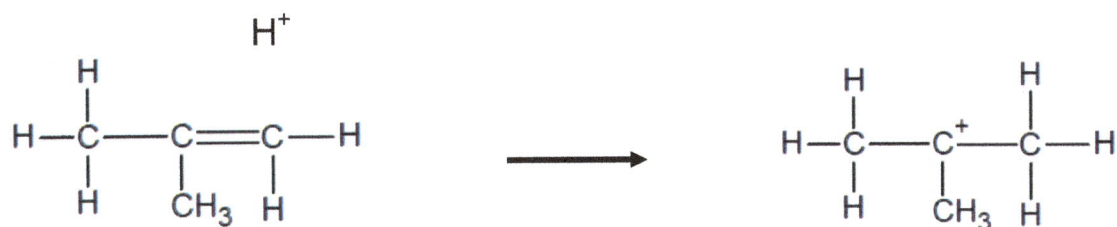

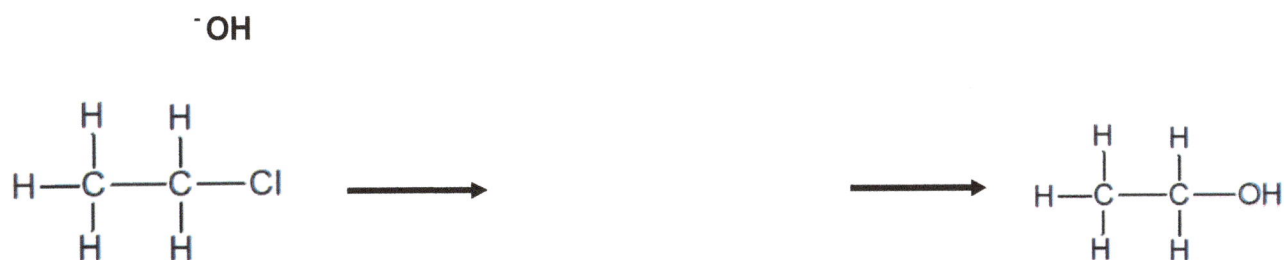

Boiling Point of Alcohols

Use your knowledge of bonding to predict the order of increasing boiling point of the following alcohols.

A

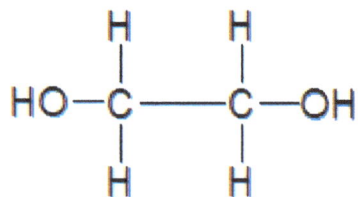

B

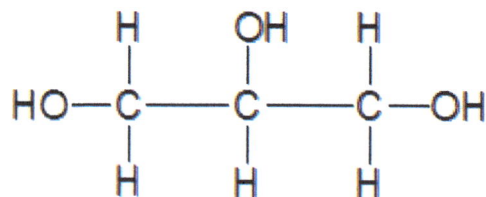

C

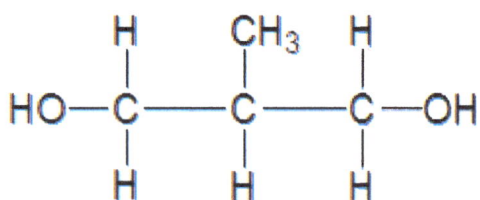

D

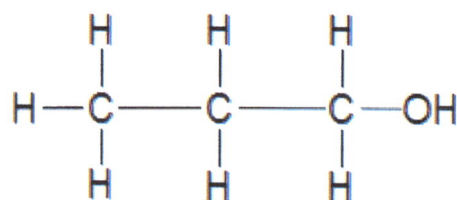

E

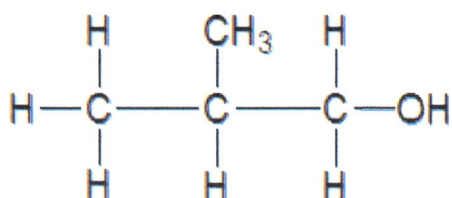

F

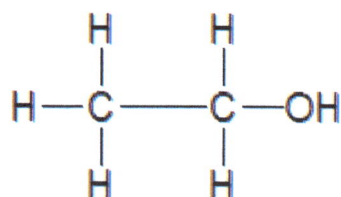

G

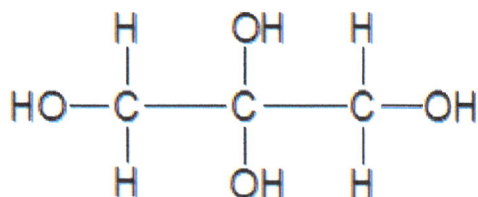

H

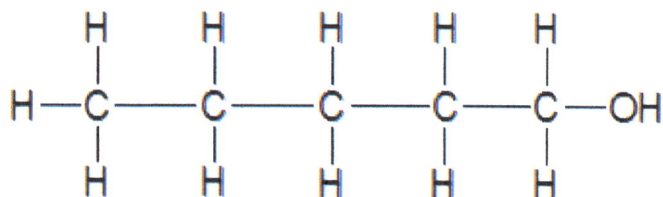

Increasing Boiling Point

Wordsearch

Complete the wordsearch below using the clues given to identify the correct words(s) that can be found in the wordsearch.

```
H P N L Y H Y K H C X P M H H
C A K O E U L U I D O X U Y E
A B L F I I C T O L K W I D N
O L X O T T Y H A U M H N R U
I A K H G L C R I W W D I O A
U A I O A E S U Y U F H M X H
G U B T X O N A D Y Z X U Y Y
M V A U L I G O A E I D L L D
M C L V B F D N A N R Q A G R
S Z E N Z U G E I L J U N R O
B N C C I Q P G S D K B A O G
T E D I R D Y H W K N A D U E
H Y D R A T I O N O I O N P N
H C D M J J A X D I U F B E R
E L B I C S I M M I K L P O W
```

1. Produced when alcohols react with metals like sodium. (9)

2. Use to make alcohols from aldehydes, ketones & carboxylic acids. (7,9,7)

3. The strongest intermolecular force that accounts for alcohols having higher boiling points than equivalent alkanes. (8,7)

4. Name of the reaction to make alcohols from an alkene. (9,9)

5. Found in all alcohols. (8,5)

6. Alcohols can help these reactants to mix and react. (10)

7. Short chain alcohols can act as this. (5,7)

8. Type of reaction used to turn aldehydes, ketones and carboxylic acids into alcohols. (9)

Types of Alcohol

There are different types of alcohols depending upon the number of hydroxyl groups and the position of the hydroxyl group. Identify the type of alcohol by putting the relevant code next to it.

Code:

A   Primary alcohol
B   Secondary alcohol
C   Tertiary alcohol

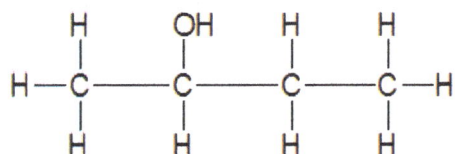

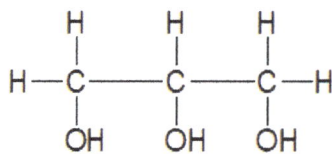

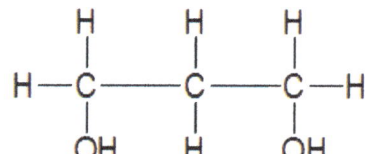

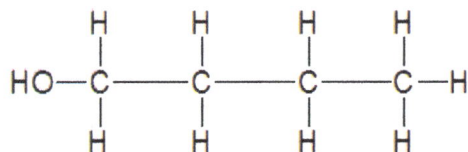

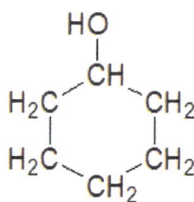

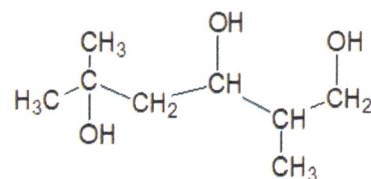

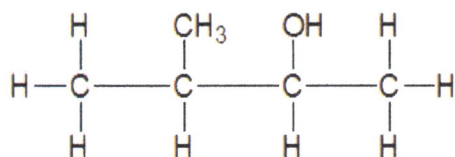

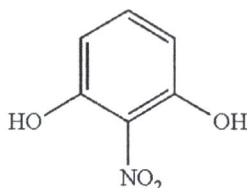

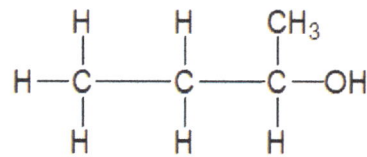

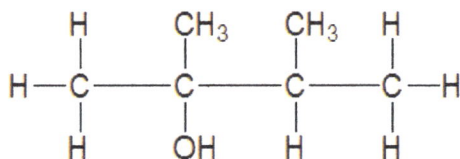

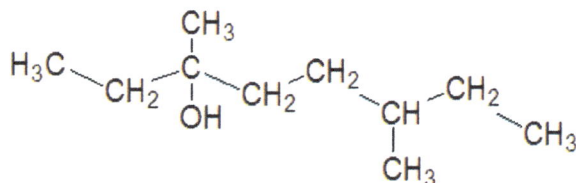

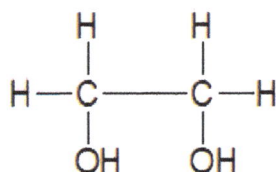

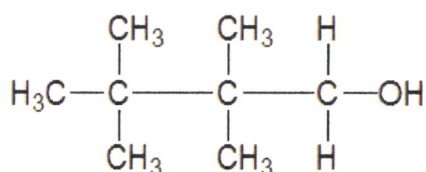

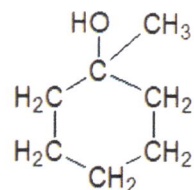

D   Diol
E   Triol

Row 1:

Structure 1: H–C(H)(H)–C(H)(OH)–C(H)(H)–C(H)(H)–H

Structure 2: H–C(H)(OH)–C(H)(OH)–C(H)(OH)–H

Structure 3: H–C(H)(OH)–C(H)(H)–C(H)(OH)–H

Row 2:

Structure 4: HO–C(H)(H)–C(H)(H)–C(H)(H)–C(H)(H)–H

Structure 5: Cyclohexane ring: HO–CH, H_2C, CH_2, H_2C, CH_2, CH_2

Structure 6: H_3C–C(CH$_3$)(OH)–CH$_2$–CH(OH)–CH(CH$_3$)–CH$_2$–OH

Row 3:

Structure 7: H–C(H)(H)–C(CH$_3$)(H)–C(OH)(H)–C(H)(H)–H

Structure 8: Benzene ring with HO, OH, and NO$_2$ substituents

Structure 9: H–C(H)(H)–C(H)(H)–C(CH$_3$)(H)–OH

Row 4:

Structure 10: H–C(H)(H)–C(CH$_3$)(OH)–C(CH$_3$)(H)–C(H)(H)–H

Structure 11: H_3C–CH$_2$–C(CH$_3$)(OH)–CH$_2$–CH$_2$–CH(CH$_3$)–CH$_2$–CH$_3$

Row 5:

Structure 12: H–C(H)(OH)–C(H)(OH)–H

Structure 13: H_3C–C(CH$_3$)(CH$_3$)–C(CH$_3$)(CH$_3$)–C(H)(H)–OH

Structure 14: Cyclopentane ring: HO–C–CH$_3$, H_2C, CH_2, H_2C, CH_2

Practice Questions

1. Step 5 involving several reactions, shown below, is the final stage in turning aspirin into salbutamol:

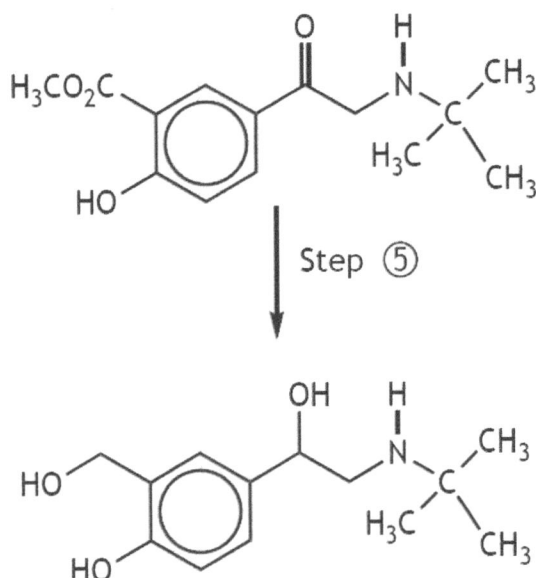

   Name a reagent that could be used to convert the carbonyl group into the hydroxyl group.

2. Pectin is a natural polymer found in apples which helps jam to thicken.

   Part of the structure of pectin is shown:

   Pectin binds to itself to help jam thicken.

   Suggest how the hydroxyl groups allow pectin molecules to bind.

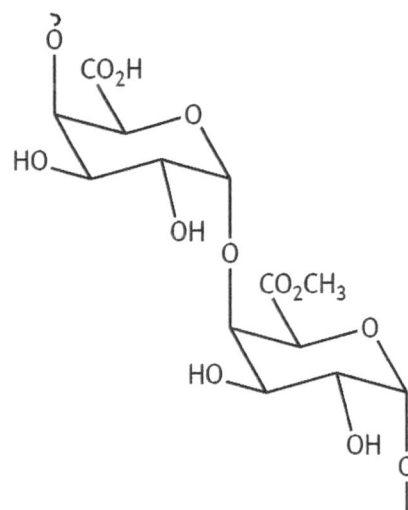

3. Alcohols can be made in a number of ways. Using your knowledge of chemistry discuss how propan-1-ol could be made.

Unit 3   Organic Synthesis - Ethers & Acids

Ethers

Ethers are made by the nucleophilic substitution of a halogenoalkane with a metal alkoxide (made by reacting an alkali metal with the appropriate alcohol).

e.g.

$$CH_3Br \ + \ Na^{+-}OC_2H_5 \ \rightarrow \ CH_3OC_2H_5 \ + \ NaBr$$

sodium ethoxide   methoxyethane

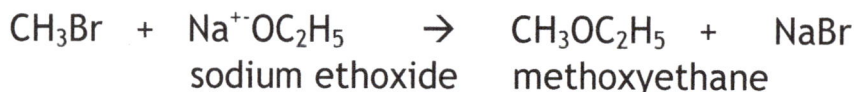

Uses of ethers:

They are very volatile and flammable so burn easily, but can act as good non-polar solvents which can be easily evaporated to leave the desired product.

Naming ethers:

Ethers are alkoxyalkanes, and are named by looking at the length of the carbon chains either side of the oxygen atom. The shorter chain is the alkoxy part and the longer chain the alkane part.

e.g.

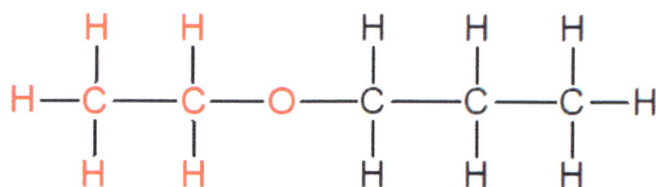

ethoxypropane

For branched ethers the alkoxy part is named as you would any branch.

e.g.

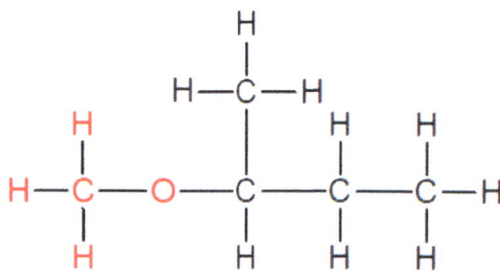

2-methoxybutane

Carboxylic Acids

Making carboxylic acids:

Oxidation of primary alcohols and aldehydes

$$CH_3CH_2OH \xrightarrow{\text{acidified } K_2Cr_2O_7} CH_3CHO \xrightarrow{\text{Tollen's reagent}} CH_3COOH$$

Acid hydrolysis of nitriles

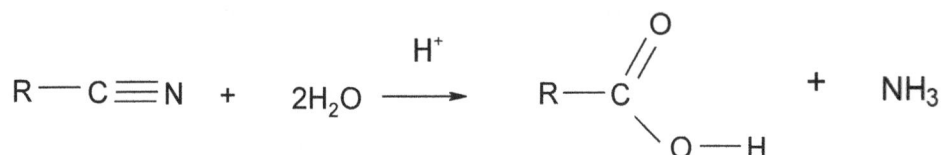

$$R-C\equiv N \ + \ 2H_2O \ \xrightarrow{\ H^+\ } \ R-C\underset{O-H}{\overset{O}{\Big\langle}} \ + \ NH_3$$

Hydrolysis of esters

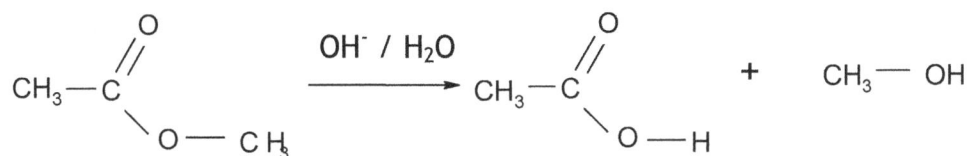

$$CH_3-C\underset{O-CH_3}{\overset{O}{\Big\langle}} \ \xrightarrow{\ OH^-/H_2O\ } \ CH_3-C\underset{O-H}{\overset{O}{\Big\langle}} \ + \ CH_3-OH$$

Hydrolysis of amides

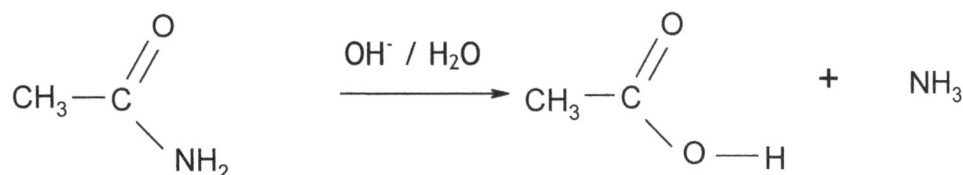

$$CH_3-C\underset{NH_2}{\overset{O}{\Big\langle}} \ \xrightarrow{\ OH^-/H_2O\ } \ CH_3-C\underset{O-H}{\overset{O}{\Big\langle}} \ + \ NH_3$$

Reactions of carboxylic acids:

Carboxylic acids react in the same way as any acid forming alkanoate salts, e.g

ethanoic acid + sodium hydroxide → sodium ethanoate + water

Reaction with alcohols to form esters

ethanoic acid   +   propanol   ⇌   propyl ethanoate   +   water

Reaction with amines to form amides

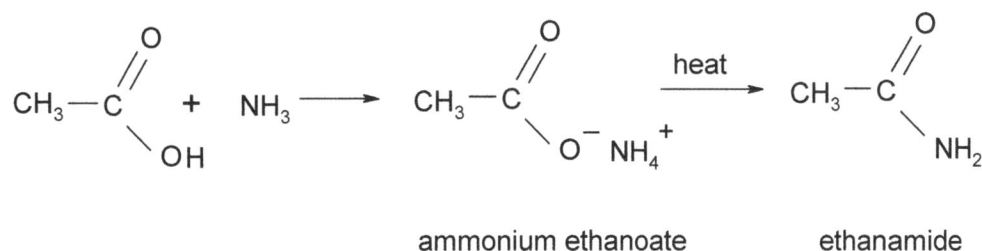

$$CH_3-C\underset{OH}{\overset{O}{\Big\langle}} \ + \ NH_3 \ \longrightarrow \ CH_3-C\underset{O^-\ NH_4^+}{\overset{O}{\Big\langle}} \ \xrightarrow{\ heat\ } \ CH_3-C\underset{NH_2}{\overset{O}{\Big\langle}}$$

ammonium ethanoate   ethanamide

Properties of carboxylic acids:

Due to the carboxyl functional group carboxylic acids are very soluble in water and have higher boiling points than comparable alkanes or indeed alcohols. The formation of dimers causes the boiling points to be significantly higher than expected.

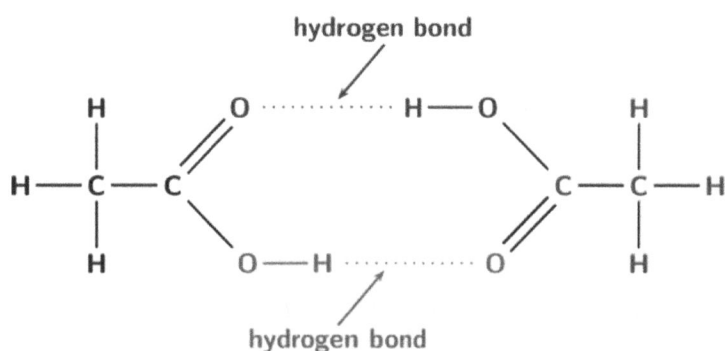

hydrogen bond

hydrogen bond

Systematic Naming

Match the following ether compounds to the correct systematic name.

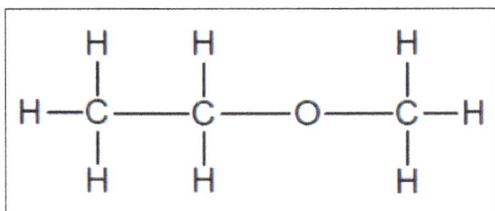 | 2-ethoxypropane

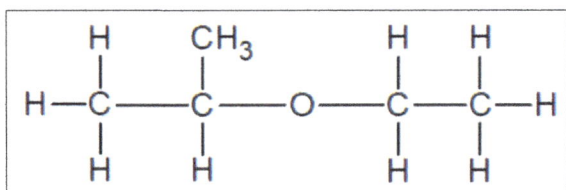 | 3-methoxypentane

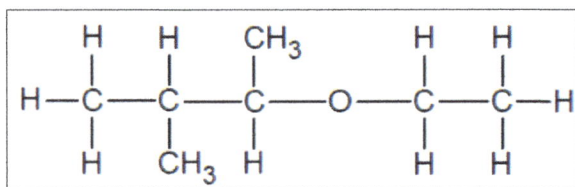 | methoxyethane

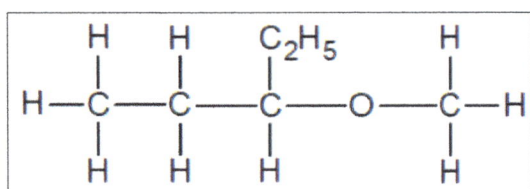 | 2-methyl-2-propoxybutane

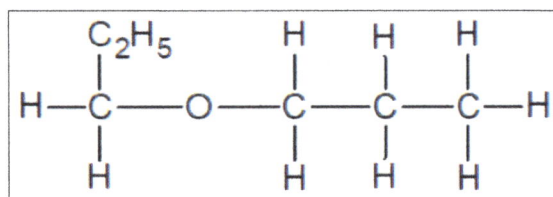 | 3-methyl-2-ethoxybutane

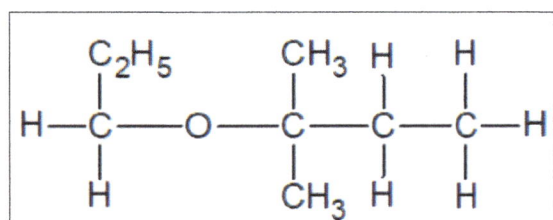 | propoxypropane

Systematic Naming

Match the following carboxylic acid compounds to the correct systematic name.

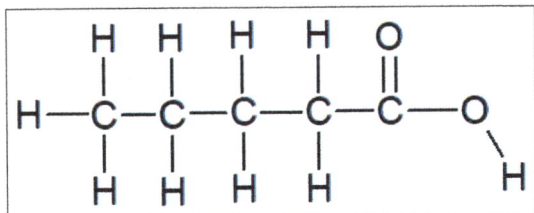

2-methylbutanoic acid

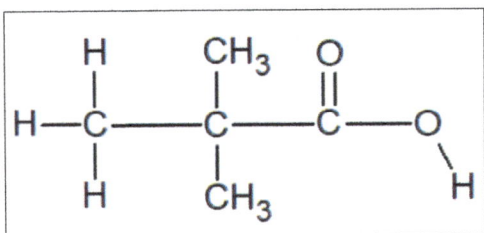

butanoic acid

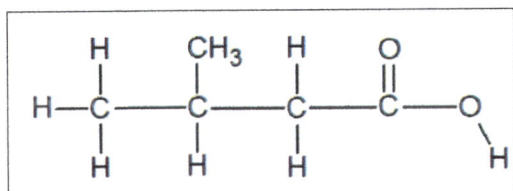

methylpropanoic acid

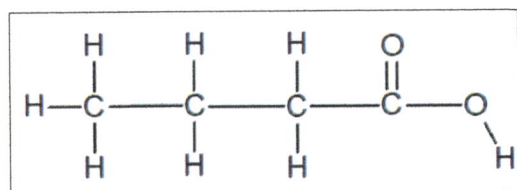

pentanoic acid

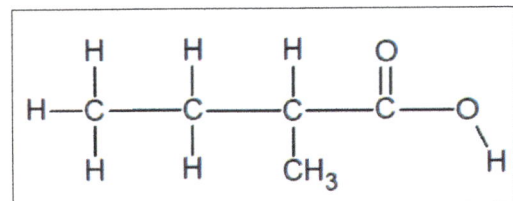

3-methylbutanoic acid

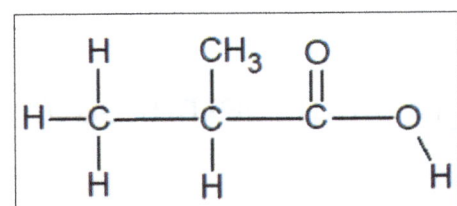

2,2-dimethylpropanoic acid

Naming Salts

Match the following carboxylic acid reactions to the correct name of the salt formed.

ethanoic acid + zinc	calcium ethanoate
butanoic acid + sodium hydroxide	sodium propanoate
methanoic acid + magnesium	zinc methanoate
propanoic acid + sodium carbonate	zinc ethanoate
ethanoic acid + calcium oxide	sodium butanoate
methanoic acid + zinc	magnesium propanoate
propanoic acid + magnesium carbonate	magnesium methanoate

Naming Esters

Match the following ester compounds to the correct systematic name.

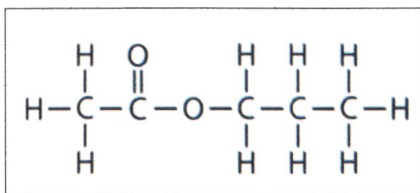

ethyl propanoate

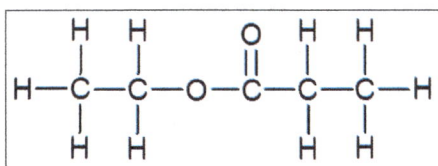

ethyl butanoate

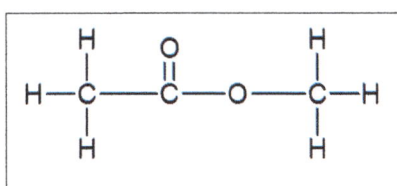

methyl ethanoate

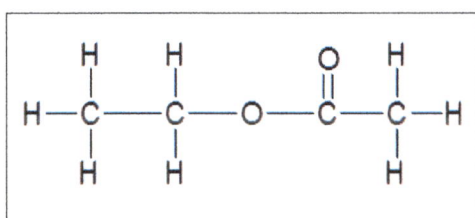

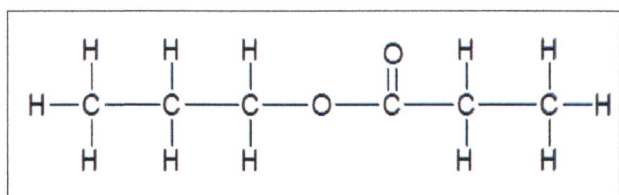

propyl ethanoate

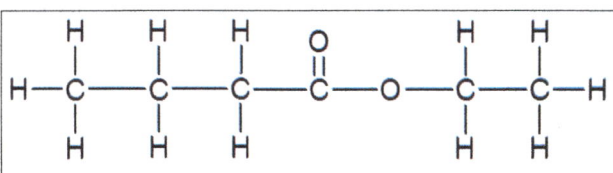

methyl methanoate

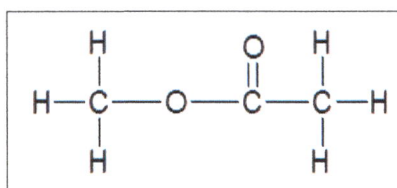

propyl propanoate

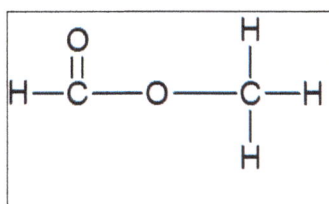

ethyl ethanoate

methyl ethanoate

Chemical Misconceptions

A student has written a note on the properties of ethers & carboxylic acids. They have made **nine** mistakes, can you find them and write the correct note in the space below:

Ethers

Ethers are made by reacting a hydroxide with a halogenoalkane in a nucleophilic addition reaction. An example is shown below:

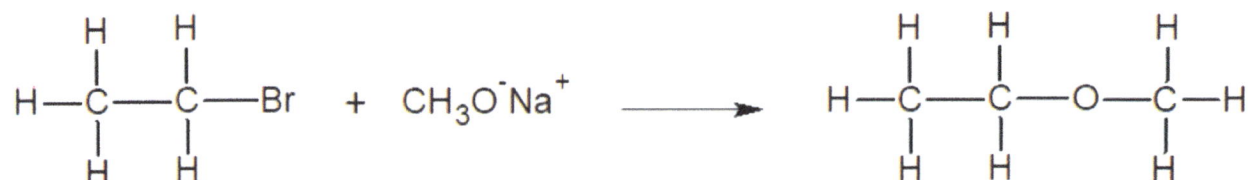

The ether formed is called ethoxymethane. Ethers are used as solvents as they don't evaporate very easily and are non-flammable.

Carboxylic acids

Carboxylic acids are made by the oxidation of a ketone. They are called acids as they contain a carboxyl group which can react to form the carboxylate ion.

They react to form bases with a variety of compounds like alkalis, carbonates and oxides. They can also react with alcohols to form amides and amines to form esters.

Quiz Word

Answer the following questions to complete the quiz word and then try to work out what the key phrase in the **bold** boxes should be.

1. Nucleophile used to make ethers. (5,8)
2. Reaction used to make carboxylic acids. (9)
3. Functional group found in carboxylic acids. (8)
4. Formed by the reaction of a carboxylic acid and an amine. (5)
5. Ethers are often used as these. (8)
6. A problem found with ethers. (4,6)

Practice Questions

1. Mandelic acid, 2-hydroxy-2-phenylethanoic acid, is a component of skin care products.

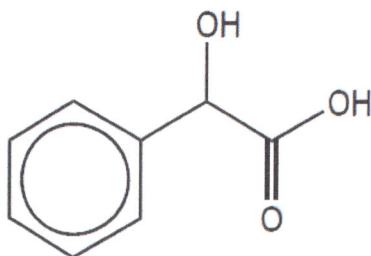

mandelic acid

a) Circle the carboxyl functional group.

b) When mandelic acid reacts with sodium hydroxide it forms a salt. Give the systematic name of the salt formed.

2. 1-chloro-1-methylcyclohexane can be used to make an ether.

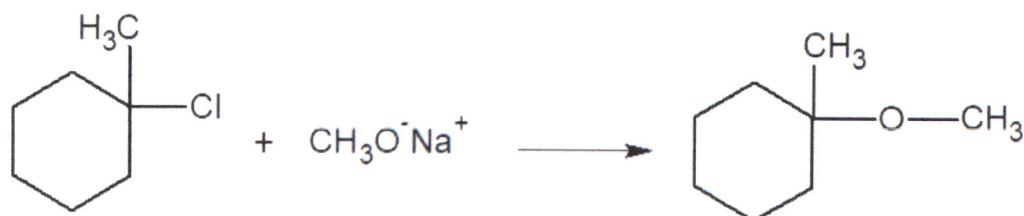

a) Using structural formula and curly arrows show the mechanism for the reaction.

b) Name the ether formed.

c) Suggest a use for the ether.

Unit 3   Organic Synthesis - Amines & Aromatics

Amines can be classed as primary, secondary or tertiary

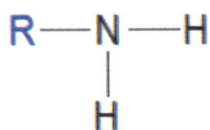

primary	secondary	tertiary
1 carbon attached	2 carbons attached	3 carbons attached

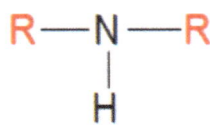

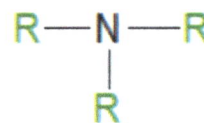

Where R is alkyl chains or branch

Naming amines:

There are two ways to name amines

Remove the ending 'e' from alkane name and add amine

e.g. $C_2H_5NH_2$ ethanamine   or $C_4H_9NH_2$ butanamine

Describe the alkane chain as an alkyl branch followed by amine.

e.g. $C_2H_5NH_2$ ethylamine   or $C_4H_9NH_2$ butylamine

Making primary amines:

Nucleophilic substitution of halogenoalkanes with ammonia (see p110).

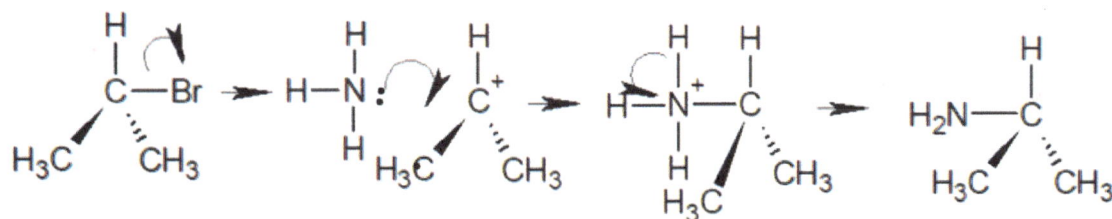

Properties of amines:

The presence of a N—H bond in primary and secondary amines gives rise to hydrogen bonding between the molecules and so an elevated boiling point and excellent solubility.

Amines can act as bases as the lone pair of electrons on the nitrogen is able to accept a proton from water forming an alkylammonium ion and a hydroxide ion.

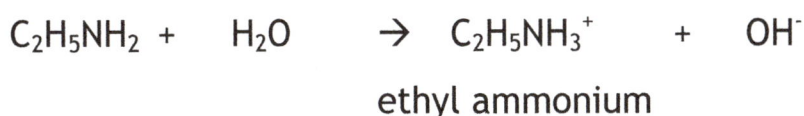

$C_2H_5NH_2$ + H_2O → $C_2H_5NH_3^+$ + OH^-

ethyl ammonium

Reactions of amines:

Amines can act like bases and neutralise acids forming an alkylammonium salt.

Amines react with carboxylic acids forming amides (see carboxylic acids)

Benzene & Aromatic Hydrocarbons

Benzene has the following structure, C_6H_6. Compounds containing a benzene ring often called a phenyl ring were originally called aromatic hydrocarbons on account of their strong smells.

sp^2 hybridisation is best used to describe the bonding in benzene:

This means that the six carbon atoms in the ring each have 3 δ bonds one to a hydrogen & one each to the adjacent carbons and 2 Π bonds one to each adjacent carbon atom.

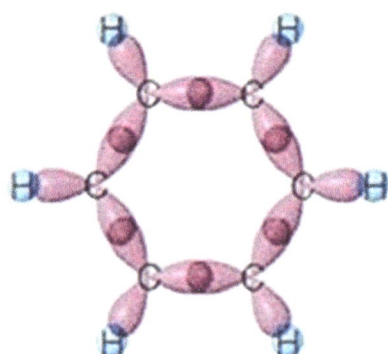 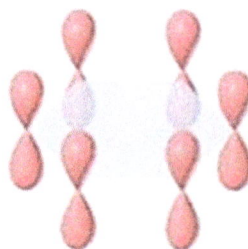 

δ—bonds	Π—bonds	molecular orbital

Due to the ring of delocalised electrons the 6 carbon atoms are very stable and they are surrounded by the **delocalised electrons which are very attractive to ions and molecules with a positive charge, called electrophiles**.

Benzene undergoes electrophilic substitution where an electrophile replaces one of the hydrogen atoms.

Reactions of benzene:

Bromination

In the presence of a catalyst such as iron(III) bromide the bromine molecule is polarised.

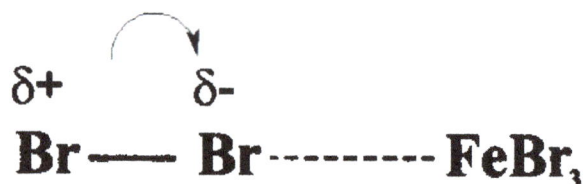

The positive charge on the bromine atom is attracted to the delocalised electrons of the benzene ring and a bond forms as it breaks away from the other bromine atom.

The positive charge on the bromine atom is attracted to the delocalised electrons and a bond forms as it breaks away from the other bromine atom.

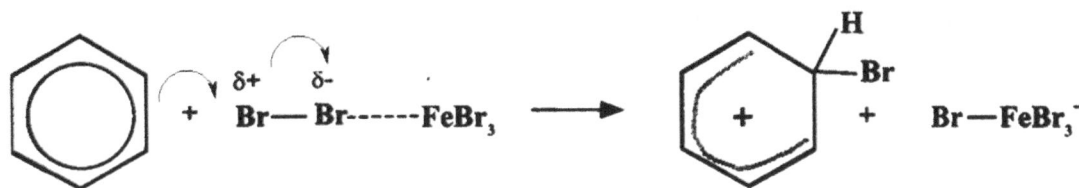

The hydrogen then leaves to bind to the negative bromide that was attached to the catalyst.

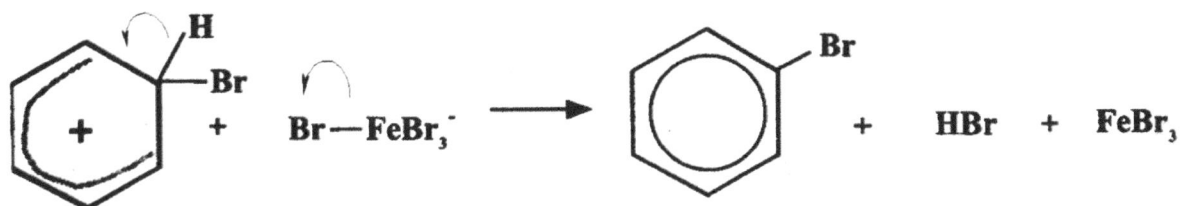

The same mechanism works for other electrophiles, like the nitronium ion.

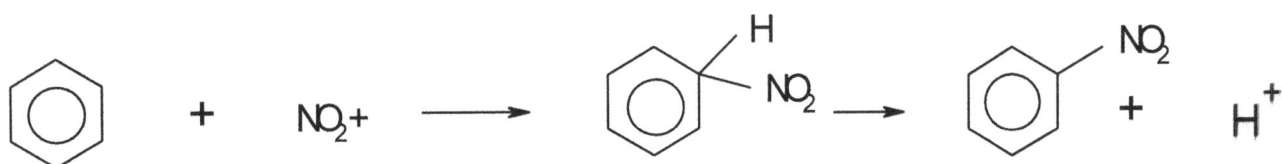

Or a halogenoalkane.

Or sulfuric acid

Primary, Secondary or Tertiary Amines

Look at the following amines and decide whether they are primary, secondary or tertiary using the following code:

1 = Primary

2 = Secondary

3 = Tertiary

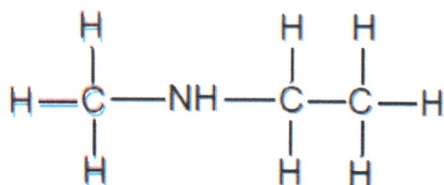

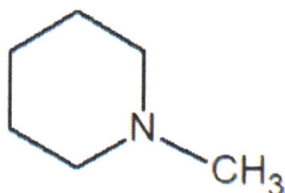

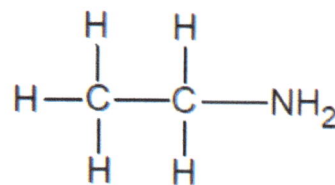

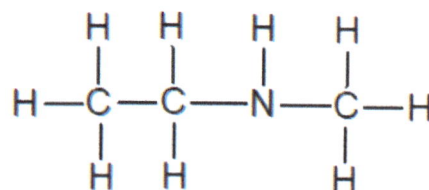

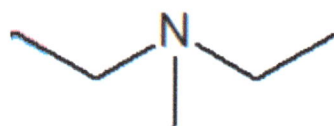

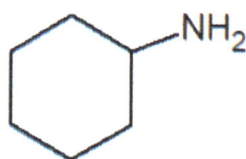

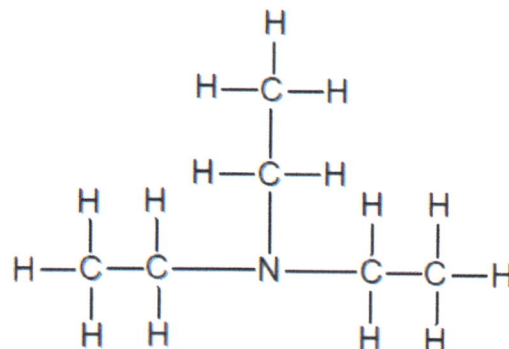

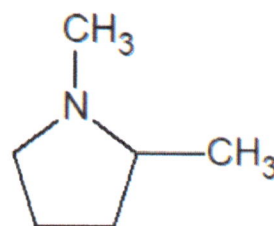

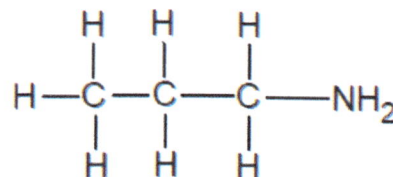

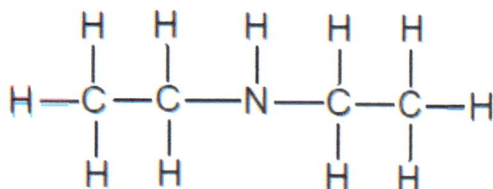

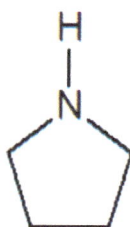

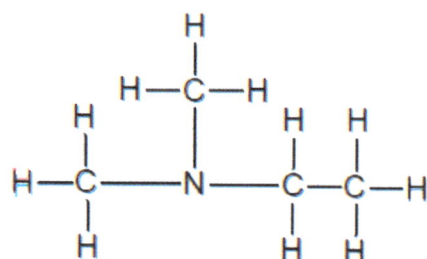

Systematic Naming

Match the following carboxylic acid compounds to the correct systematic name.

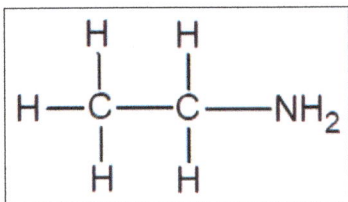

hexanamine

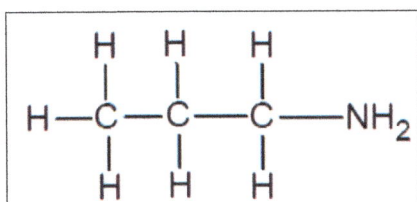

ethylmethylamine

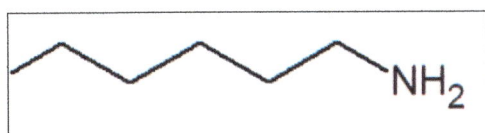

ethylamine

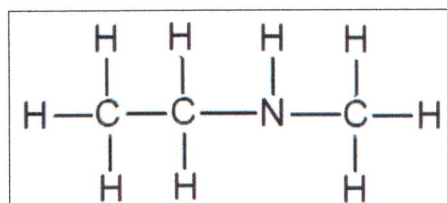

propylamine

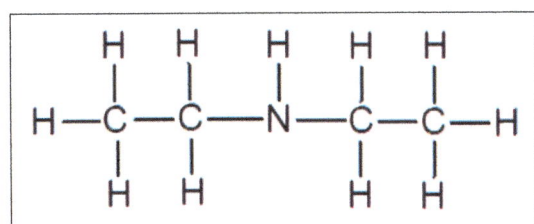

heptanamine

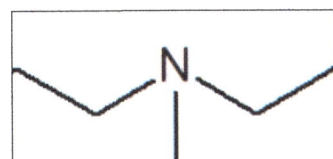

diethylamine

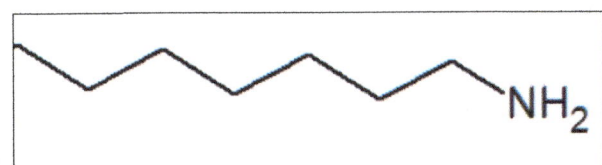

diethylmethylamine

Quiz Word

Answer the following questions to complete the quiz word and then try to work out what the key phrase in the **bold** boxes should be.

1. Formed when an amine reacts with a carboxylic acid. (5)
2. Type of amine with three carbon atoms bonded to the nitrogen. (8)
3. Type of bonds found between primary or secondary amine molecules. (8)
4. Name given to a compound containing a benzene ring. (8)
5. Type of reaction that benzene undergoes. (13,12)
6. Amines dissolved in water form these.(5)

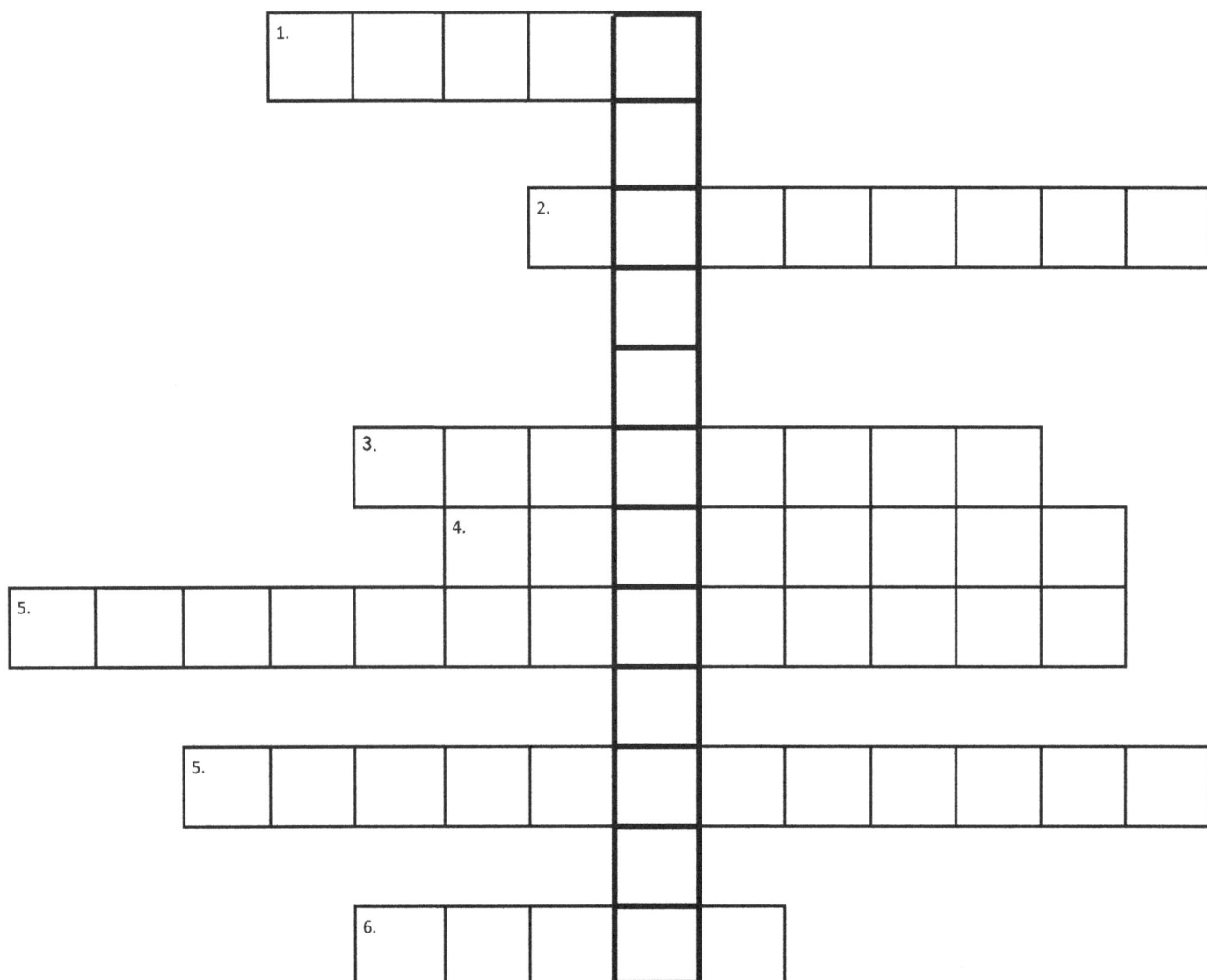

Quiz Word Clue: Type of reactant that attacks benzene.

Naming Salts

Match the following amine reactions to the correct name of the salt formed.

methylamine + hydrochloric acid	phenylammonium nitrate
ethylamine + sulfuric acid	hexylammonium propanoate
phenylamine + nitric acid	ethylammonium sulfate
butanamine + hydrochloric acid	methylammonium chloride
ethylmethylamine + ethanoic acid	dimethylammonium sulfate
hexanamine + propanoic acid	ethylmethylammonium ethanoate
dimethylamine + sulfuric acid	butylammonium chloride

Reactions of Benzene

Complete the summary chart showing the reaction mechanism of benzene with a number of electrophiles using curly arrows and structural formulae.

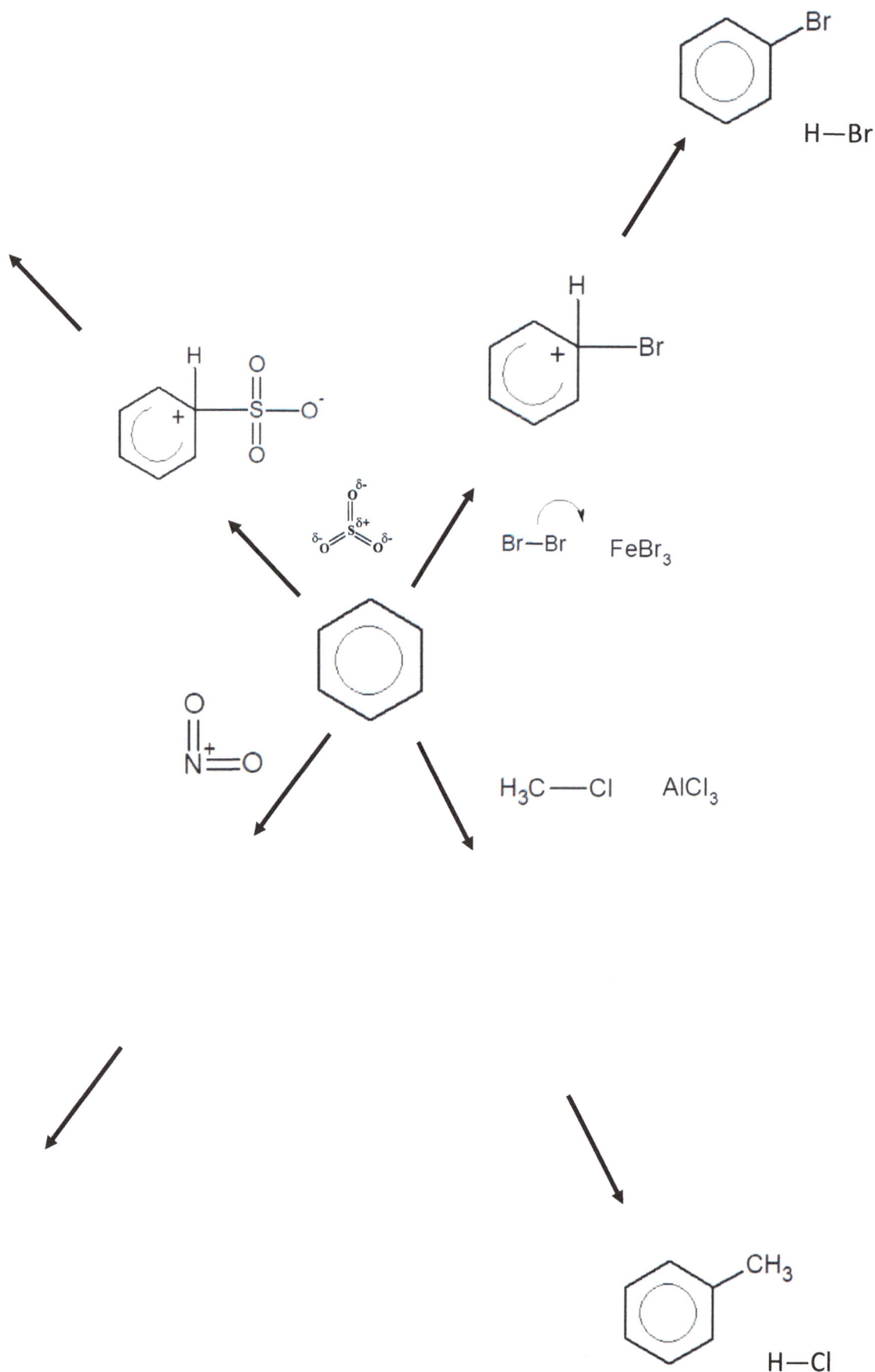

Chemical Misconceptions

A student has written a note on benzene. They have made **ten** mistakes, can you find them and write the correct note in the space below:

Benzene

Benzene is a five membered ring with sp^3 hybridisation of the carbon atoms. This results in the carbon atoms bonding to two adjacent carbon atoms and a hydrogen atom with pi π bonds. This then leaves a sigma σ bond which means you have delocalised electrons moving around above and below the ring. These delocalised electrons weaken the structure of the ring making benzene susceptible to nucleophilic substitution. Where a carbon atom is substituted for another atom or group of atoms.

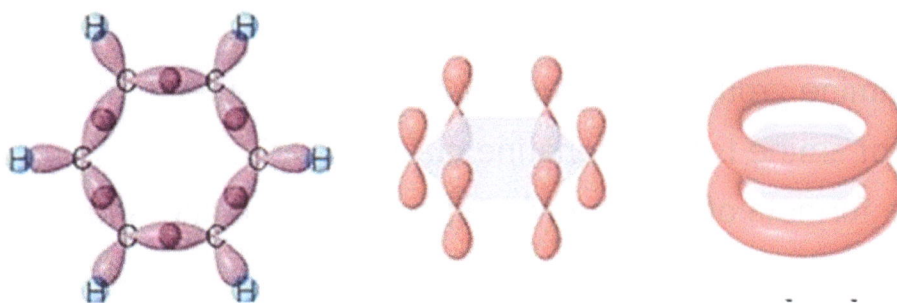

Good nucleophiles that react with benzene are halogens (with $AlCl_3$ or $FeBr_3$ as a catalyst), NO_2^+ nitronium ion made by reacting concentrated nitric acid with concentrated sulfuric acid, halogenoalkanes with $AlCl_3$ catalyst and concentrated sulfuric acid.

Another name for the benzene ring when it is acting as a branch is an alkyl ring. Its drawn as shown

Practice Questions

1. Noradrenaline, phenylephrine and amphetamine are all drugs that interact with our bodies.

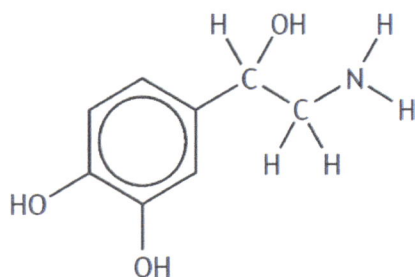

Noradrenaline

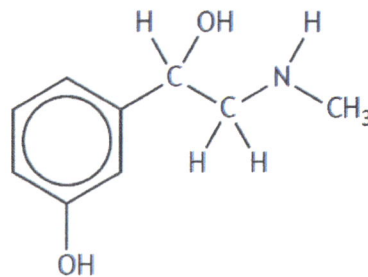

Phenylephrine

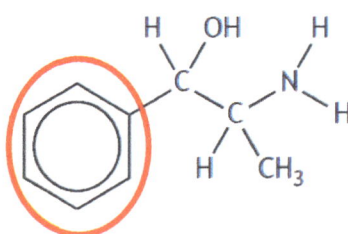

Amphetamine

a) Circle the amine group in the phenylephrine molecule.

b) What type of amine is noradrenaline classified as?

c) What is the formula of the phenyl ring circled in amphetamine.

2. Acetyl salicylic acid is the starting point for making salbutamol. The first step is shown below:

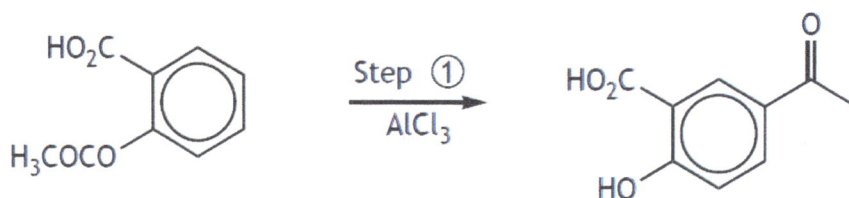

a) 1-chloropropanone is the reagent used in this step. What reaction does it undergo with the acetyl salicylic acid?

b) What is the role of the $AlCl_3$ in this reaction?

c) State the type of hybridisation which is adopted by the carbon atoms in the aromatic ring.

d) Salbutamol is shown below circle the amine group and state what class of amines this molecule belongs to.

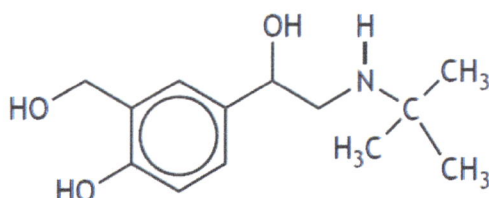

Unit 3   Organic Synthesis - Summary

CH_3CH_2COOH Carboxylic acid

Condensation CH_3CH_2OH / H^+

$CH_3CH_2OCOCH_2CH_3$ Esters

Acid Hydrolysis dil. HCl or dil. NaOH

Hydrolysis H_2O / OH^-

CH_3CH_2CN Nitriles

Nucleophilic Substitution KCN

Condensation CH_3CH_2COOH / H^+

CH_3CH_2OH Alkohols

Nucleophilic Substitution Alkali OH^-

$CH_3CH_2NH_2$ Amines

Nucleophilic Substitution NH_3

$CH_3CH_2OCH_3$ Ethers

Nucleophilic Substitution $CH_3O^-Na^+$

CH_3CH_3Cl Halogenoalkanes

Elimination Alcoholic KOH

Hydration H_2O / c.H_3PO_4

Dehydration Al_2O_3 / heat

Electrophilic addition HCl

$CH_2 = CH_2$ Alkenes

Cracking Al_2O_3 / heat

Hydrogenation H_2 / Ni

Radical Substitution Cl_2 / UV light

CH_3CH_3 Alkanes

CH_3CH_2OH Alkanols (primary)

Oxidation $K_2Cr_2O_7$ / H^+

Reduction $LiAlH_4$

CH_3CHO Aldehydes

Oxidation $K_2Cr_2O_7$ / H^+

Reduction $LiAlH_4$

CH_3COOH Carboxylic Acid

$CH_3CH(OH)CH_3$ Alkanols (secondary)

Oxidation $K_2Cr_2O_7$ / H^+

Reduction $LiAlH_4$

CH_3COCH_3 Ketones

General Mechanism for Electrophilic Substitution

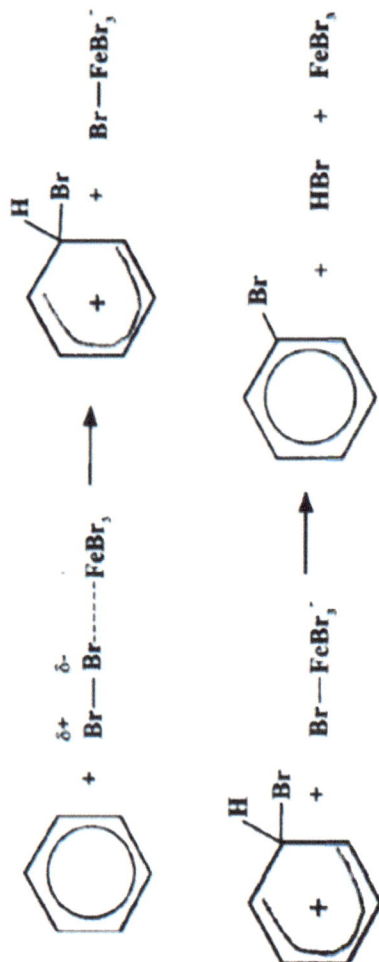

$$\overset{\delta+}{Br} — \overset{\delta-}{Br} ----- FeBr_3$$

$$Br—FeBr_3^-$$

$$\longrightarrow \quad H \; Br \quad + \quad Br—FeBr_3^-$$

$$\longrightarrow \quad Br \quad + \quad HBr \quad + \quad FeBr_3$$

Other electrophiles:

Nitronium ion used to make nitrobenzene.

$$NO_2^+$$

Sulfur trioxde formed by sulfuric acid to make detergents.

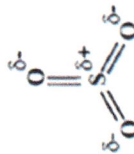

$$\overset{\delta-}{O} = \overset{\delta+}{S} \overset{\delta-}{=O}$$ (with $\overset{\delta-}{O}$)

Halogenoalkanes with aluminium chloride as a catalyst

$$\overset{\delta+}{R} — \overset{\delta-}{Cl} ----- \overset{\delta-}{AlCl_3}$$

Organic Reaction Summary Sheet

Reactions of Benzene

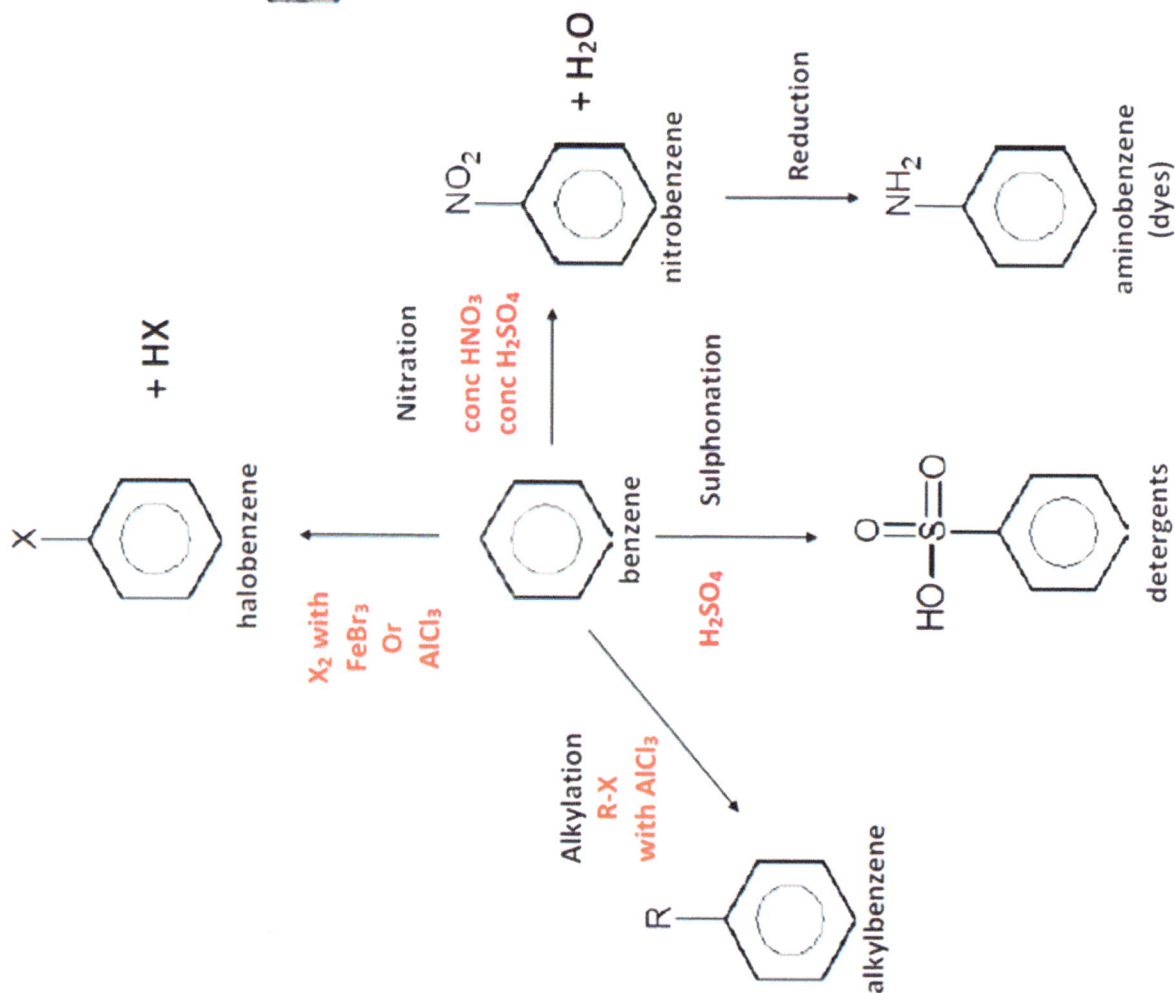

Alkylation
R-X
with AlCl₃ → alkylbenzene (R—)

X₂ with FeBr₃ Or AlCl₃ → halobenzene (X—) + HX

Nitration
conc HNO₃
conc H₂SO₄ → nitrobenzene (NO₂—) + H_2O

→ **Reduction** → aminobenzene (NH₂—) (dyes)

Sulphonation
H₂SO₄ → detergents (HO—S(=O)(=O)—)

benzene

Reagents

Link the reagents to the different type of reactions that they are used for in organic synthesis, using the diagrams on p149-150 to help.

Reagents	Reaction types
Br_2 / $FeBr_3$	nucleophilic substitution
CH_3CH_2OH / H^+	electrophilic substitution
KCN	catalytic hydration
HBr	acid hydrolysis
H_2O / HCl	condensation
CH_3Cl / $AlCl_3$	oxidation
$K_2Cr_2O_7$ / H^+	reduction
H_2O / conc. H_3PO_4	addition
$LiAlH_4$	radical substitution
H_2O / NaOH	nucleophilic substitution
NH_3	electrophilic substitution
Cl_2 / UV light	hydrolysis

Reaction Types (I)

Link the reaction type to the correct reaction shown, using the diagrams on p149-150 to help.

| nucleophilic substitution |

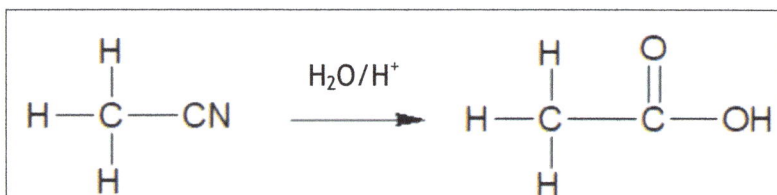

| electrophilic substitution |

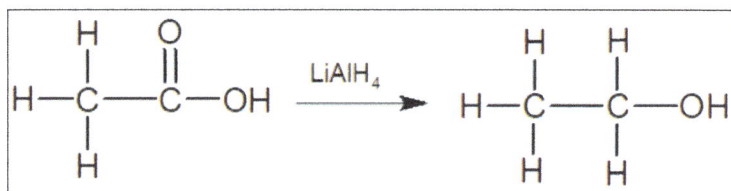

| catalytic hydration |

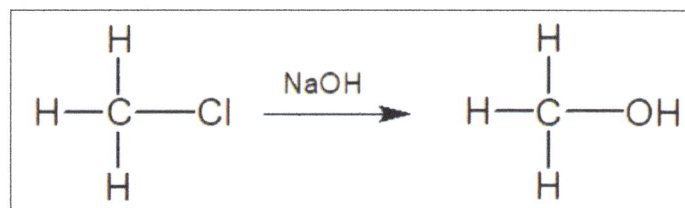

| acid hydrolysis |

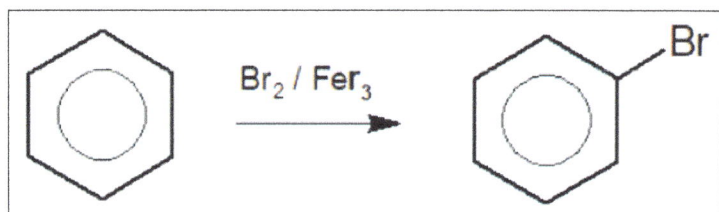

| condensation |

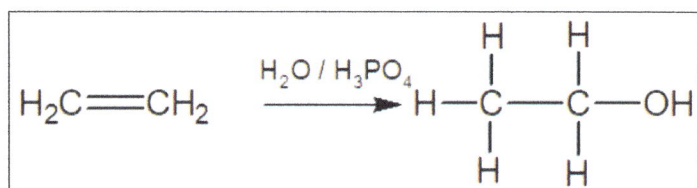

| oxidation |

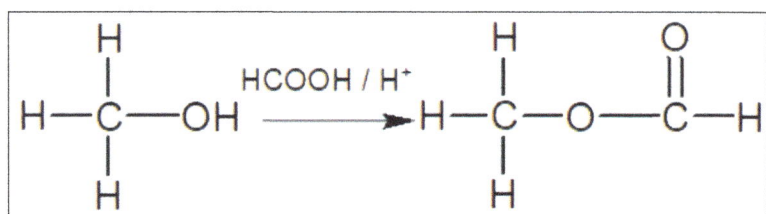

| reduction |

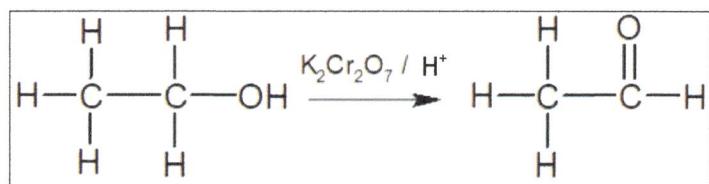

Reaction Pathways (I)

Identify the reagents and reaction types for each of the sequences of reactions given below, using the diagram on p149 to help:

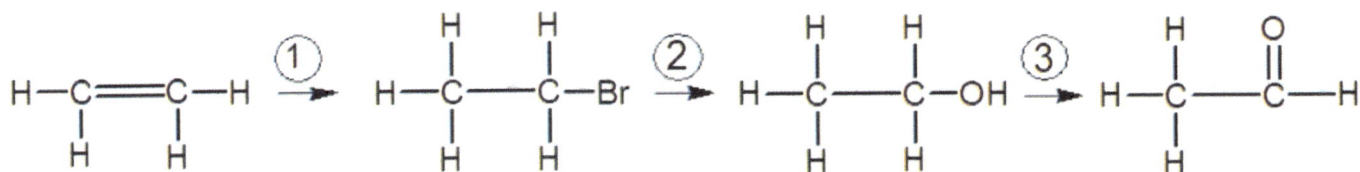

$$H_2C=CH_2 \xrightarrow{1} CH_3-CH_2-Br \xrightarrow{2} CH_3-CH_2-OH \xrightarrow{3} CH_3-CHO$$

1. reagents   reaction type

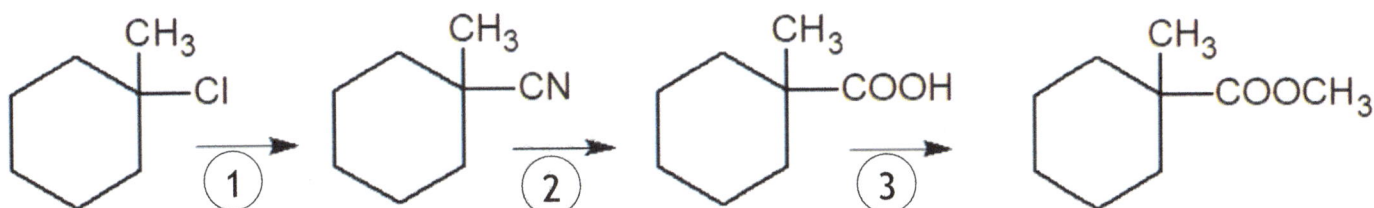

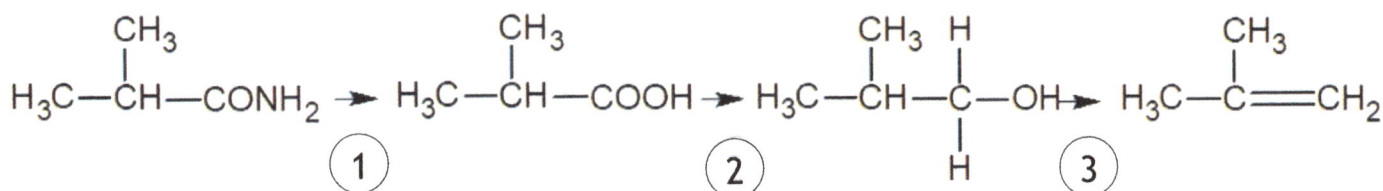

2. reagents   reaction type

3. reagents   reaction type

$$C_6H_{10}(CH_3)-Cl \xrightarrow{1} C_6H_{10}(CH_3)-CN \xrightarrow{2} C_6H_{10}(CH_3)-COOH \xrightarrow{3} C_6H_{10}(CH_3)-COOCH_3$$

1. reagents   reaction type

2. reagents   reaction type

3. reagents   reaction type

$$H_3C-CH(CH_3)-CONH_2 \xrightarrow{1} H_3C-CH(CH_3)-COOH \xrightarrow{2} H_3C-CH(CH_3)-CH(H)-OH \xrightarrow{3} H_3C-C(CH_3)=CH_2$$

1. reagents   reaction type

2. reagents   reaction type

3. reagents   reaction type

Quiz Word

Answer the following questions to complete the quiz word and then try to work out what the key phrase in the **bold** boxes should be.

1. Compound that undergoes electrophilic substutution reactions. (7)

2. Reaction that converts an alcohol into a carbonyl. (9)

3. LiAlH$_4$ is used as a reagent in this reaction. (9)

4. Type of compound that undergoes acid hydrolysis to form a carboxylic acid. (7)

5. Starting point of many organic synthesis reactions. (6)

6. Radical, electrophilic and nucleophilic are examples of this type of reaction. (12)

7. Negative ion or molecule with a lone pair of electrons.(11)

Quiz Word Clue: Reaction used to make alkenes from halogenoalkanes.

154

Reaction Types (II)

Link the reaction type to the correct definition shown.

nucleophilic substitution	H^+ ions along with water create a carboxylic acid from a nitrile.
electrophilic substitution	H^+ ions help water add across a double bond.
catalytic hydration	A positive charged ion replaces a hydrogen atom in benzene
acid hydrolysis	A positively charged carbon atom is attacked by a negative charged ion or molecule.
condensation	The hydrogen to oxygen ration is increased.
oxidation	Two molecules join together and eliminate a small molecules like H_2O or HCl.
reduction	The oxygen to hydrogen ratio is increased.

Reaction Pathways (II)

Connect the starting molecule to the reaction steps and the final product, using p149 to help, the first one has been done for you:

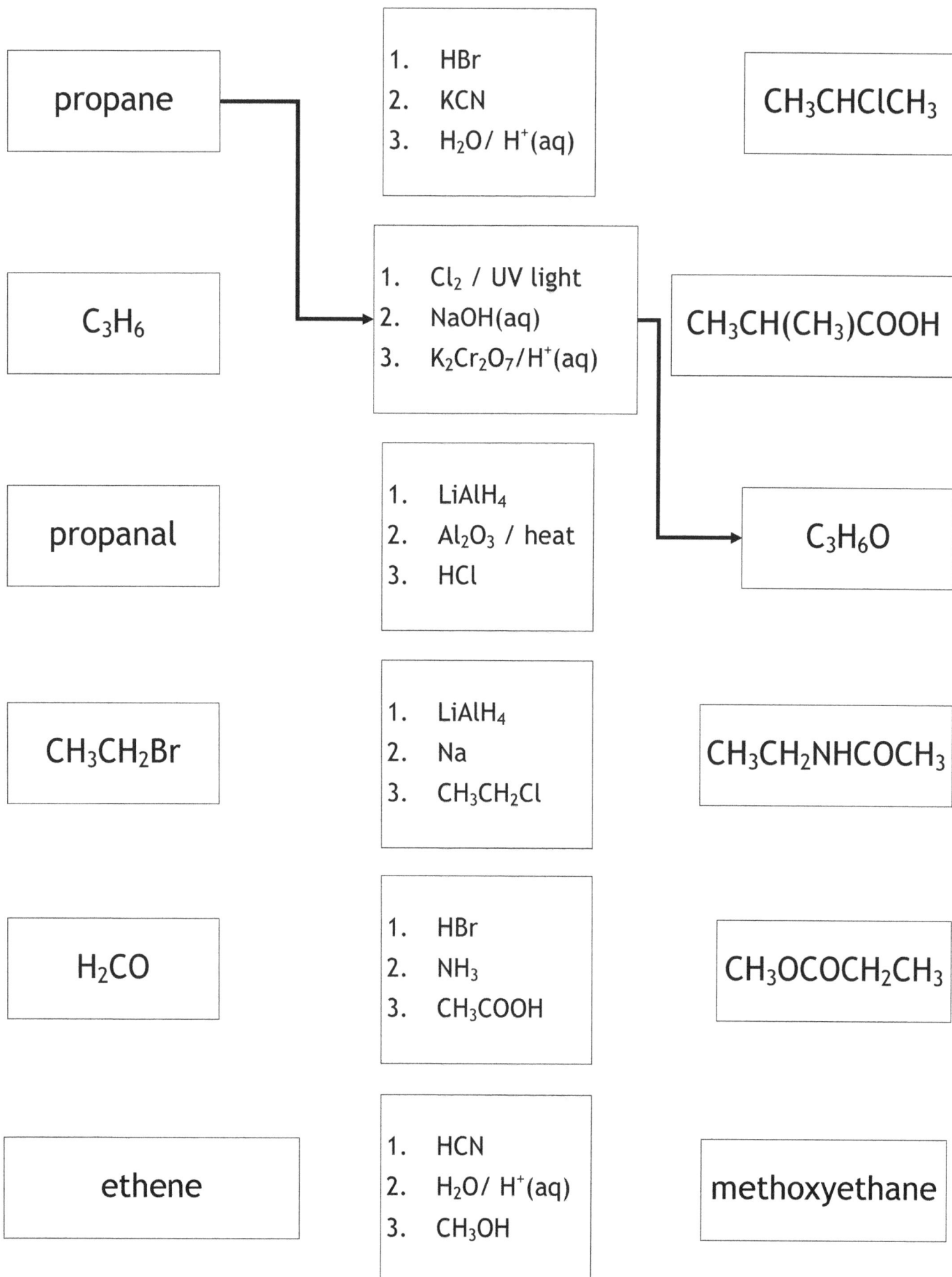

| propane | 1. HBr
2. KCN
3. $H_2O/ H^+(aq)$ | $CH_3CHClCH_3$ |

| C_3H_6 | 1. Cl_2 / UV light
2. NaOH(aq)
3. $K_2Cr_2O_7/H^+(aq)$ | $CH_3CH(CH_3)COOH$ |

| propanal | 1. $LiAlH_4$
2. Al_2O_3 / heat
3. HCl | C_3H_6O |

| CH_3CH_2Br | 1. $LiAlH_4$
2. Na
3. CH_3CH_2Cl | $CH_3CH_2NHCOCH_3$ |

| H_2CO | 1. HBr
2. NH_3
3. CH_3COOH | $CH_3OCOCH_2CH_3$ |

| ethene | 1. HCN
2. $H_2O/ H^+(aq)$
3. CH_3OH | methoxyethane |

Practice Questions

1. A chemist performed the following sequence of reactions to make a natural chemical found in the body called adrenaline:

    Step 1

    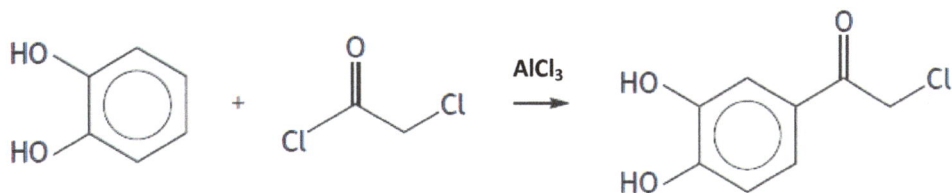

    Step 2

    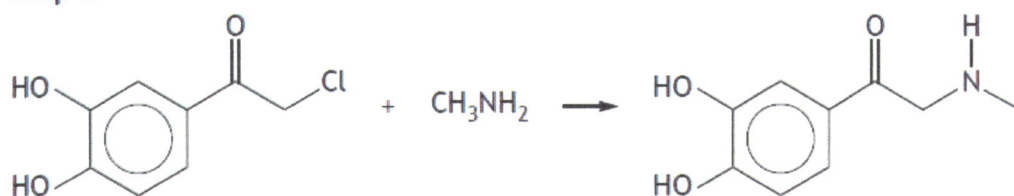

    Step 3

    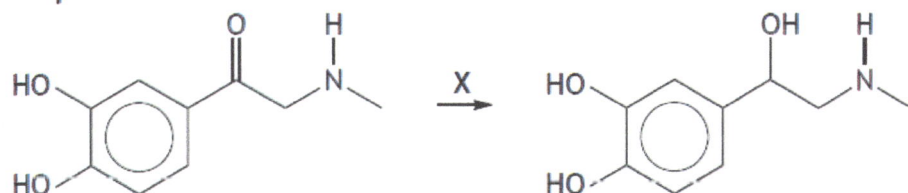

    a) What type of reaction does the benzene ring undergo in step 1.

    b) Draw the structural formula of the amine used in step 2.

    c) What type of reaction is occurring in step 2?

    d) Identify reagent X in step 3.

2.

    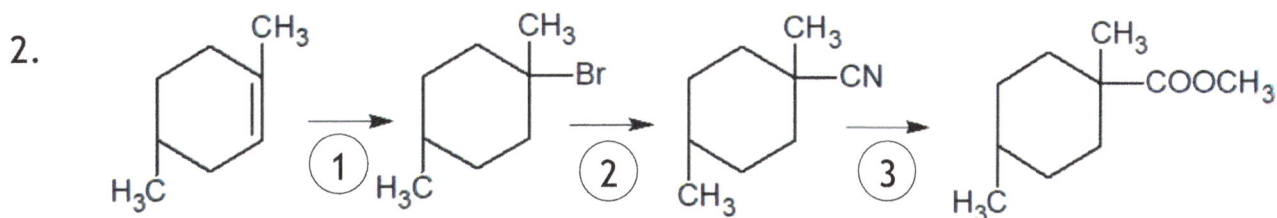

    a) Identify the reagent used in step 1.

    b) Step 2 follows a S_N1 mechanism, using curly arrows and structural formulae show this process.

    c) Step 3 involves two reactions, the first is called acid hydrolysis, identify the reagent used in the second.

3. Compound Z can be produced by the reaction of compound X with compound Y as shown in the synthesis outlined below.

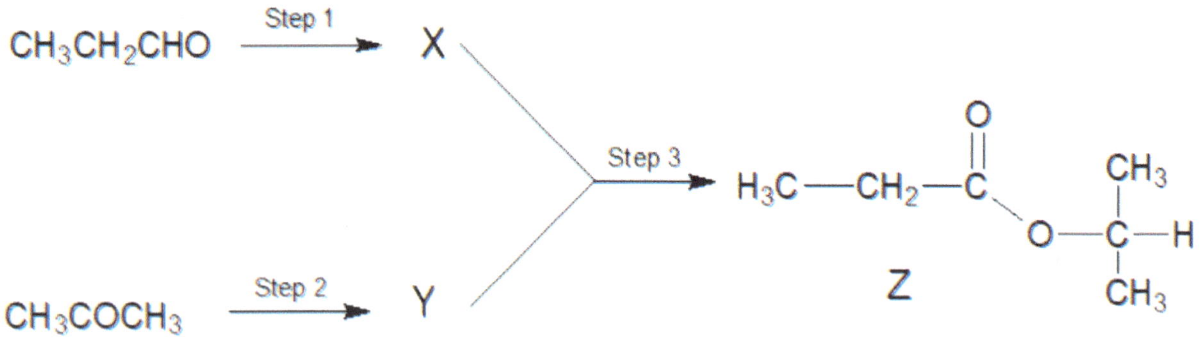

CH_3CH_2CHO —Step 1→ X

CH_3COCH_3 —Step 2→ Y

X and Y —Step 3→ Z: $H_3C-CH_2-\overset{\displaystyle O}{\overset{\displaystyle \|}{C}}-O-\overset{\displaystyle CH_3}{\underset{\displaystyle CH_3}{C}}-H$

a. Identify compounds X and Y.

b. Give the name of the type of reaction in

i. Step 1

ii. Step 2

iii. Step 3

c. Suggest a suitable reagent for

i. Step 1

ii. Step 2

4. A student carried out the following reaction sequence:

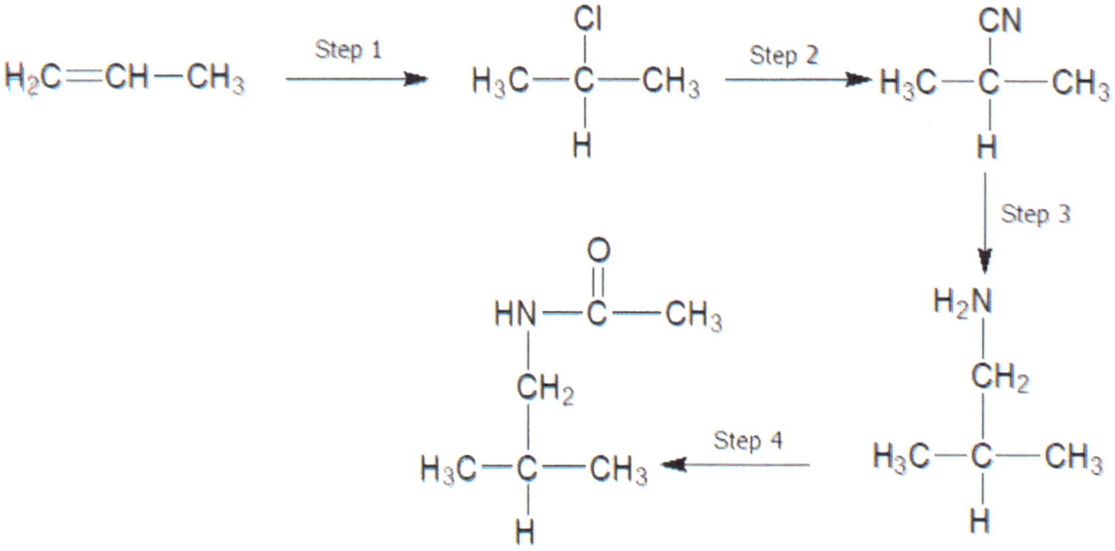

$H_2C=CH-CH_3$ —Step 1→ $H_3C-\overset{\displaystyle Cl}{\underset{\displaystyle H}{C}}-CH_3$ —Step 2→ $H_3C-\overset{\displaystyle CN}{\underset{\displaystyle H}{C}}-CH_3$

Step 3 ↓

$H_3C-\overset{\displaystyle H_2N}{\underset{\displaystyle H}{C}}-CH_3$ with CH_2 chain: $H_3C-\overset{\displaystyle CH_2}{\underset{\displaystyle H}{C}}-CH_3$

—Step 4→ structure with $HN-\overset{\displaystyle O}{\overset{\displaystyle \|}{C}}-CH_3$, CH_2, $H_3C-\overset{}{\underset{\displaystyle H}{C}}-CH_3$

a. Suggest a suitable reagent for step 1.

b. What type of reaction is step 2?

c. Step 3 produces an amine, what type of amine is being formed?

Unit 3 Stereoisomers

Structural isomers have the same chemical formula but different structural formula.

e.g. propan-1-ol and propan-2-ol

They look different and have different systematic names.

Stereoisomers on the other hand have the same chemical formula and chemical structure. They only differ in the 3D arrangement of atoms around an atom or bond.

There are two types of stereoisomers, geometric and optical or chiral isomers.

Geometric Isomers

These occur when there is a double bond or ring structure preventing rotation. This causes two possible arrangements of atoms around the bond. The atoms can be opposite each other (TRANS) or adjacent to each other (CIS).

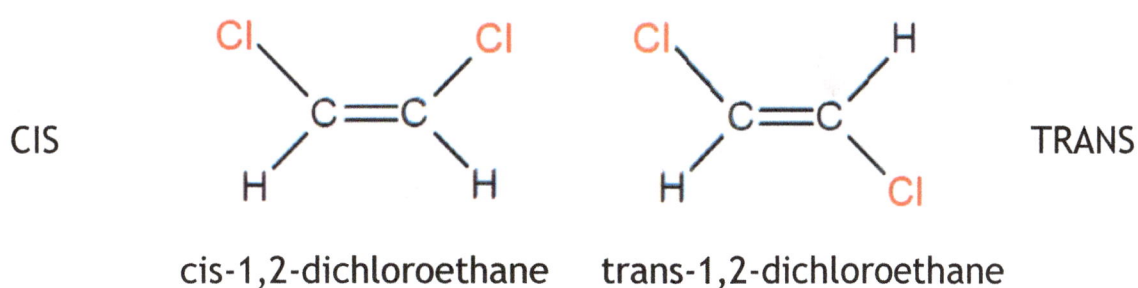

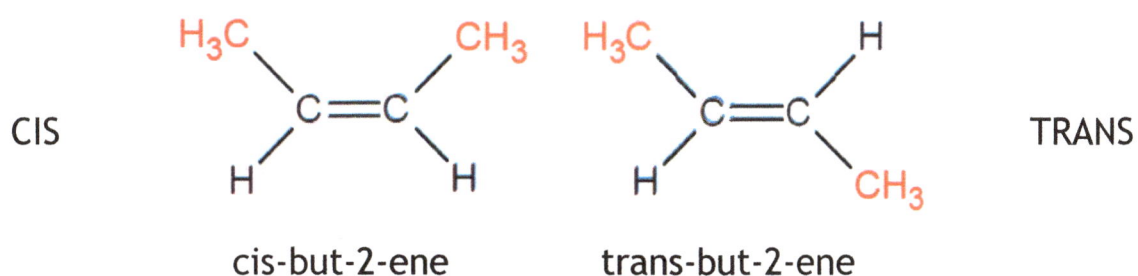

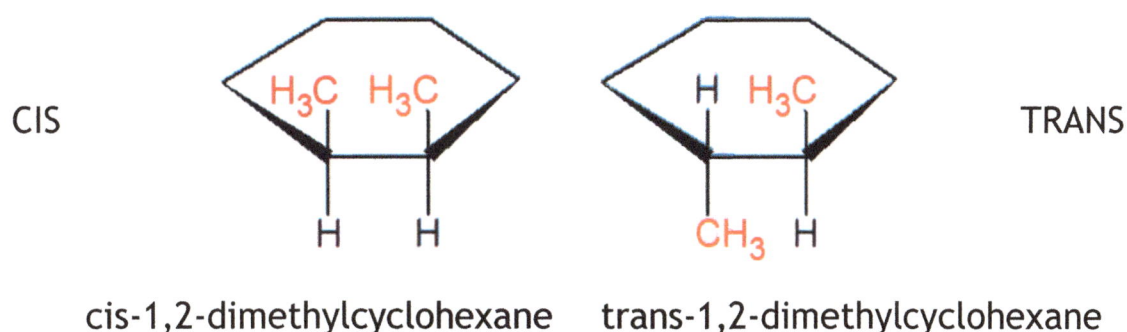

CIS

cis-1,2-dichloroethane

TRANS

trans-1,2-dichloroethane

CIS

cis-but-2-ene

TRANS

trans-but-2-ene

CIS

cis-1,2-dimethylcyclohexane

TRANS

trans-1,2-dimethylcyclohexane

Cis and trans isomers can have different physical and chemical properties.

Optical isomers

If a carbon atom has 4 different atoms or groups of atoms attached, then a **chiral centre** occurs.

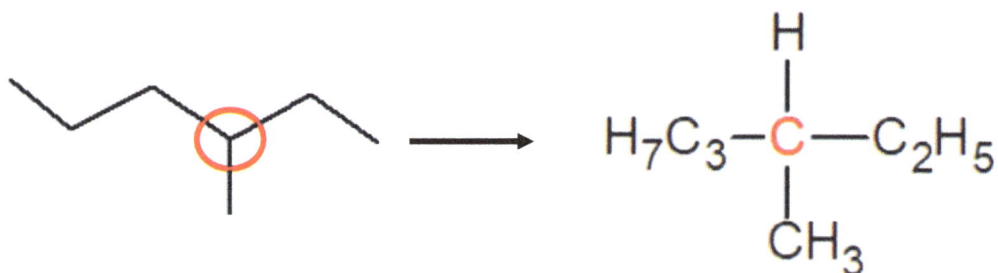

$$H_7C_3 - \overset{\displaystyle H}{\underset{\displaystyle CH_3}{C}} - C_2H_5$$

Like a pair of gloves you get a left hand and right hand form. The two isomers are **identical mirror images** of one another but are **non-superimposable**. They are called the L-enantiomer and the D-enantiomer. Amino acids apart from glycine are always chiral.

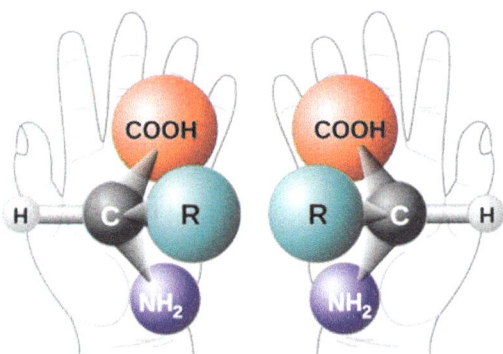

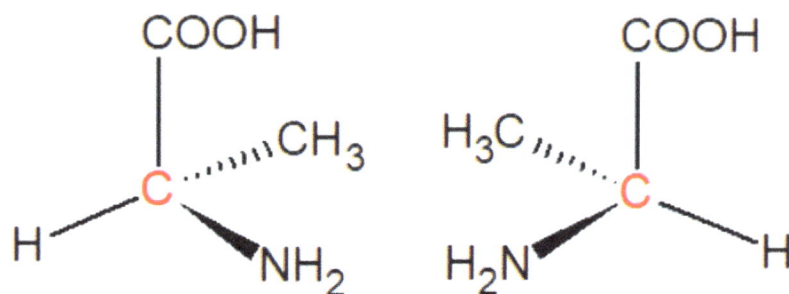

They are called optical isomers because the two isomers rotate plane polarised light by 45⁰ in opposite directions.

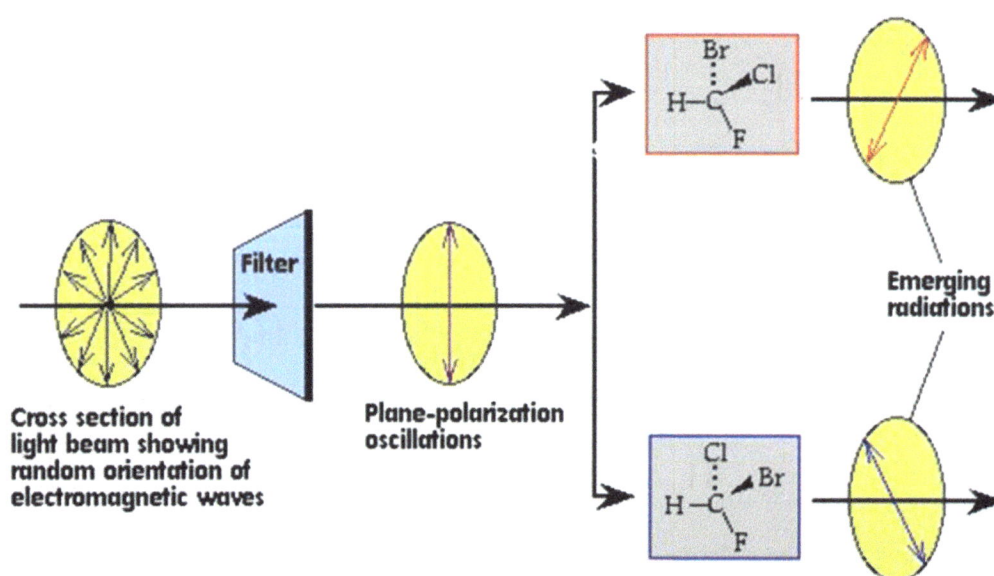

Cross section of light beam showing random orientation of electromagnetic waves

Plane-polarization oscillations

Filter

Emerging radiations

If there **are equal concentrations of each enantiomer, then a racemic mixture** is present and there is **no observable rotation of plane polarised light**.

Geometric & Optical Isomers

Identify all the compounds that will have geometric or optical isomers, use the code given below:

1   Geometric isomer

2   Optical isomer

3   No stereoisomers

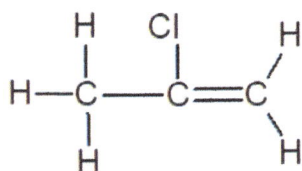

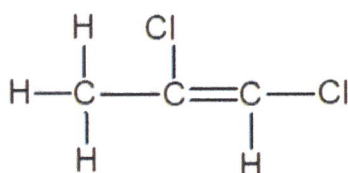

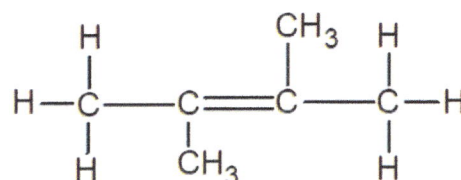

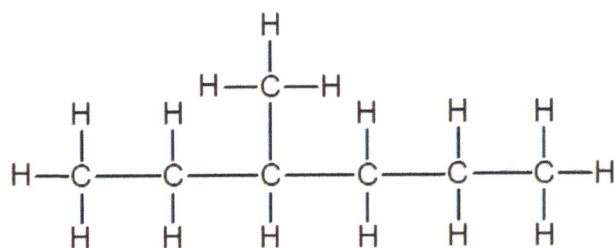

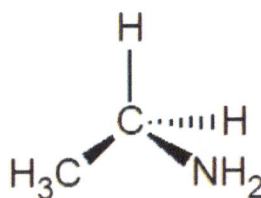

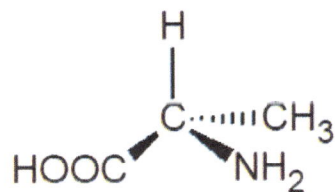

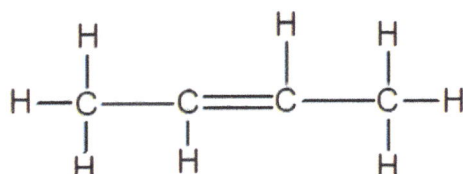

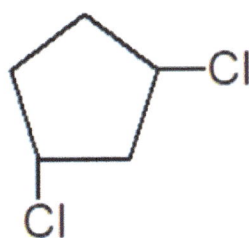

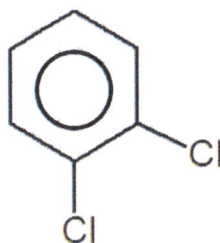

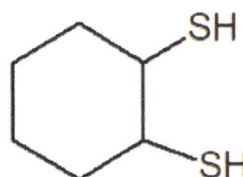

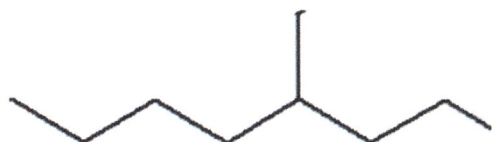

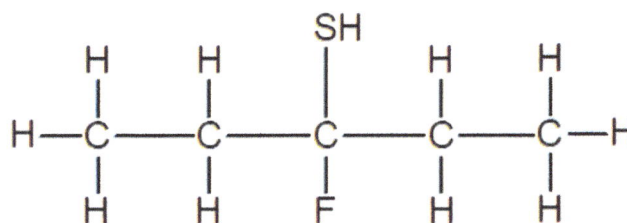

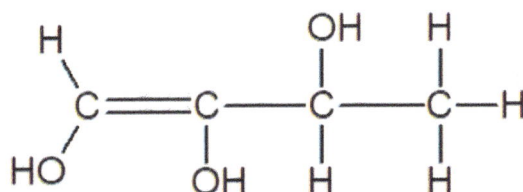

Cis & Trans Isomers

Work out what type of isomer is shown in the examples below and in the space next to it draw out the opposite geometric isomer.

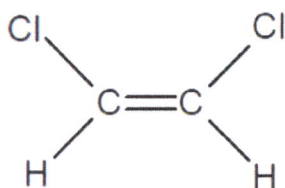

Type =

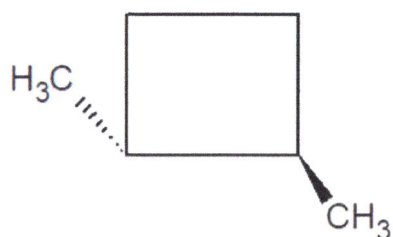

Type =

Type =

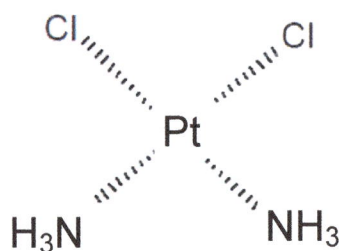

Type =

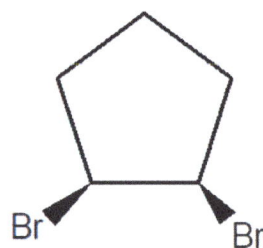

Type =

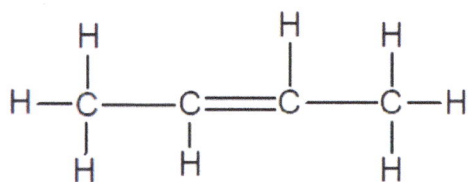

Type =

Quiz Word

Answer the following questions to complete the quiz word and then try to work out what the key phrase in the **bold** boxes should be.

1. Type of hydrocarbon that can have geometric isomers. (6)
2. Type of geometric isomer. (3)
3. Light used to identify optical isomers. (5,9)
4. Type of isomer where rotation of two carbon atoms is prevented. (9)
5. Type of fat where the hydrogen atoms are on opposite sides of a C=C bond. (5)
6. The two types of isomers with a chiral centre are called this. (11)
7. A mixture of two optical isomers in equal concentrations. (7)

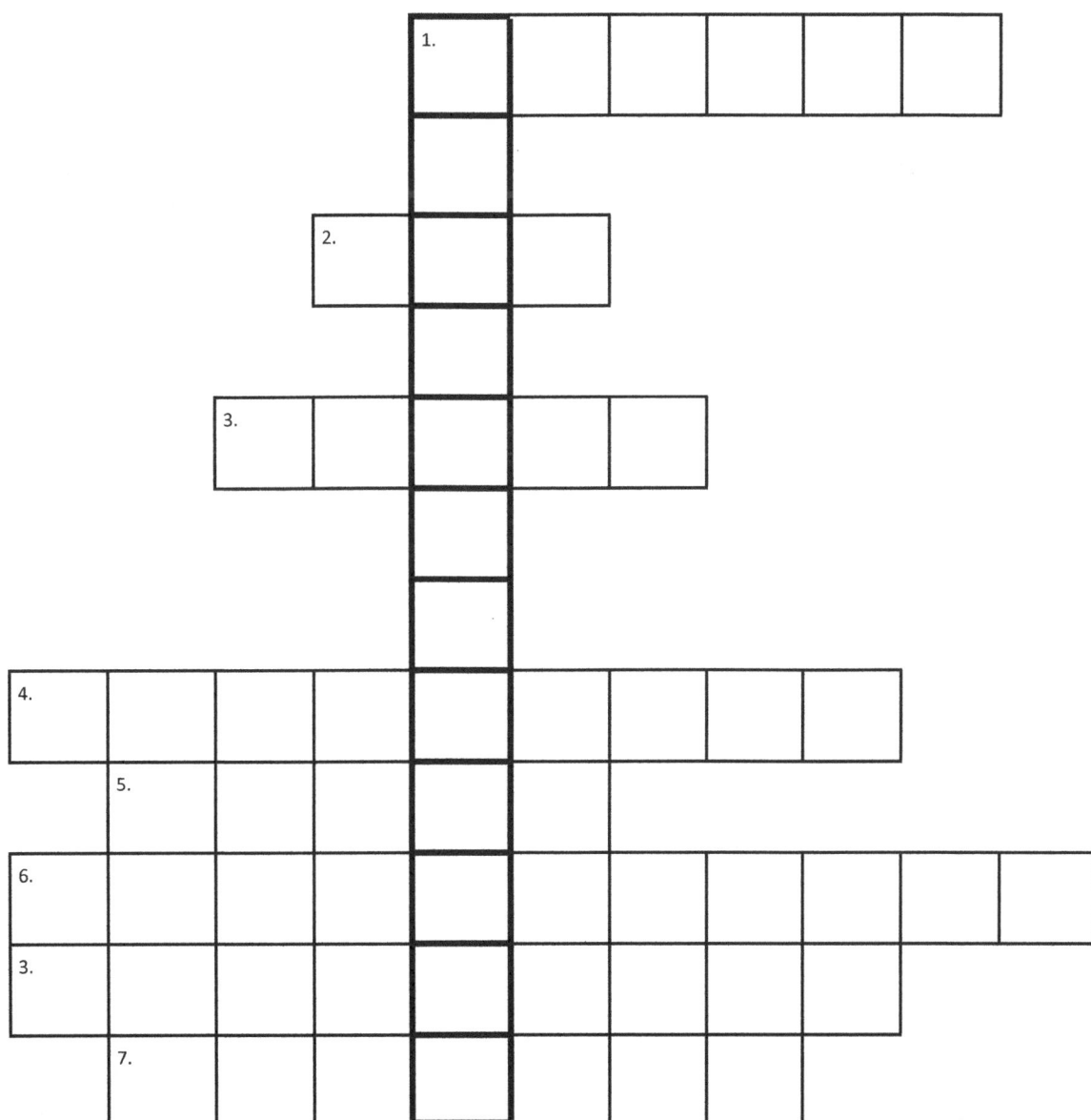

Optical Isomers

Connect the matching enantiomers.

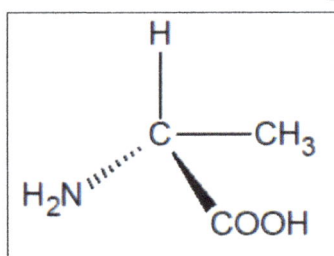

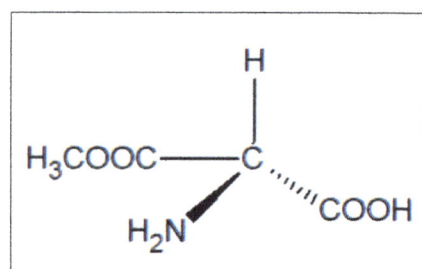

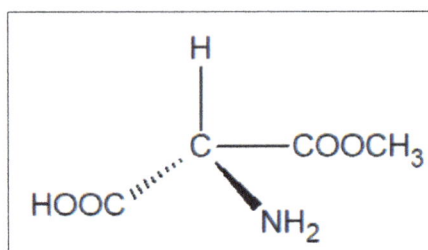

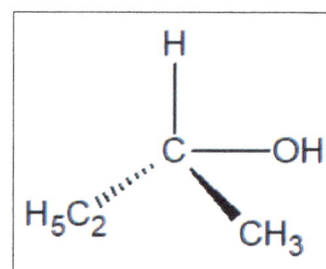

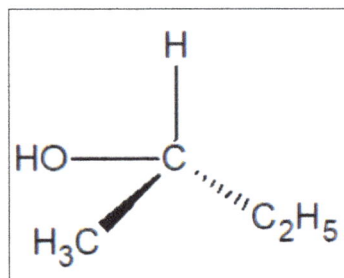

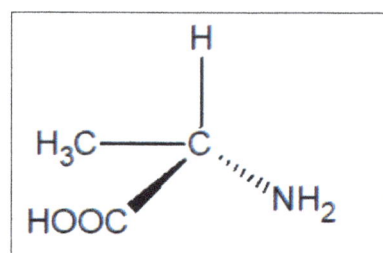

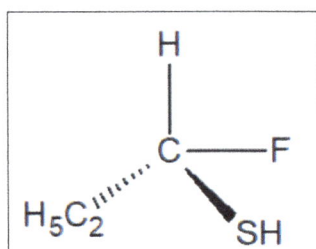

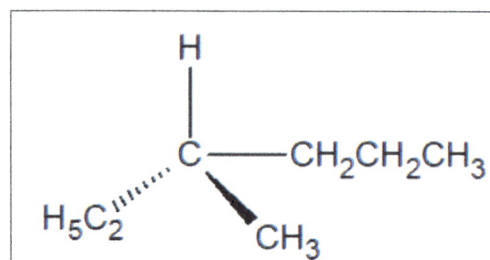

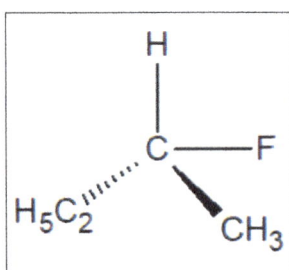

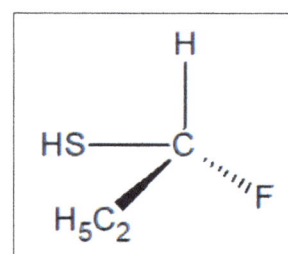

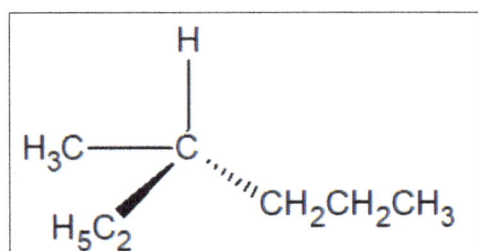

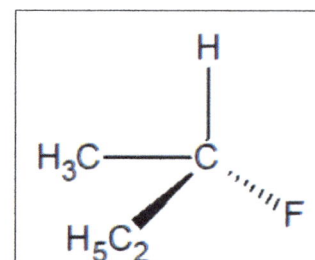

Chemical Misconceptions

A student has written a note on the properties of ethers & carboxylic acids. They have made **12** mistakes, can you find them and write the correct note in the space below:

Geometric Isomers

These occur when a carbon to carbon single bond prevents rotation. This leads to two types of geometric isomers L and D:

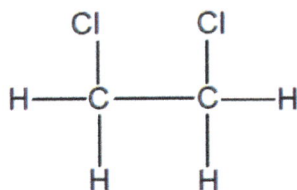 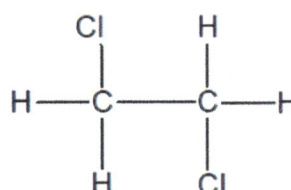

L isomer   D isomer

Geometric isomers also occur in cycloalkanes.

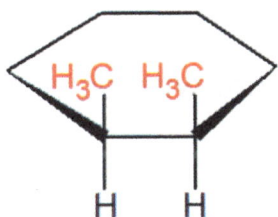 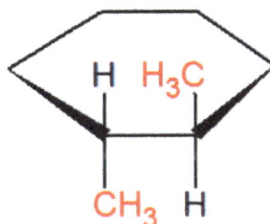

Optical Isomers

These occur when a carbon atom has 3 different groups attached to it, this is called a choral centre. They are called optical isomers because they can rotate normal light by 45° in opposite directions and are superimposable mirror images. An equal mixture of each racemic is called an enantiomer mixture.

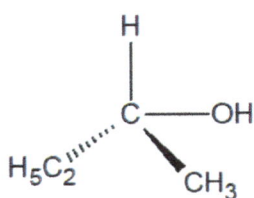 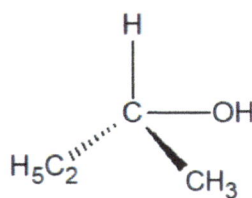

Practice Questions

1. Adrenaline is a natural chemical found in the body, it is part of our fight or flight response to danger.

ADRENALINE

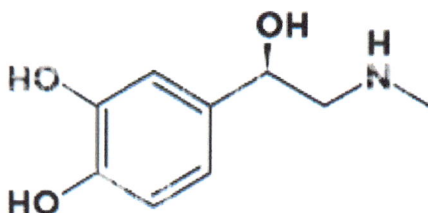

a. Circle the chiral centre present in this molecule.

b. There are two forms of adrenaline and they are referred to as optical isomers. What does the term optical isomer mean?

c. What is the term used to describe a mixture with equal concentrations of each isomer?

2. In the reaction sequence shown below, 2-chloropentane reacts with sodium hydroxide in different ways depending on the solvent used.

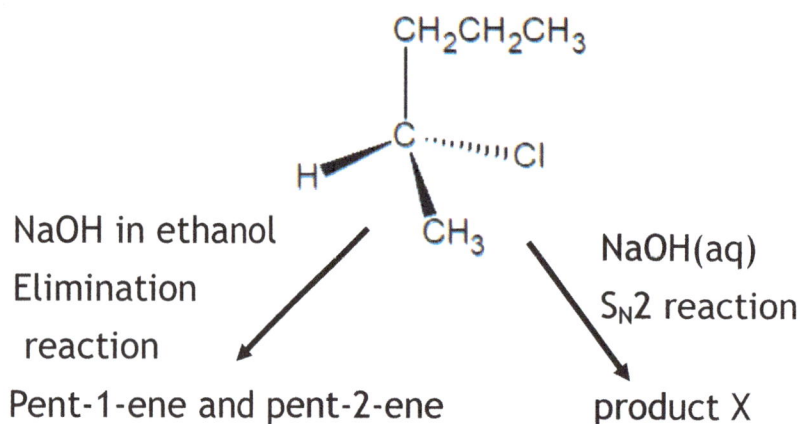

NaOH in ethanol
Elimination
reaction

Pent-1-ene and pent-2-ene

NaOH(aq)
S_N2 reaction

product X

a. One of the alkenes formed in the elimination reaction is present as two **geometric isomers**. Draw the structure of both geometric isomers and name each one.

b. 2-chloropentane has a chiral centre, draw the other enantiomer that is possible.

Unit 3   Instrumental Analysis

Elemental Microanalysis

Completely burn the organic compound and weigh the mass of carbon dioxide, water and any other oxides. The empirical formula can then be deduced.

e.g. Compound X was subjected to elemental analysis. Complete combustion of 0.210g of X gave 0.478g of carbon dioxide and 0.196g of water. No other product was formed.

Step 1: Work out number of moles of carbon and hydrogen **atoms**:

Number moles C = mass CO_2 / 44   number moles H = mass H_2O / 9*

$\qquad\qquad$ = 0.478 / 44 $\qquad\qquad\qquad\qquad\qquad$ = 0.196 / 9

$\qquad\qquad$ = <u>0.011</u> $\qquad\qquad\qquad\qquad\qquad\qquad$ = <u>0.022</u>

(* H_2O has a mass of 18, but there are 2 H atoms so therefore need to divide by 2.)

Step 2: Work out total mass of C and H atoms in the sample:

Total mass = [0.011 x 12] + 0.022

$\qquad\qquad$ = 0.154g

Step 3: Work out mass of O atoms in the sample:

Mass O = mass of sample – mass of C & H

$\qquad\qquad$ = 0.21 – 0.154

$\qquad\qquad$ = 0.056g

Step 4: Work out number of moles of O atoms:

Number of moles of O = mass / GFM

$\qquad\qquad\qquad$ = 0.056 / 16

$\qquad\qquad\qquad$ = <u>0.0035</u>

Step 5: Work out the simplest ratio of C:H:O by dividing smallest number of moles into the other two:

C	:	H	:	O
0.011	:	0.022	:	0.0035
3	:	6	:	1

The empirical formula of X is therefore **C_3H_6O**

Sometimes the masses of each element are given as a percentage. In this case assume the mass of the sample is 100g and therefore you know the mass of each element and their respective number of moles can be calculated by diving by the relative atomic mass.

Mass Spectrometry (MS)

Here the sample is bombarded by a beam of electrons to ionise it and also break it up into positively charged fragments. The charged fragments are passed through a magnetic field and detected according to their mass/charge ratio. A mass spectrum shows the abundance of each fragment. **The peak corresponding to the largest mass/charge ratio will give the molecular mass of the sample.**

When drawing possible ion fragments the positive charge must be shown either outside square brackets or on the carbon atom. It <u>must not</u> be on a hydrogen atom i.e. $[CH_3]^+$ or $^+CH_3$.

e.g.

$CH_3 — CH_2 — \overset{|}{CH} — O — \overset{+}{CH_2}$ $\overset{|}{CH_3}$ (M=87)

$CH_3 — CH_2 — \overset{+}{CH} — O — CH_2 — CH_3$ (M=87)

$CH_3 — CH_2 — \overset{|}{CH} — O — CH_2 — \overset{+}{CH_3}$ $\overset{|}{CH_3}$ (M=102)

$HO — \overset{+}{CH} — CH_3$ (M=45)

$CH_3 — CH_2 — \overset{+}{CH}$ $\overset{|}{CH_3}$ (M=57)

$CH_3 — \overset{+}{CH_2}$ (M=29)

$\overset{+}{CH} — O — CH_2 — CH_3$ $\overset{|}{CH_3}$ (M=73)

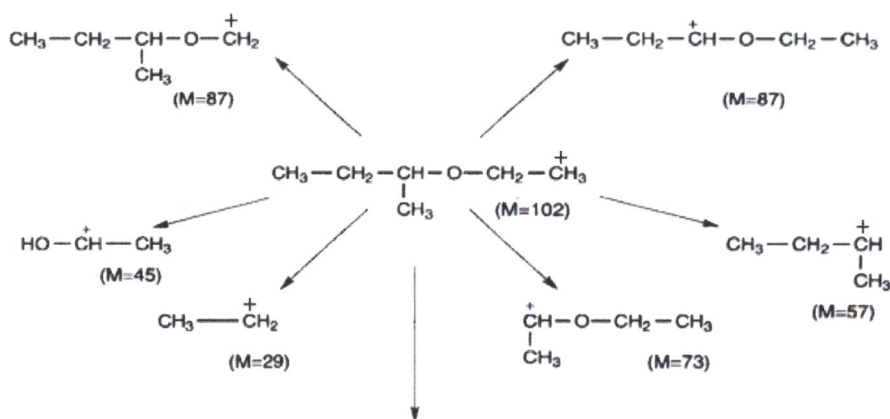

Gives this mass spectrum

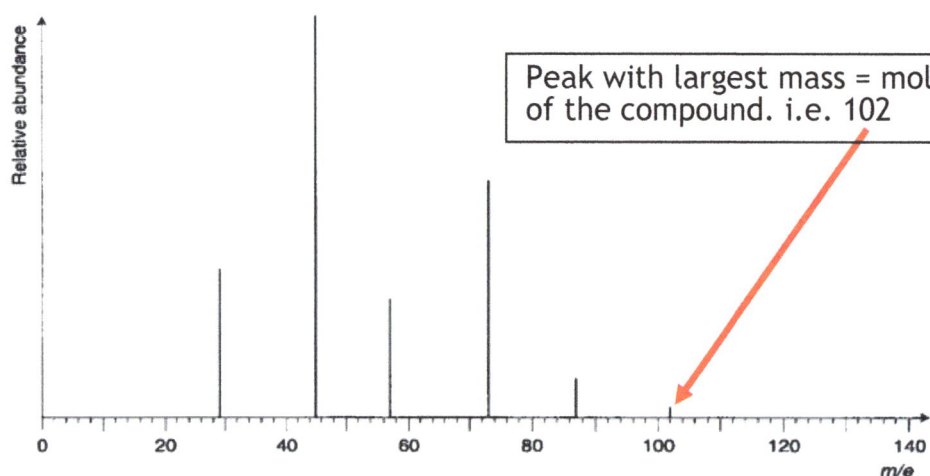

Peak with largest mass = molecular mass of the compound. i.e. 102

The different masses of the fragments can be used to help deduce the structure of the sample.

Normally the mass spectrum of all known compounds are stored on a database and a computer can accurately match the mass spectrum of the unknown sample with that of known structures to find a match.

Infrared Spectroscopy (IR)

Bonds vibrate naturally but when infrared radiation is passed through a sample, certain wavelengths are absorbed by different bonds causing the bonds to bend, wag, stretch or twist.

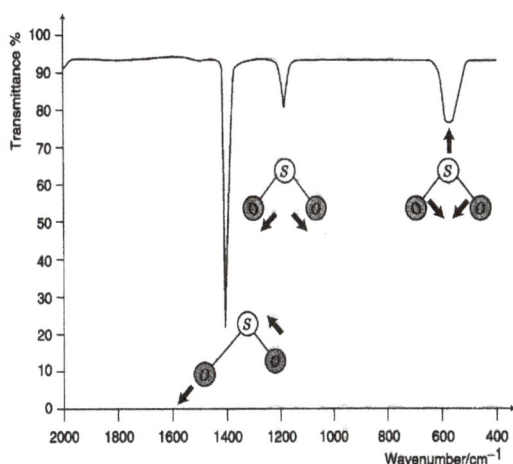

Each functional group gives rise to its own particular absorbance measured by wavenumbers in cm^{-1} and so IR spectroscopy is very good for identifying functional groups in the unknown sample.

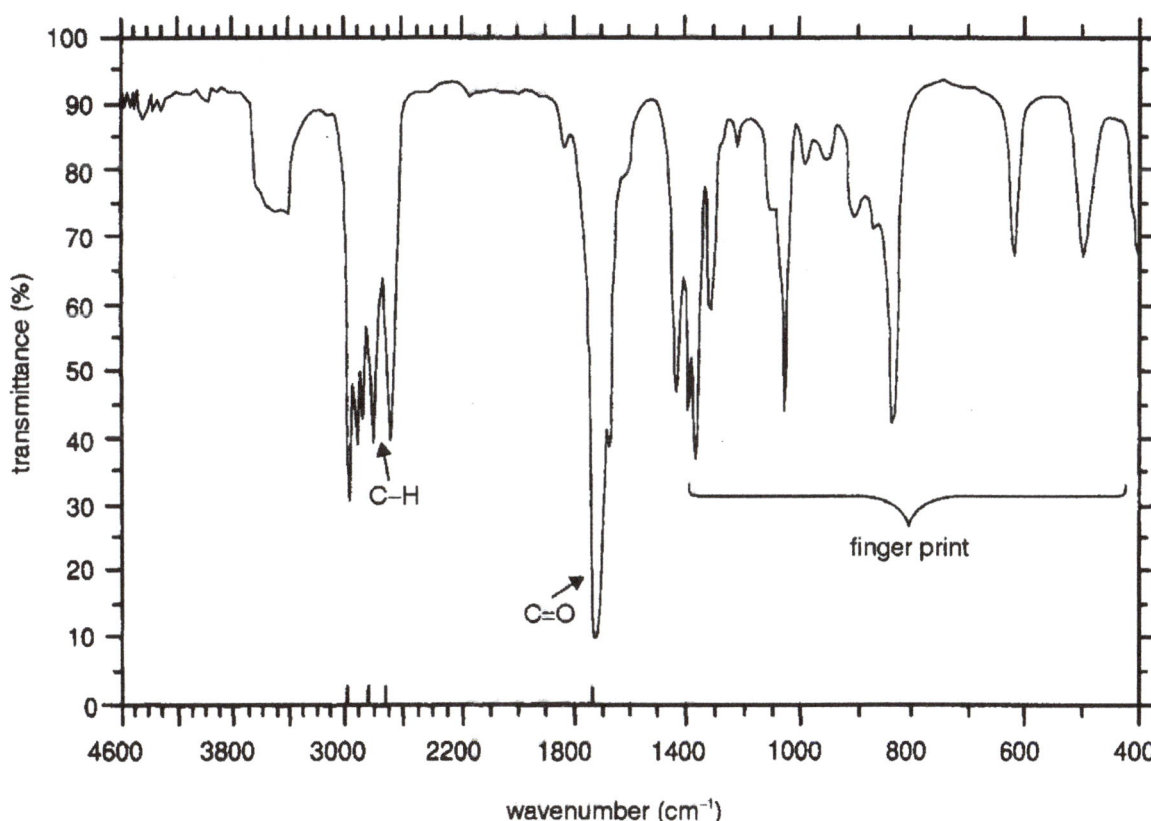

Page 14 in your data booklet gives a table of wave number ranges caused by the absorption of infrared radiation by a particular bond stretching and the compound type it is found in.

If asked in a question; make sure you give the bond within the functional group given in the righthand column of the table that is absorbing the particular wavenumber i.e. an absorbance of 1710cm^{-1} is caused by the C=O (carbonyl bond) stretch within the carboxylic acid functional group.

Nuclear Magnetic Resonance (NMR)

The nuclei of hydrogen atoms spin randomly, but if they are placed in a strong magnetic field they align with or against the direction of the field. Those aligned with the field have slightly less energy than those aligned against it. Radio waves can cause those aligned with the field to flip and align against it. When the proton flips back a corresponding frequency of radiation is released and this can be detected. **The molecular environment the proton is in affects the radiation emitted and is called the chemical shift**. The table on p16 of your data booklet gives these for a range of structural environments. **Tetra Methyl Silane (TMS) is used as a reference and always has a value of zero.**

The area of the peak corresponds to the number of H atoms in that particular environment and so the number of hydrogens can be deduced. An integration curve is often given to make the comparison easier.

e.g. ethanol CH_3CH_2OH

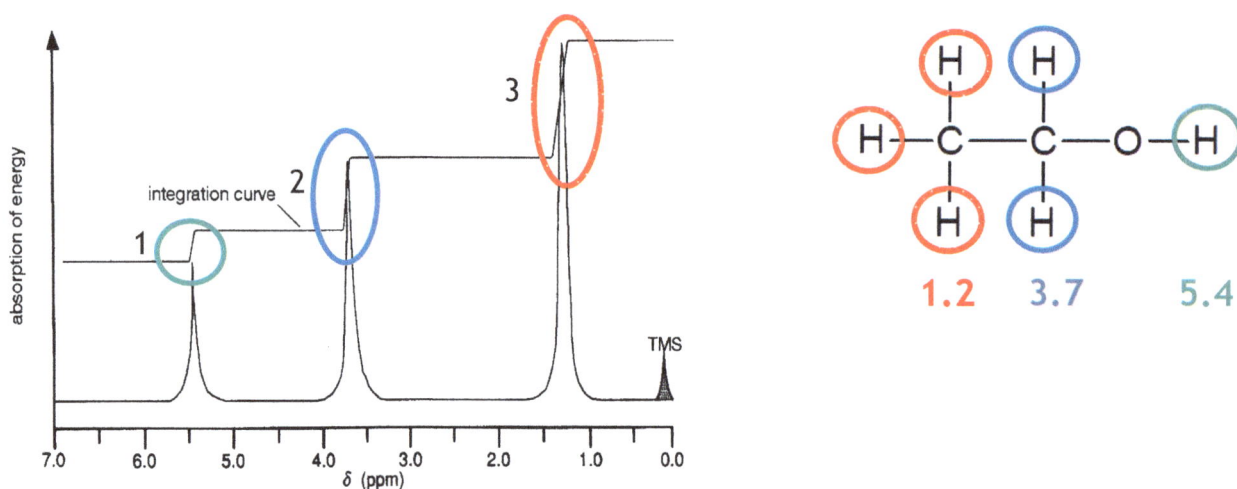

High resolution NMR involves the analysis of multiple peaks caused by spin coupling. Hydrogen atoms on adjacent carbon atoms cause multiple peaks to appear depending on the number of hydrogen atoms involved: The number of adjacent hydrogen atoms is given by n where n + 1 = number of peaks at a particular chemical shift e.g. 3 peaks = triplet caused by 2 adjacent hydrogens.

e.g. ethanol

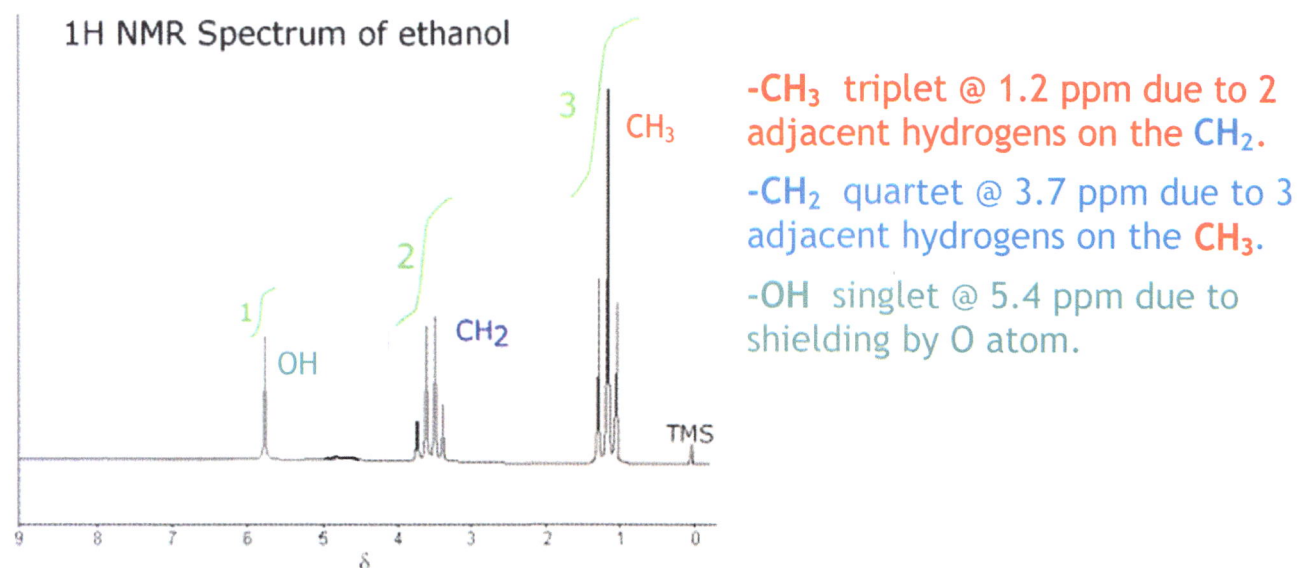

1H NMR Spectrum of ethanol

-CH$_3$ triplet @ 1.2 ppm due to 2 adjacent hydrogens on the **CH$_2$**.

-CH$_2$ quartet @ 3.7 ppm due to 3 adjacent hydrogens on the **CH$_3$**.

-OH singlet @ 5.4 ppm due to shielding by O atom.

Empirical Formulae

Use the information given to work out and then connect it to the correct empirical formula for each compound. Each compound was analysed using elemental microanalysis and they all contain only carbon, hydrogen and oxygen.

Compound A
0.21g burnt
0.478g CO_2 & 0.196g H_2O produced

C_2H_4O

Compound B
By mass found 68.9% C, 4.9% H and 26.2% O

$C_4H_{10}O$

Compound C
1.76g burnt
3.52g CO_2 & 1.44g H_2O produced

$C_7H_6O_2$

Compound D
5.00g burnt
11.89g CO_2 & 6.08g H_2O produced

C_3H_6O

Compound E
By mass found 50% C, 5.6% H and 44.4% O

C_6H_6O

Compound F
By mass found 76.6% C, 6,4% H and 17% O

$C_3H_6O_2$

Compound G
1.5g burnt
2.64g CO_2 & 1.08g H_2O produced

$C_3H_4O_2$

Mass Spectroscopy

Use the following mass spectra to identify the molecular mass of each compound and draw the selected ion fragments.

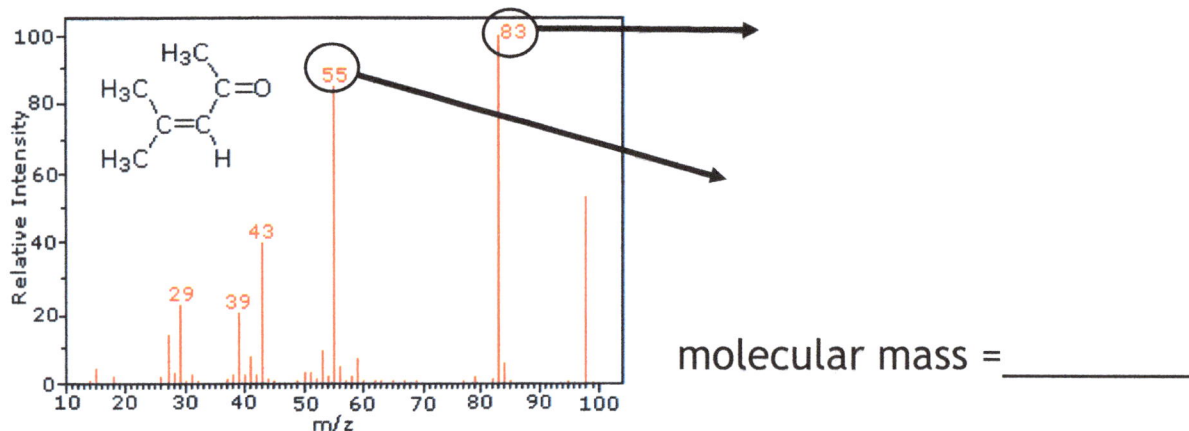

molecular mass = _____

ethanol

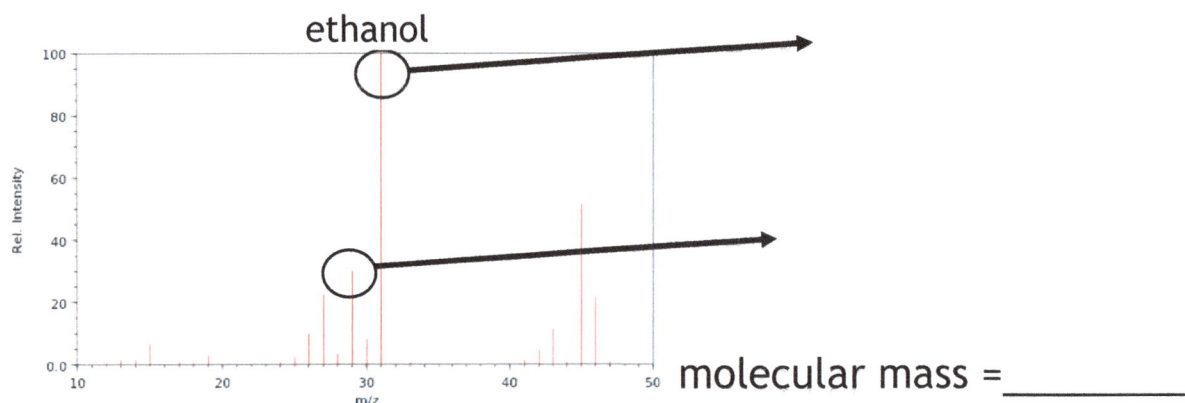

molecular mass = _____

butanal

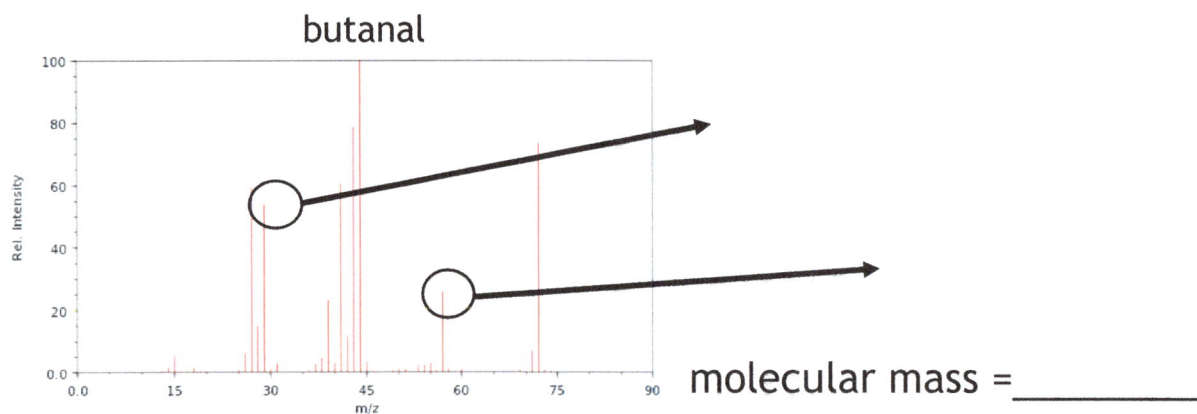

molecular mass = _____

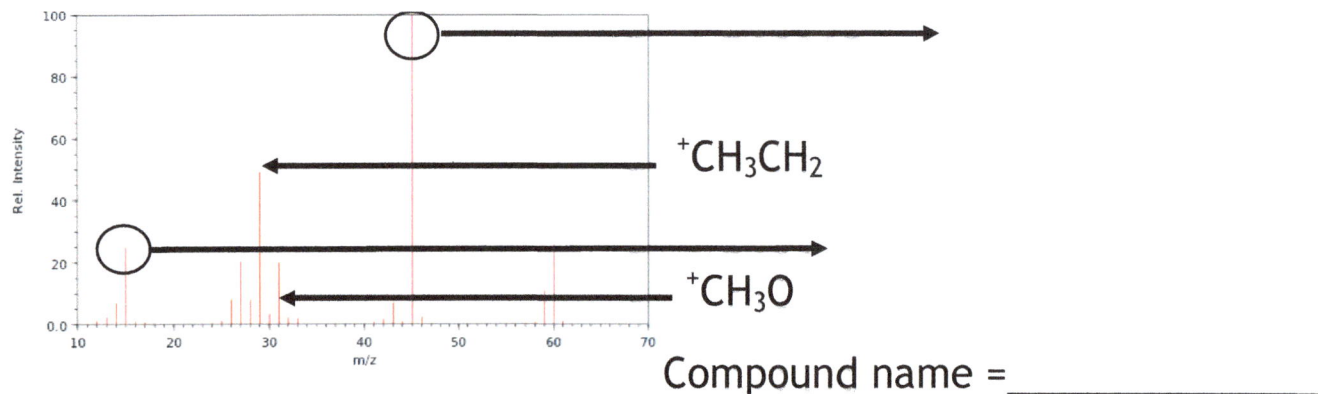

$^+CH_3CH_2$

$^+CH_3O$

Compound name = _____

Quiz Word

Answer the following questions to complete the quiz word and then try to work out what the key phrase in the **bold** boxes should be.

1. Ratio used in mass spectrometry to identify peaks. (4, 6)
2. Spectroscopy technique used to identify functional groups. (5,3)
3. Common absorption at around 1700cm^{-1} for a C=O bond. (7)
4. Elemental microanalysis uses this to work out an empirical formula. (10)
5. Radio waves do this to the spin of H nuclei in a magnetic field. (4)
6. Two H atoms on adjacent atoms would form this in high resolution NMR. (7)
7. Used to give an indication of the area under the peaks in NMR. (11,5)

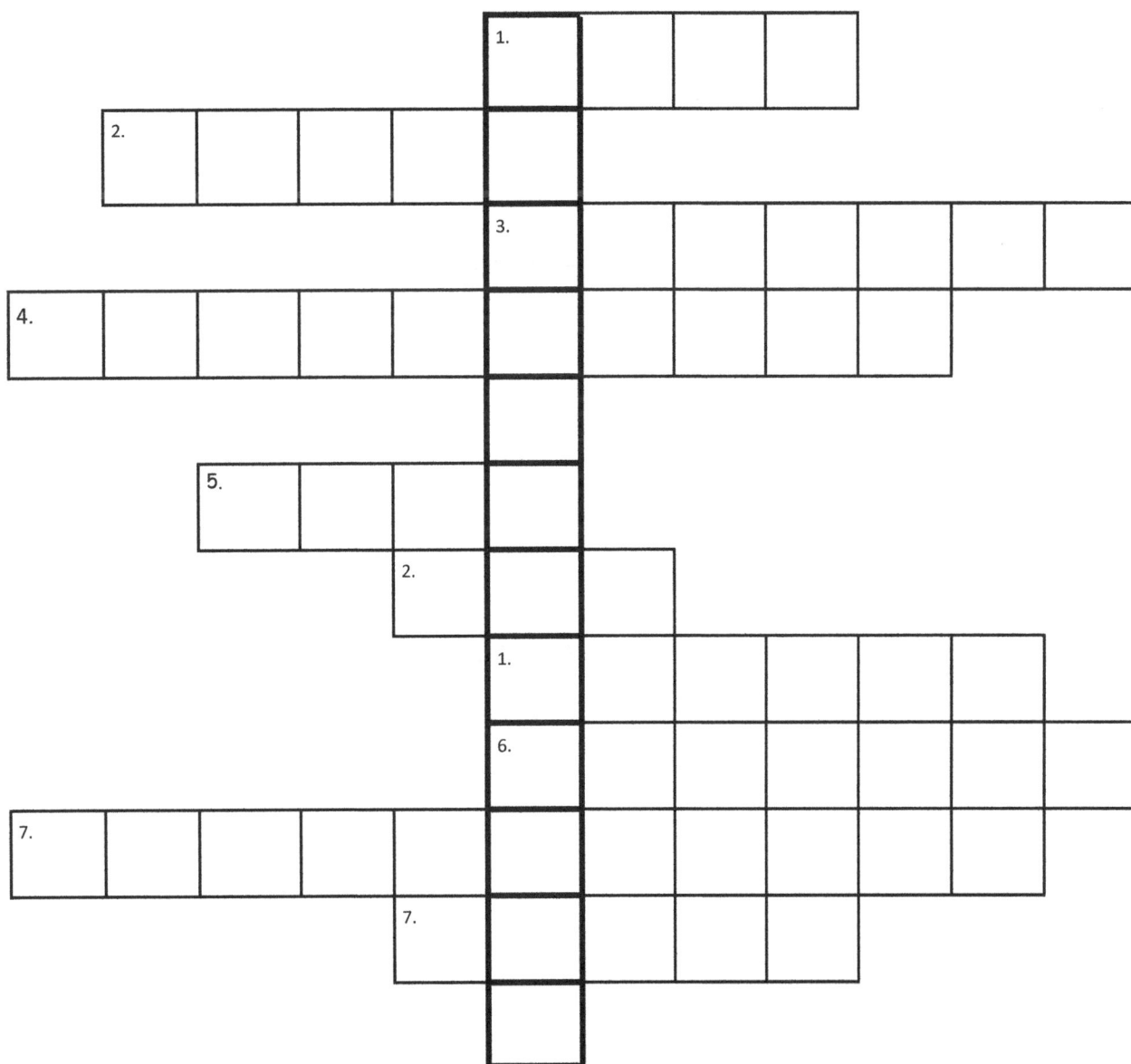

Quiz Word Clue: Formed by ionising a sample and passing them through a magnetic field.

© P & L Johnson 2021

173

Infrared Spectroscopy

Circle and name, on the following infrared spectra, the absorption caused by the only functional group found in each compound, using p14 of your data booklet to help.

methanol

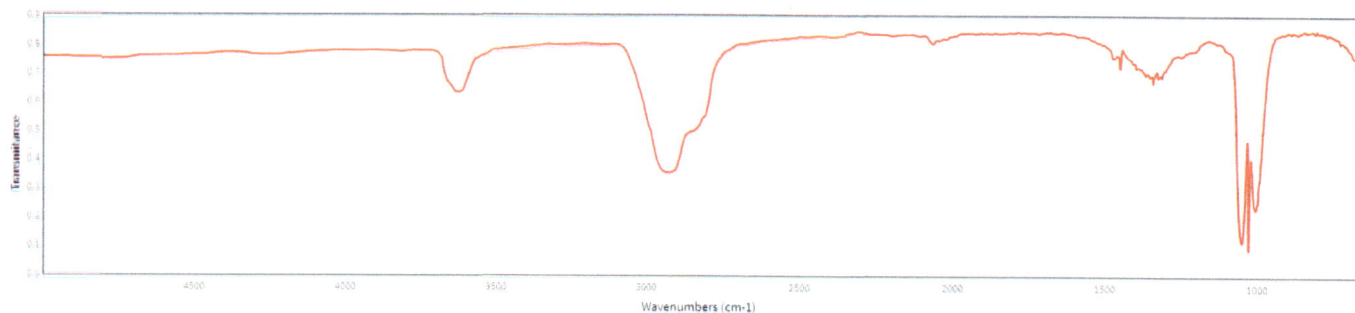

propanone

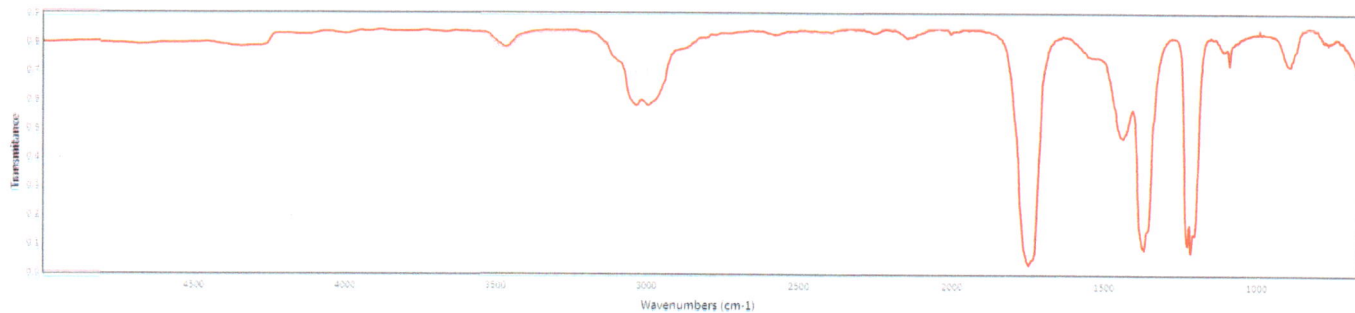

ethyl methanoate

ethyne

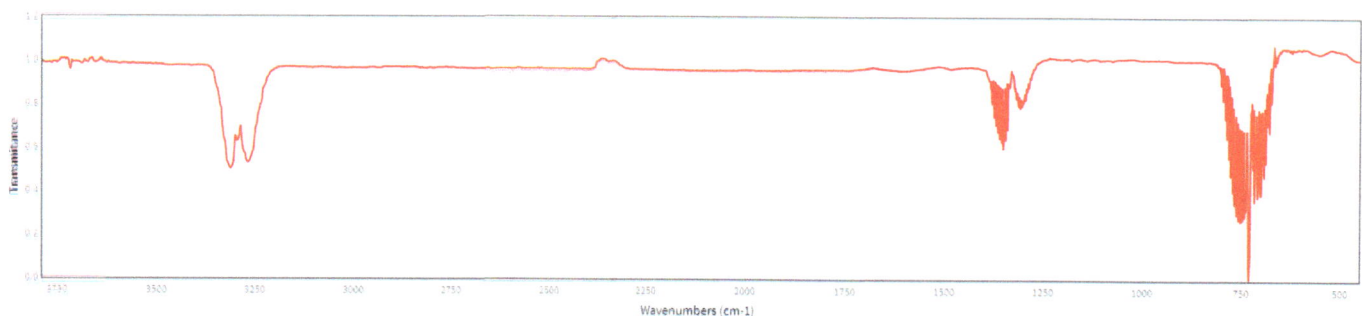

NMR Spectroscopy

Link the compounds to their correct low or high resolution NMR spectra, using p16 of your data booklet to help. Integration curve data is given above each peak.

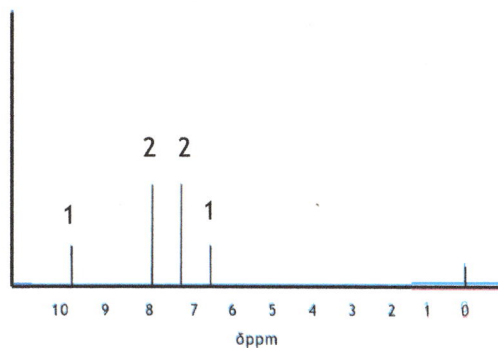

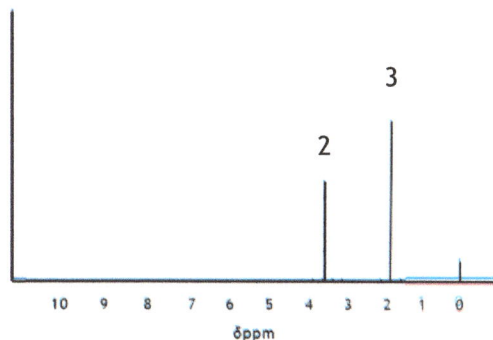

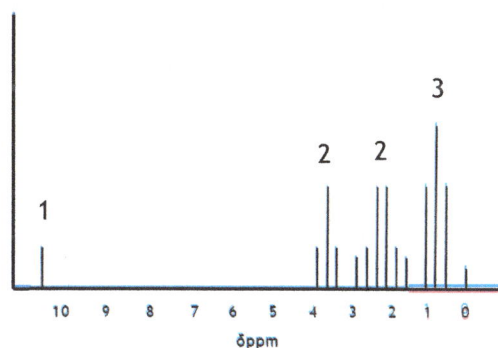

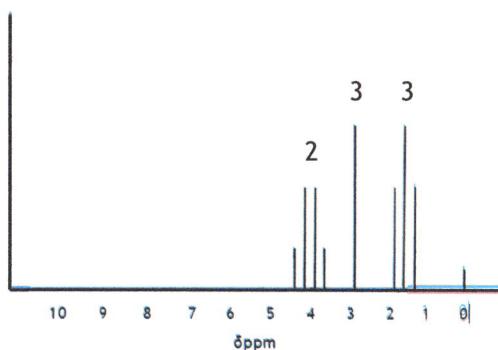

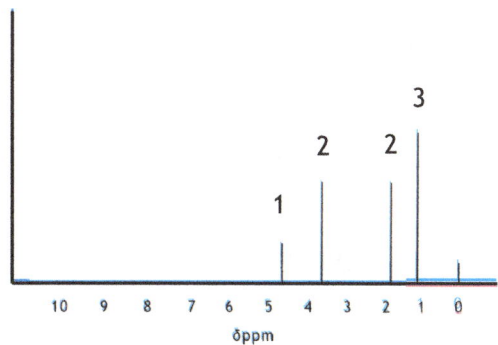

$CH_3CH_2OCOCH_3$

$CH_3CH_2CH_2OH$

C_6H_5OH

$CH_3CH_2CH_2COOH$

CH_3NH_2

Practice Questions

1. 5.00g of an organic compound was completely burnt in oxygen and found to produce 11.378g of CO_2 and 4.655g of H_2O. The compound did not react with Tollen's reagent and produced the following mass and IR spectra.

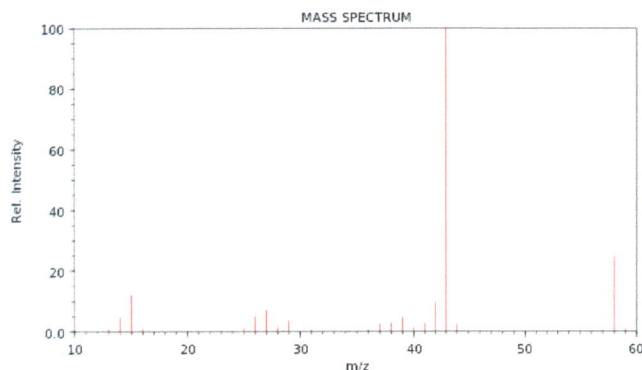

MASS SPECTRUM

NIST Chemistry WebBook (https://webbook.nist.gov/chemistry)

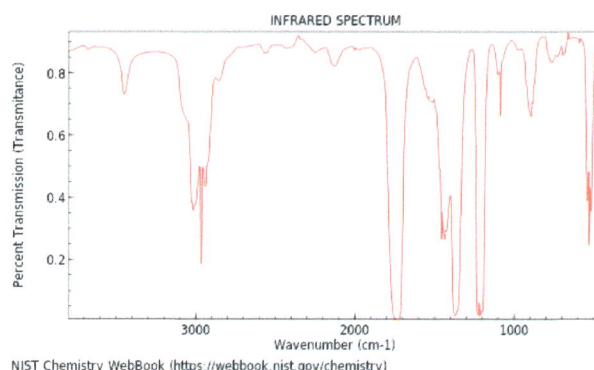

INFRARED SPECTRUM

NIST Chemistry WebBook (https://webbook.nist.gov/chemistry)

a. Work out the empirical formula for this compound.

b. Write the formula of the ion fragment with a mass/charge ratio of 43.

c. What functional group is shown by the absorption at $1700cm^{-1}$?

d. Use all the information to identify the name of the compound.

2. An organic compound, that smells of vomit, consisted of 54.5% C, 9.1% H and 36.4% O. The compound reacted easily with lithium aluminium hydride to form a flammable liquid. Its IR and NMR spectra are shown below:

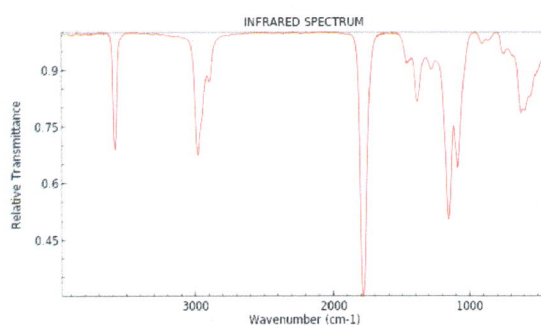

INFRARED SPECTRUM

NIST Chemistry WebBook (https://webbook.nist.gov/chemistry)

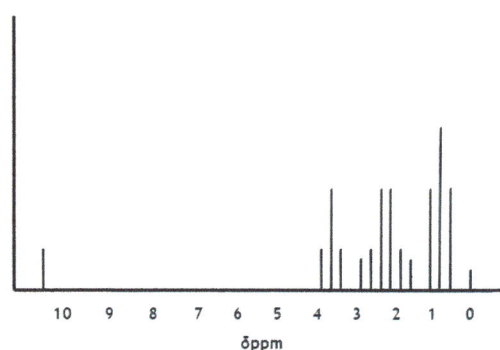

a) Work out the empirical formula of the compound.

b) What functional group causes the absorption at $3500cm^{-1}$ in the IR spectra?

c) Mass spectroscopy finds that the compound has a molecular mass of 88. Using the information given identify the unknown compound.

d) Draw the full structural formula of the compound and circle the part that causes the sextuplet at 2.2ppm in the NMR spectra.

3. An organic compound had the empirical formula C_6H_6O. The compound did not react with bromine solution and produced the following mass, IR and low resolution NMR spectra.

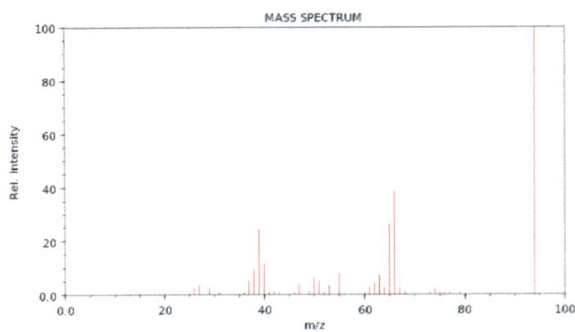
MASS SPECTRUM
NIST Chemistry WebBook (https://webbook.nist.gov/chemistry)

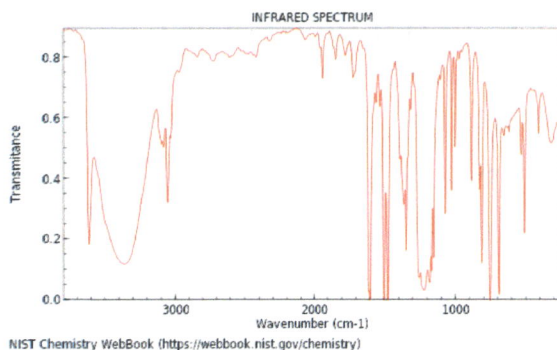
INFRARED SPECTRUM
NIST Chemistry WebBook (https://webbook.nist.gov/chemistry)

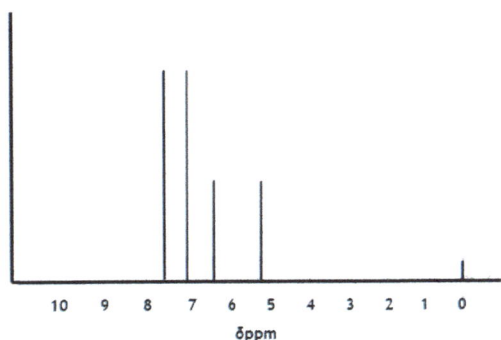

a. Using the mass spectrum what is the chemical formula for this compound?.

b. Write the formula of the ion fragment with a mass/charge ratio of 72.

c. Circle the peaks in the IR spectra that show that this molecule is aromatic?

d. Use all the information to draw a structural formula for this molecule.

e. Use your answer to part d to explain why there are only 4 peaks in the NMR spectra.

2. Methanol CH_3OH is a relatively simple organic compound. Using your knowledge of mass spectroscopy, infra red spectroscopy and high resolution NMR spectroscopy and pages 14 & 16 of your data booklet complete the following three spectra:

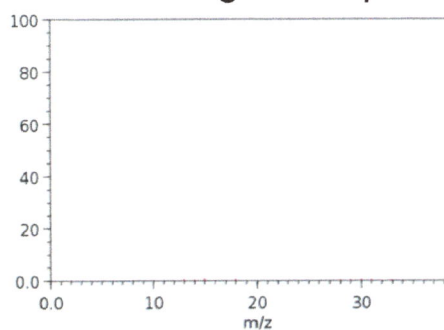

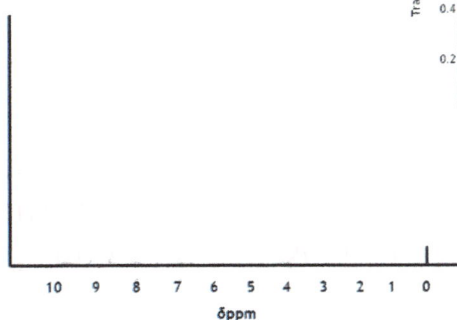
INFRARED SPECTRUM

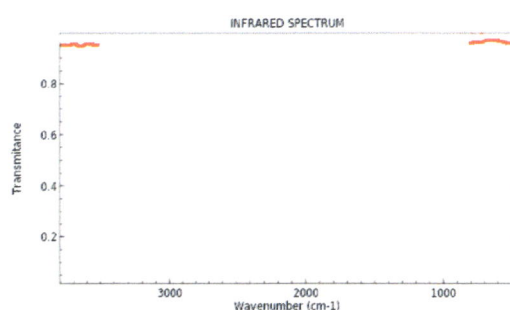

Unit 3   Pharmaceutical Industry

Drugs are substances which alter the biochemical processes in the body. Drugs which have beneficial effects are used in medicines. A medicine usually contains the drug plus other ingredients.

Classification of drugs

Many drugs can be classified as agonists or as antagonists at receptor sites, according to whether they enhance or block the body's natural responses.

An agonist will produce a response similar to the body's natural active compound.

An antagonist produces no response but prevents the action of the body's natural active compound.

Many drugs that act on enzymes are classified as enzyme inhibitors and act by binding to the active site of the enzyme and blocking the reaction normally catalysed there.

How drugs work

Most drugs work by binding to receptors. Receptors are usually protein molecules on the surface of cells where they interact with small biologically active molecules, or are enzymes that catalyse chemical reactions (catalytic receptors).

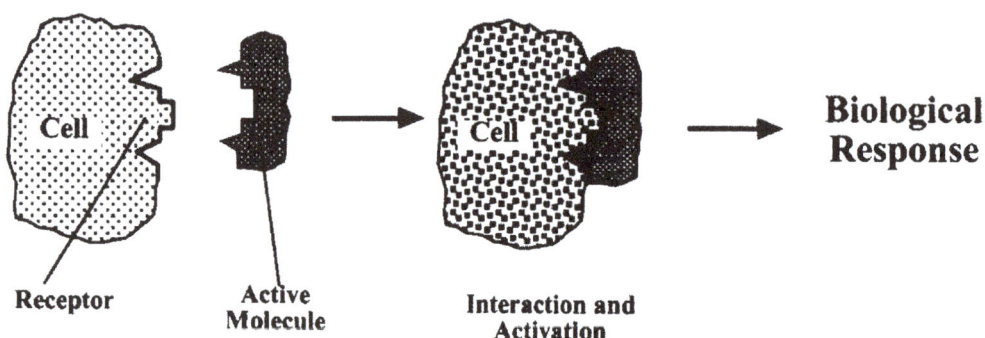

Receptor   Active Molecule   Interaction and Activation   Biological Response

The structural fragment of a drug molecule which confers pharmacological activity upon it normally consists of different functional groups correctly orientated with respect to each other. This is called the pharmacophore. The overall shape and size of the drug has to be such that it fits a binding site. The functional groups on both the drug and the receptor are positioned such that the drug can interact with and bind to the receptor. This is often described as being like a lock and key mechanism.

The main types of interaction between drugs and binding sites are hydrogen bonding and dipole-dipole interactions. Look for the presence of -OH or -NH groups in drugs as these are usually where the drug binds to the receptor site.

178

Many drugs act as enzyme inhibitors by binding to the enzyme's active site and blocking the reaction normally catalysed there.

Using adrenaline like compounds as drugs:

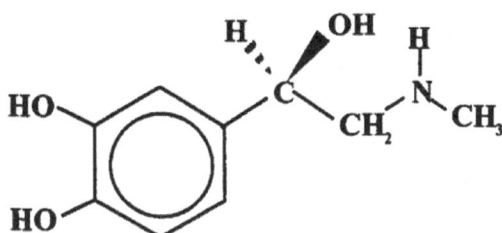

Adrenaline, shown above, is a compound produced naturally by our bodies usually when we are scared or stressed, it is responsible for the "fight or flight" response to a threat. It can interact with three receptor sites shown below:

Receptor	Effect
α	Increases blood pressure
β_1	Increases heart rate and force
β_2	Dilates the bronchial tubes

Salbutamol:

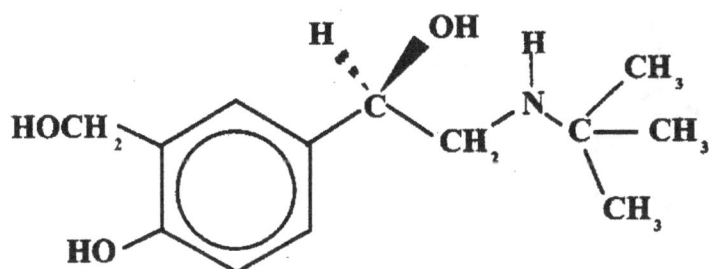

Salbutamol acts as a β_2 agonist in order to open up the airways of those suffering from an asthma attack.

Propranolol:

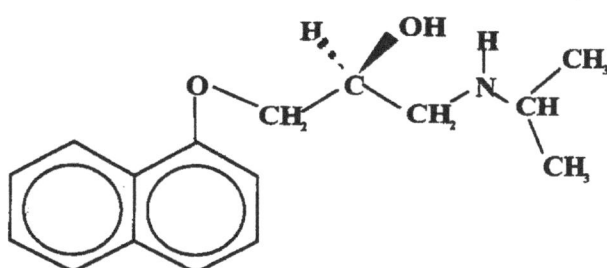

Propranolol acts as a β_1 antagonist preventing adrenaline being able to bind to the site and are used in the treatment of high blood pressure, they are often called beta-blockers.

By comparing the structures of drugs that have similar effects on the body, the structural fragment that is involved in the drug action can be identified.

A good example of how chemist try to alter the properties of drugs by adding or changing the groups attached to the pharmacophore, is morphine. Morphine is very good at relieving pain but is very addictive and has other unpleasant side effects. The aim was to create drugs with less side effects but keep the pain-relieving properties.

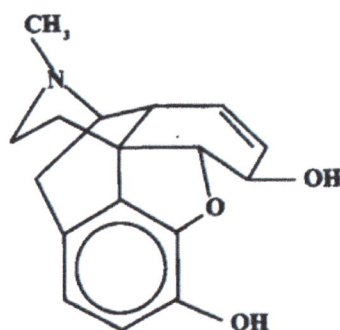

(a) morphine

The pharmacophore is shown in bold below:

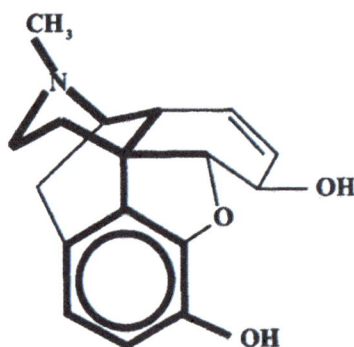

Chemist made a number of changes to try and increase the pain relieving properties but also to reduce the side effects. Codeine is much less addictive but isn't as good at pain relief, but it was also found to be a cough suppressant. Heroin was better at relieving pain but is even more addictive and has a number of other unpleasant side effects.

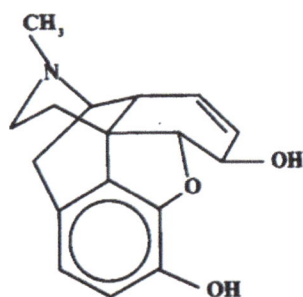 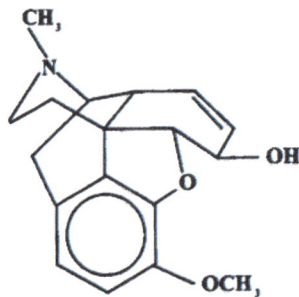 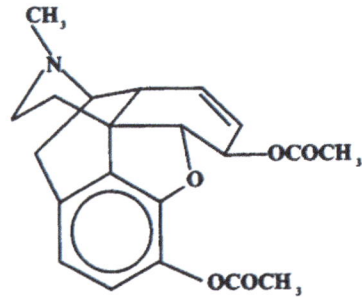

(a) morphine   (b) codeine   (c) heroin

Drug Calculations

Often, when dealing with drugs and dispensing them, it is more convenient/traditional to quantify them in terms of

% solution by mass

% by volume

ppm (parts per million)

% solution by mass:

The % solution is the mass of solute made up to $100cm^3$ of solution.

% by mass = $\dfrac{\text{mass of solute (g)}}{\text{volume of water(cm}^3)}$ x100%

<u>Example</u>

4g of sugar was dissolved in $250cm^3$ of water. Its % solution by mass is,

$\dfrac{4}{250}$ x 100%

= **1.6%**

% by volume:

The % by volume is the number of cm^3 of solute made up to $100cm^3$ of solution.

<u>Example</u>

40ml ethanol dissolved in water and made up to 240ml

$\dfrac{40}{240}$ x 100%

= **16.7%**

Parts per million (ppm):

The unit ppm stands for parts per million and refers to 1mg (0.001g) per kg (1000g). They are often used to quantify very dilute solutions.

<u>Example</u>

A solution has a concentration of 1.25g/L.

What is its concentration in ppm?

Convert the mass in grams to a mass in milligrams:
1.25g = 1.25 x 1000mg = 1250mg

Re-write the concentration in mg/L = 1250mg/L = **1250ppm**

Agonist, Antagonist or Enzyme Inhibitor

Use the information given to work out whether each drug acts as an agonist, antagonist or enzyme inhibitor:

THC in cannabis =

Activates the cannabinoid receptor site interfering with the normal functioning of the brain, resulting in the cannabis high.

Fentanyl =

Binds to Mu opioid receptor site stimulating the release of pain inhibiting chemicals in the body.

Aspirin =

Binds to COX-2 enzymes preventing them from binding to receptor sites that make prostaglandins that inform our brain we are in pain.

Prozac =

Blocks the reabsorption of serotonin into neurons. This can help prevent depression.

Salbutamol =

Binds to beta2-adrenergic receptor site causing it to open up airways in the lungs.

Propranolol =

Prevent adrenaline from making contact with your heart's beta receptors. This prevents your heart pump harder or faster.

Penicillin =

Works by inactivating an enzyme necessary for the cross linking of bacterial cell walls. The enzyme is known as transpeptidase.

LSD =

A synthetic molecule mimicking the actions of the neurotransmitter serotonin at one of its many receptors – the 5HT2A receptor.

Quiz Word

Answer the following questions to complete the quiz word and then try to work out what the key phrase in the **bold** boxes should be.

1. A drug that mimics a natural chemical in the body to promote a response. (7)

2. Receptor sites are usually made up of these types of compounds. (8)

3. An antagonist drug will block this.(8,4)

4. This morphine based molecule was modified by making it a methyl ester; making it a stronger pain killer but with more addictive side effects. (6)

5. This agonist stimulates the β_2 receptor site to open up their airways. (10)

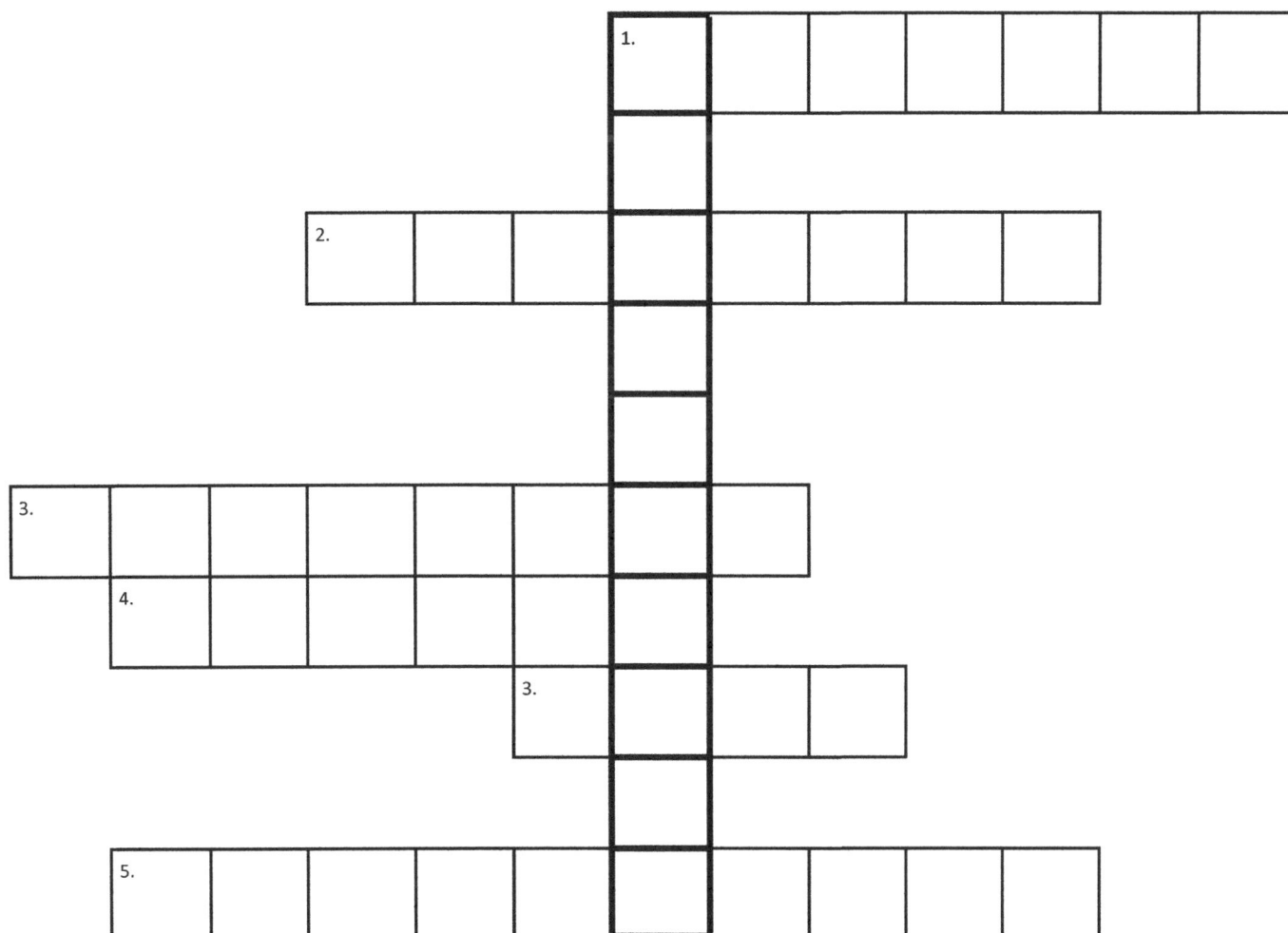

Pharmacophore

Below is the section of molecule that causes a biological response called the pharmacophore. Put a tick next to any of the drugs that would be expected to give a similar response:

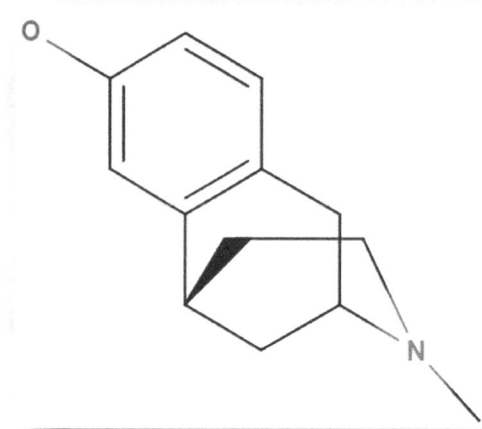

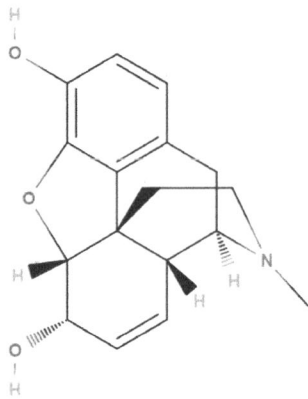

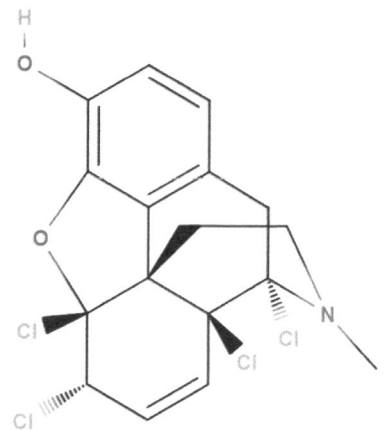

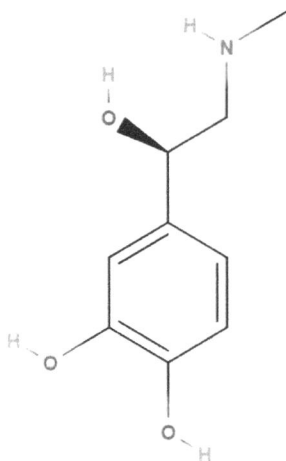

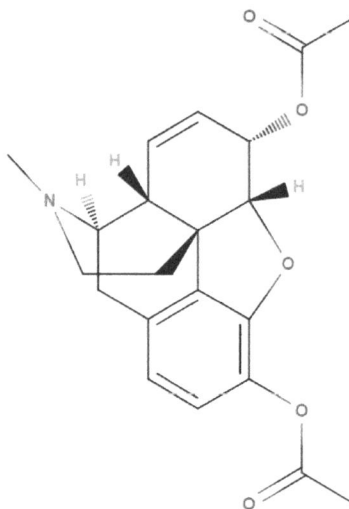

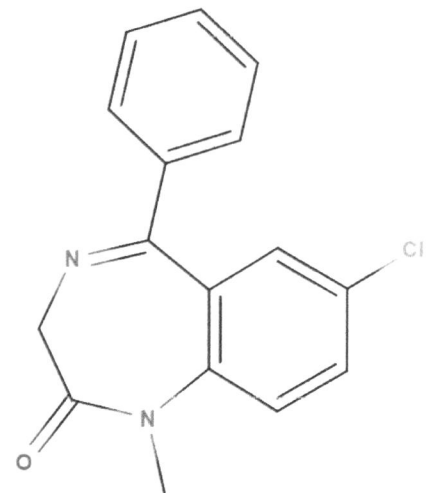

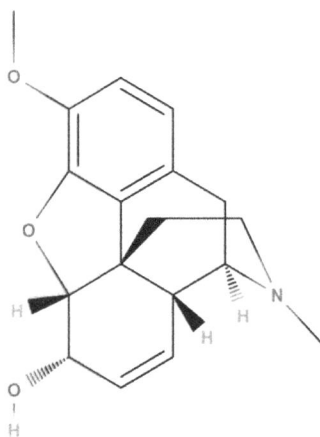

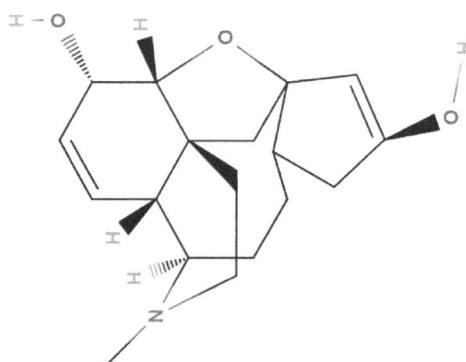

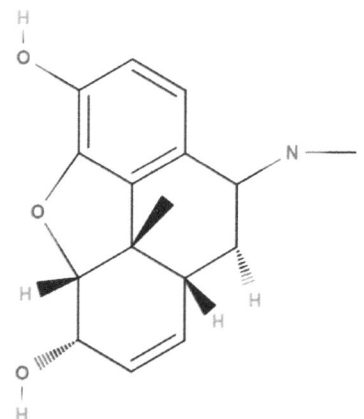

Wordsearch

Complete the wordsearch below using the clues given to identify the correct words(s) that can be found in the wordsearch.

```
Q R F T T F Z G Y T J K Y X N
C O N C E N T R A T I O N O R
B F K C F U H S J V V P I G E
D S I F B S Z O I T T L R X C
M O R G C U E H J N L B M N E
I N W N H I J W X I O A Y I P
H B S Q D T X I M S N G L E T
Y W K R R Q O R K T A R A T O
V Q F T R Z E R A S T P U O R
Y F T B G P M G F V G J C R S
C H Z I S N O S T L A M C P I
H Q H T V N T Q N Z I E Z Y T
P U R A I I B R P A X G R I E
A A R S M D G C A F C R H F Y
P C T Y E K D N A K C O L T H
```

1. % solution by mass or % solution by volume are both measures of drug _____. (13)

2. Drugs act as this when they produce a response similar to a natural active compound. (7)

3. This is the place where the drug interacts with the body. (8,4)

4. Usually abbreviated to ppm.(5,3,7)

5. Adrenaline is famous for activating this response when we feel threatened. (5,2,6)

6. Drugs act as this when they block a natural response. (10)

7. Most receptor sites are made up of this type of large molecule. (7)

8. This is the way drug molecules are described as interacting with the receptor site. (4,3,3)

Chemical Misconceptions

A student has completed an exercise on calculating drug concentrations. Unfortunately they have made a number of mistakes. Work out which calculations are correct, then identify by circling where they went wrong with the others and put the correct value next to the incorrect answer.

1. 10g of the drug was dissolved in 100cm³ of water, what is the concentration expressed as % by mass?

   10/100 x 100 = 10%

2. 20cm³ of a cough syrup was dissolved in ethanol and made up to 400cm³. What is the concentration expressed as % by volume?

   20/0.4 = 50%

3. 0.5g of iodine was dissolved in a 500cm³ of water, what is the concentration in ppm?

   0.5 x 1000 / 0.5 = 1000ppm

4. A 0.1 moll⁻¹ solution of iodine was made up. What is the concentration expressed as % by mass?

   0.1/1000 x 100 = 0.01%

5. If 5 tablets weigh 10g and each contains 1mg of the drug, what is the quantity of the drug in **each tablet** expressed in ppm?

   1 tablet = 10/5 = 2g = 0.002kg

   1 x 0.002 = 0.002ppm

Practice Questions

1. The following structures show a range of common street drugs:

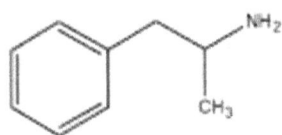

amphetamine

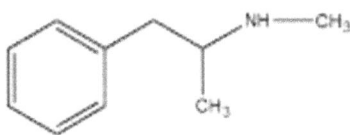

methamphetamine

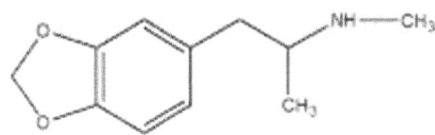

3,4-methylenedioxy-methamphetamine
(MDMA or "ecstasy")

a. Circle the site that is most likely to bind to the receptor site they stimulate.

b. What type of bonding is likely to be used to bind to the receptor site.

c. The following similar molecule does not have any appreciable effect:

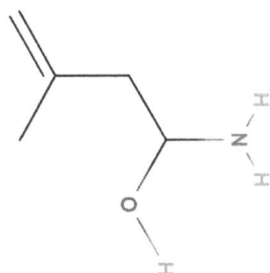

Draw a structural section of the molecule (pharmacophore) that will need to be present to stimulate the receptor site.

2. If 50 cm^3 of 2 moll^{-1} sodium hydroxide solution is diluted by making it up to 250cm^3 in a standard flask. What is the concentration of the diluted sodium hydroxide solution in gl^{-1}?

3a. Naloxone is used as a treatment for drug overdoses. A typical dose contains 0·3 cm^3 of 500 ppm adrenaline solution. Calculate the mass of adrenaline, in mg, delivered in one dose.

b. Naloxone stimulates the receptor sites that increase the rate of breathing. What term is used to describe how Naloxone acts?

4. Carbon monoxide poisoning is easy to miss as the gas is colourless and odourless. Poorly ventilated rooms with old heaters inside are a particular hazard. The maximum short term exposure limit is 800ppm per hour.

   If a person breathes in 600g of air per hour, what is the mass of carbon monoxide that is breathed in at the maximum short term exposure limit?

Researching Chemistry

Common chemical apparatus

- conical flask
- digital balance
- pipette with safety filler
- burette
- volumetric (standard) flask
- distillation (round-bottomed) flask
- condenser
- thermometer
- Buchner or Hirsch or sintered glass funnel
- glassware with ground glass joints ('Quickfit' or similar)
- thin-layer chromatography apparatus
- colorimeter
- melting point
- separating funnel

Skills involved in experimental work

- tabulate data using appropriate headings and units of measurement
- represent data as a scatter graph with suitable scales and labels
- sketch a line of best fit (straight or curved) to represent the trend observed in the data
- calculate average (mean) values
- identify and eliminate rogue points
- qualitatively appreciate the relative accuracy of apparatus used to measure the volume of liquids
- comment on the reproducibility of results where measurements have been repeated
- carry out quantitative stoichiometric calculations
- interpret spectral data
- appropriately use a positive control, for example a known substance, to validate a technique or procedure

Gravimetric analysis

This is used to determine the mass of an element or compound in a substance.

The substance is converted into a solid substance of known chemical composition, which can be readily isolated and purified.

The conversion can occur either through precipitation or volatilisation.

In precipitation conversion the substance undergoes a precipitation reaction. The precipitate is separated from the filtrate and the filtrate tested to ensure the reaction has gone to completion. The precipitate is washed, dried to constant mass (weighed, heated, cooled then reweighed & repeated until there is no change in mass) and then weighed.

In volatilisation conversion the substance is heated and any volatile products (often water) are evaporated. The substance is heated to constant mass and the final mass recorded.

The number of moles of water in hydrated $BaCl_2.nH_2O$ can be calculated using this technique.

Gravimetric Analysis of hydrated $BaCl_2.nH_2O$:

A sample of hydrated $BaCl_2.nH_2O$ is weighed by difference and the mass recorded. The sample is heated to constant mass by heating and then cooling in a desiccator repeatedly until there is no further change in mass. The change in mass is recorded.

Mass of $BaCl_2.nH_2O$ = 2.799g
Mass of $BaCl_2$ = 2.385g
Mass of H_2O removed = 0.414g

n of $BaCl_2$ = 2.385/208.4 (GFM of $BaCl_2$) = 0.011

n of H_2O = 0.414 /18 (GFM of H_2O) = 0.022

Therefore the ratio of $BaCl_2$: H_2O is 1:2

So number of moles of water = 2

Correct formula for hydrated barium chloride is $BaCl_2.2H_2O$

Important considerations:

Heating to constant mass ensures that all the water has been removed.

The sample must be cooled in a desiccator so no moisture can be reabsorbed as the $CaCl_2$ or silica in the desiccator keeps the atmosphere dry.

Weighing by difference ensures the exact mass in the crucible is recorded and takes into account any solid left in the weigh boat.

Gravimetric analysis can be more accurate than volumetric analysis as there are fewer measurements being taken so less sources of error.

Volumetric Analysis

You must be familiar with use of the technique of volumetric analysis, including:

- preparing a standard solution
- accurate dilution
- standardising solutions to determine accurate concentration
- titrating to obtain concordance using burettes, pipettes and volumetric flasks
- choosing an appropriate indicator

EDTA is a hexadentate ligand so binds octahedrally to a metal ion, with a coordination number of 6.

The advantage of using EDTA is that it always reacts 1:1 with a metal.

EDTA is also an excellent primary standard as it has the following characteristics:

High purity

Low reactivity

Doesn't absorb moisture

Relatively high molecular mass

Complexometric determination of nickel using EDTA

A known mass of nickel salt is dissolved in a small volume of water. Quantitatively transferred to a $100cm^3$ standard flask and a $20cm^3$ portion titrated against a $0.10moll^{-1}$ EDTA solution until concordant results were obtained.

Example 2.620g of $NiSO_4$ was dissolved and the average titre was $19.90cm^3$.

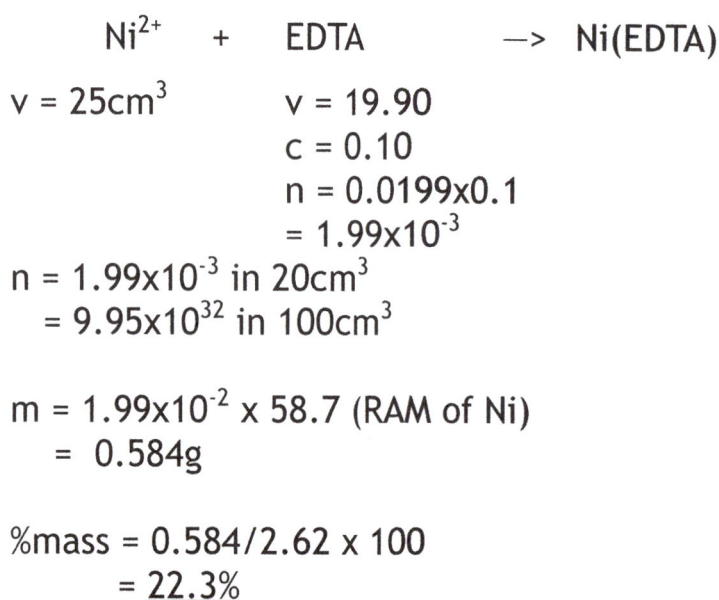

$$Ni^{2+} \quad + \quad EDTA \quad \longrightarrow \quad Ni(EDTA)$$

$v = 25cm^3$

$v = 19.90$
$c = 0.10$
$n = 0.0199 \times 0.1$
$= 1.99 \times 10^{-3}$

$n = 1.99 \times 10^{-3}$ in $20cm^3$
$= 9.95 \times 10^{32}$ in $100cm^3$

$m = 1.99 \times 10^{-2} \times 58.7$ (RAM of Ni)
$= 0.584g$

%mass $= 0.584/2.62 \times 100$
$= \underline{22.3\%}$

Possible sources of error:
Impurities in the salt or the salt is damp

Colorimetry

Many transition metal ions are coloured and so can be analysed by colorimetry. If light of the wavelength of light corresponding to the light absorbed by the coloured ion is shone at a sample solution some of that light is absorbed, depending on the concentration of the ion in the solution. **Colorimetry relies upon Beer-Lamberts law; that at low concentrations the absorbance of a specific wavelength of light is directly proportional to the concentration:**

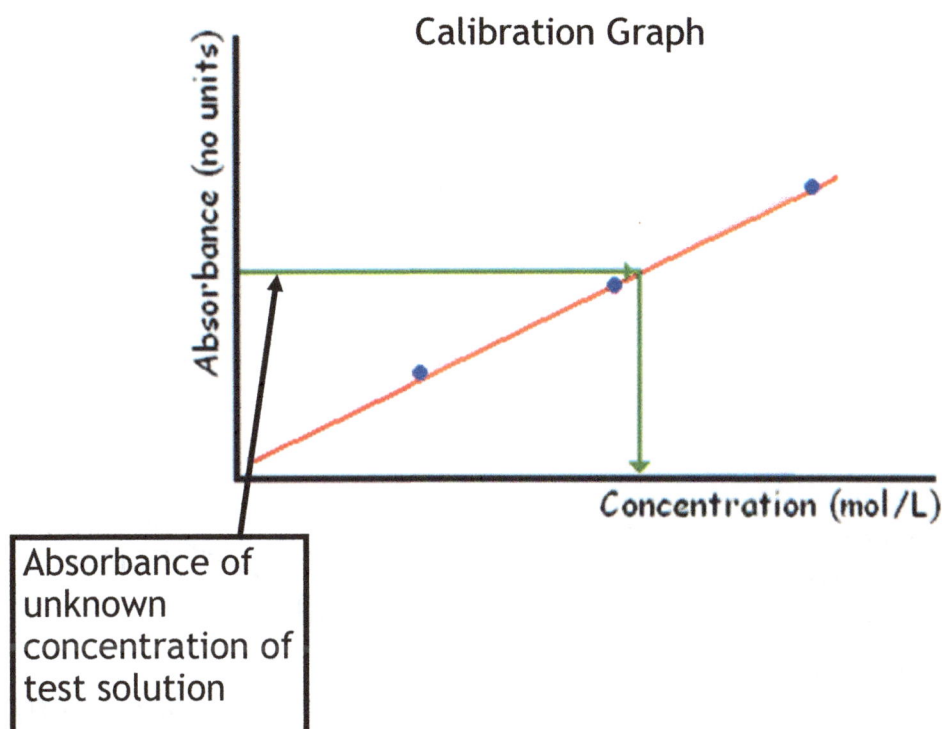

Calibration Graph

Absorbance (no units)

Concentration (mol/L)

Absorbance of unknown concentration of test solution

An unknown concentration of solution can be analysed using a colorimeter and the absorbance used to find the concentration using an appropriate calibration graph.

To make a calibration graph a series of solutions are made with varying concentrations. Its important that the range of concentrations covers the expected concentration of the sample solution.

Colorimetry is particularly useful for the analysis of transition metal ions that are coloured and of low concentration.

Common Organic Techniques

Distillation:

Used to separate liquids with different boiling points or to purify products.

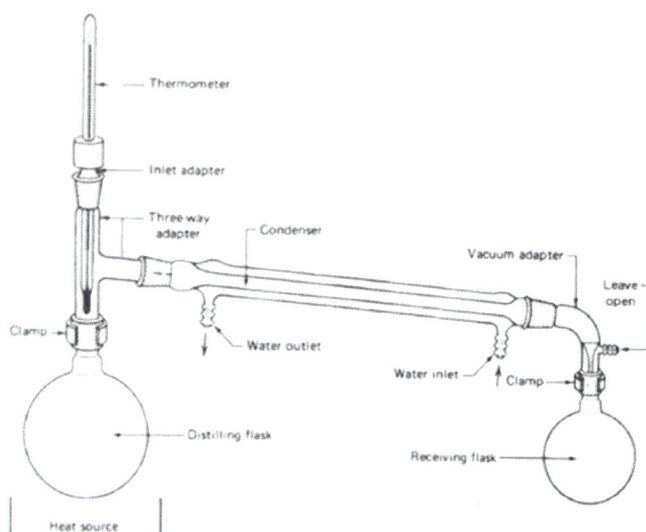

Refluxing:

Used to heat volatile liquid reactants without losing them to evaporation.

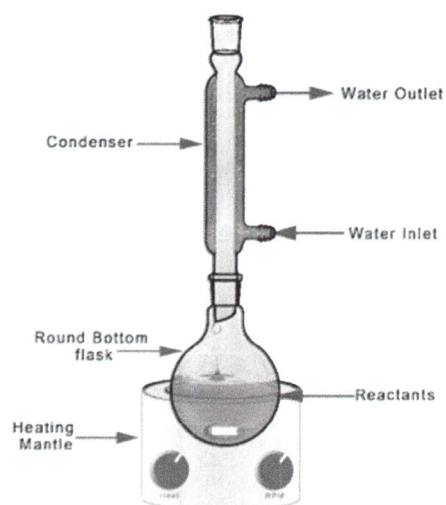

Vacuum Filtration:

Uses a vacuum pump to draw the filtrate through the filter paper at much greater speed. Works well when the solid will block the filter paper. A Buchner or Hirsch funnel is used with a vacuum flask which are designed to cope with the increased pressures involved.

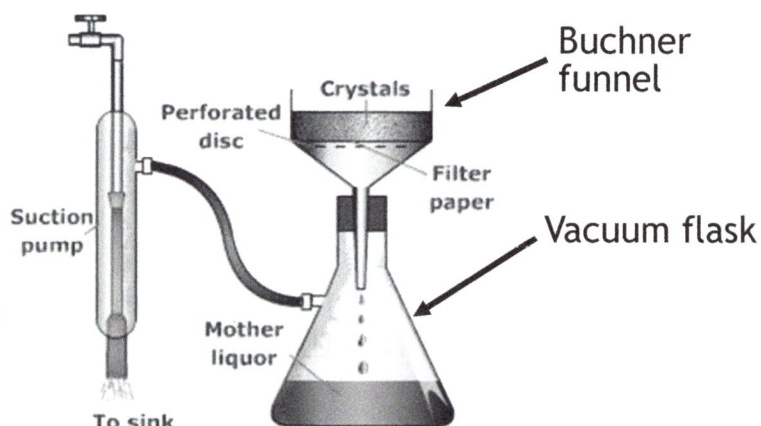

Solvent Extraction:

Based on the relative solubility of a compound in two different immiscible liquids, usually water and an organic solvent.

The two solvents form two separate layers in the separating funnel and an equilibrium exists between the two layers. The lower layer is run off into one container and the upper layer is poured out into another container. The quantity of solute extracted depends on the equilibrium constant and on the number of times that the process is repeated. The mass of solute extracted is greater if a number of extractions using smaller volumes of solvent are carried out rather than a single extraction using a large volume of solvent.

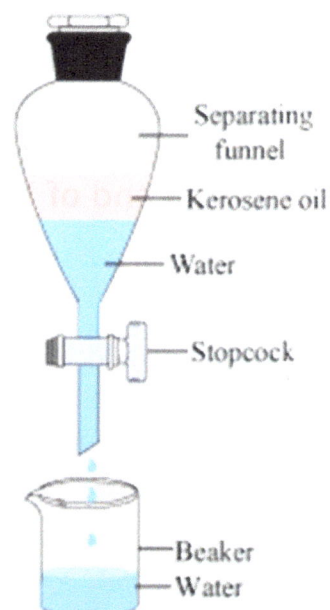

Thin-layer chromatography

Instead of chromatography paper, thin-layer chromatography (TLC) uses a fine film of silica or aluminium oxide spread over glass or plastic. Rf values can be calculated and under similar conditions a compound will always have the same Rf value within experimental error.

Since a pure substance will show up as only one spot on the chromatogram, TLC can be used to assess the purity of a product prepared in the lab.

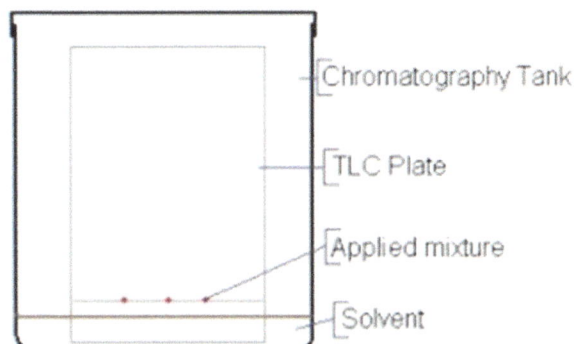

R_f values can be calculated:

$$R_f = \frac{\text{distance travelled by the sample}}{\text{distance travelled by the solvent}}$$

Under the same conditions (temperature, solvent, and saturation levels) a compound always has the same f R value (within experimental error).

The identity of a compound can be confirmed by:

- comparing the experimentally determined R_f values with a literature or known value determined under the same conditions

- making a direct comparison on a TLC plate between the compound being tested and the pure substance — a co-spot could be used

In industry and research establishments gas chromatography and/or high pressure liquid chromatography (HPLC) is used as they can accurately detect and identify very small quantities of organic compounds.

Determination of melting point and mixed melting point:

The melting point of a compound can be used to confirm its identity. Determination of the melting point can also give an indication of the purity of a compound, as the presence of impurities lowers the melting point and broadens its melting temperature range. This is because the impurities disrupt the close packing of the crystal structure and so weakens the force of attraction between the molecules.

Recrystallisation:

Recrystallisation is a laboratory technique used to purify solids, based upon solubility. The solvent for recrystallisation must be carefully selected such that the compound is insoluble at lower temperatures, yet completely soluble at higher temperatures. The impure compound is dissolved gently in the minimum volume of hot solvent then filtered to remove any insoluble impurities. The filtrate is allowed to cool slowly to crystallise the pure compound. Any soluble impurities are left behind in the solvent.

Important Equipment

Connect the correct technique name to the apparatus and connect the names of the component parts to the diagrams:

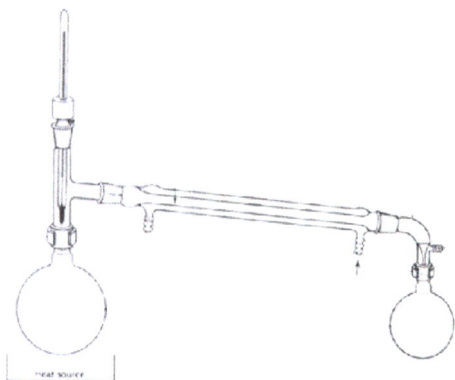

	Vacuum filtration
	Solvent extraction
	Refluxing
	Distillation
	Condenser
	Electric heating mantle
	Buchner funnel
	Separating funnel
	Suction pump

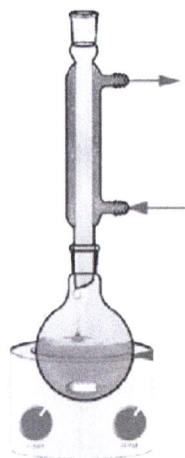

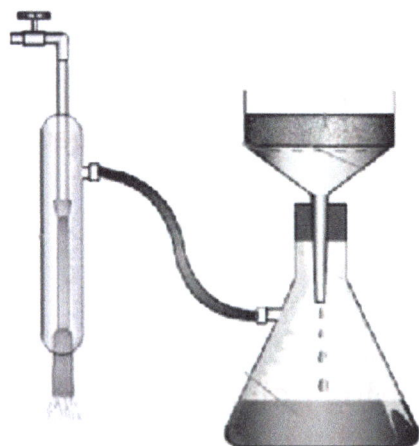

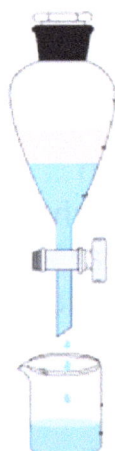

Wordsearch

Complete the wordsearch below using the clues given to identify the correct words(s) that can be found in the wordsearch.

```
S E W Y Z V V W I B O H G W C
T U X R C M I C I O H C B I Q
A K V T U X N V V X K A R E F
N K D E R M O Y H H U T N S O
D O T M Y A N V V E E E N Z C
A R N I W C C T D M I M J V Q
R C H R O M A T O G R A P H Y
D K J O Q V A I I Z N B K H Q
F P J L X P X B H O D H F S Y
L D Q O C E N Y Z E N I X O E
A R Z C L L A W L D A D D L Y
S C M P L D R N I Y B D K V W
K X M T N I O P G N I T L E M
C O E X F J G H F X I M W N R
C G R A V I M E T R I C Y T A
```

1. Technique that uses the fact that some chemicals are more soluble in the mobile phase than stationary phase. (14)

2. Technique that uses the intensity of light, of a particular wavelength, absorbed to compare concentrations. (11)

3. Technique that uses the fact that a substance can dissolve in two immiscible solvents. (7, 10)

4. Formed when a transition metal binds to a ligand in a complexometric titration. (7)

5. Type of analysis that uses masses to calculate quantities. (11)

6. Ligand that binds 1:1 to most metal ions. (4)

7. Impurities in an organic compound will lower this. (7, 5)

8. Used to make solutions of precise known concentrations. (8, 5)

Most Appropriate Analysis Technique

Connect the most appropriate technique for each of the given examples being analysed. Note more than one technique may be appropriate:

To find the water content in hydrated barium chloride.	Gravimetric analysis
To find the manganese content in a steel paperclip.	Complexometric titration
To find the calcium ion content in seawater.	Redox titration
To help determine the purity of a known organic solid.	Back titration
To help determine the purity of a known organic liquid.	Colorimetry
To find the calcium carbonate content in an eggshell.	Melting point analysis
To find the iron(II) content in a sample of iron(II) sulfate.	Chromatography (gas or HPLC)

Making a Standard Solution

Work out the correct order for making a 250 cm^3 0.10 moll^{-1} solution of sodium hydrogen carbonate (NaHCO$_3$). NOTE: Some of the steps given are incorrect and should be ignored.

A	B	C
Stopper and shake several times	Put the solid in a 100cm^3 beaker	Transfer to a 250cm^3 volumetric flask using a funnel.
D	**E**	**F**
Rinse out the beaker several times with distilled water	Add 250 cm^3 water and dissolve it	Weigh out 21.0g of sodium hydrogen carbonate
G	**H**	**I**
Make up to the mark with distilled water	Add approximately 50cm^3 distilled water to dissolve it	Stopper and invert then swirl several times
J	**K**	**L**
Pour into a 250cm^3 volumetric flask	Weigh by difference 2.10g of sodium hydrogen carbonate	Pour rinsing's into the volumetric flask

Correct Order:

☐ ☐ ☐ ☐ ☐ ☐ ☐ ☐

Practical Definitions

Connect the correct definition to the practical terms given:

Heating to constant mass	Uses silica or calcium chloride to create a dry atmosphere to store chemicals that could absorb moisture.
The mark	A solution of accurately known concentration usually of high purity; large molecular weight; unreactive and unable to absorb moisture.
Desiccator	Purification process that uses a solvent the substance to be purified is only soluble in when hot.
Weigh by difference	A sample is weighed, then heated, cooled and reweighed until there is no change in the mass.
Primary standard	An indication marked on a pipette or standard flask to indicate the level that the bottom of the meniscus should lie on.
Recrystallisation	Liquids that are not able to mix and will form two distinct layers.
Immiscible	Technique that allows volatile reactants to be heated so that they react but with out losing them as a vapour.
Refluxing	A way of making sure a technique or reaction is working correctly by using a pure form of the substance being analysed.
Positive control	An accurate way of knowing exactly how much of a solid has been used in a reaction or preparation of a standard solution.

Practice Questions

1. Seawater can be analysed for its chloride ion concentration by gravimetric analysis. Standard silver nitrate solution was added to a seawater sample to form a precipitate of silver chloride. The precipitate was filtered and dried to constant mass using an oven and a desiccator.

a. What does the term dry to constant mass mean?

b. What is the desiccator used for?

c. In the analysis of one $100 cm^3$ sample of seawater the experiment yielded 8.079g of silver(I) chloride. Calculate the concentration of chloride ions in the sample in gl^{-1}.

2. An active ingredient in many home hair dying products is the oxidising agent hydrogen peroxide, H_2O_2.

    In an experiment to determine the concentration of hydrogen peroxide present in a hair dye kit a student carried out a titration with acidified permanganate solution.

    $$2MnO_4^- + 5H_2O_2 \quad + \quad 6H^+ \quad \rightarrow \quad 2Mn^{2+} \quad + \quad 5O_2 \quad + \quad 8H_2O$$

    $25 \cdot 0 cm^3$ of the dye solution was pipetted into a $250 cm^3$ standard flask and made up to the mark with distilled water. $25 \cdot 0 cm^3$ samples were titrated with $0 \cdot 030$ mol l^{-1} permanganate solution until a permanent pink colour remained. The results are shown in the table.

	1st titration	2nd titration	3rd titration
Initial burette reading (cm^3)	0·3	19·2	0·2
Final burette reading (cm^3)	19·2	37·7	18·8
Volume used (cm^3)	18·9	18·5	18·6

i. Calculate the number of moles of hydrogen peroxide in $25 \cdot 0 cm^3$ of the diluted solution of hair dye.

ii. Calculate the concentration, in mol l^{-1}, of hydrogen peroxide in the undiluted hair dye.

3. To determine the percentage of copper in an antique copper coin a student dissolved the coin in 20 cm^3 of concentrated nitric acid and made the resulting solution up to 250 cm^3 in a volumetric flask.

   Five standard solutions were prepared by diluting a 0·10 mol l^{-1} stock solution of copper(II) nitrate with deionised water.

a. One of the standard solutions had a concentration of 0·010 mol l^{-1}. Describe fully how this 0·010 mol l^{-1} solution should be prepared in a 50 cm^3 volumetric flask from the 0·10 mol l^{-1} stock solution.

b. The colorimeter was fitted with a suitable filter and set to zero using a reference sample. The absorbance of the five standard solutions was determined and a calibration graph was drawn.

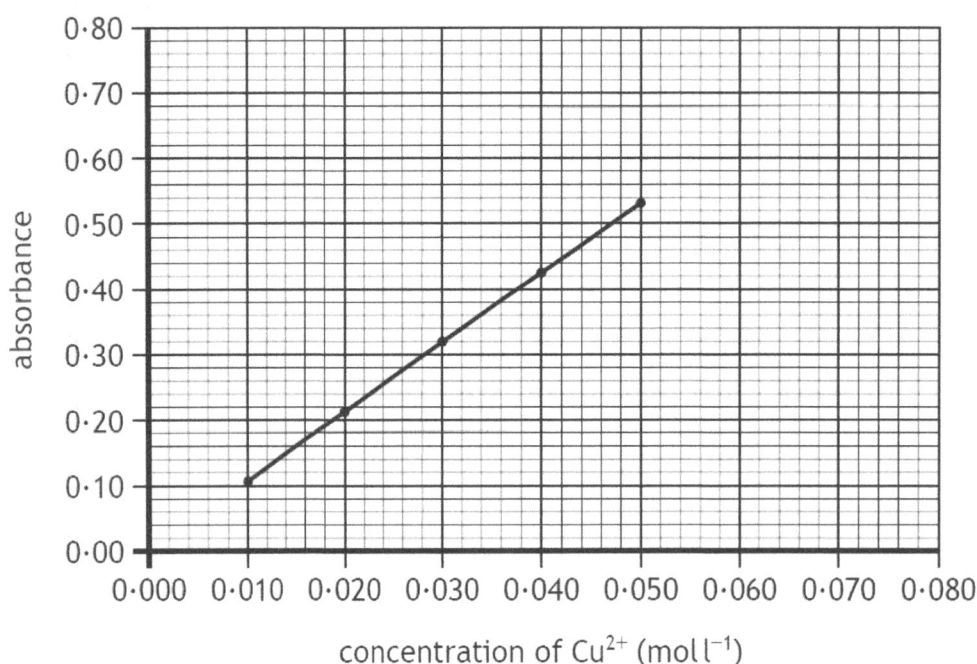

concentration of Cu^{2+} (mol l^{-1})

I. What substance is used to zero the colorimeter?

ii The copper(II) nitrate solutions are blue, suggest what wavelength in nm the filter on the colorimeter was set at.

ii. The original mass of the coin was 0.75g

   The absorbance of the coin solution was 0.42.

   Calculate the % by mass of copper in the coin.